DIVAGATING

through

THE TAROT

REBECCA FITZGERALD

iUniverse, Inc.
Bloomington

Divagating through The Tarot

iUniverse books may be ordered through booksellers or by contacting:

iUniverse
1663 Liberty Drive
Bloomington, IN 47403
www.iuniverse.com
1-800-Authors (1-800-288-4677)

ISBN: 978-1-4502-8199-7 (sc)
ISBN: 978-1-4502-8200-0 (dj)
ISBN: 978-1-4502-8201-7 (ebook)

Library of Congress Control Number: 2011901449

Printed in the United States of America

iUniverse rev. date: 01/21/2011

for Gerald

Contents

PART I
INTRODUCTION

1. WHAT IS DIVAGATING?   1

2. WHAT TO EXPECT FROM THIS BOOK   1

3. WHY ANOTHER BOOK ON TAROT CARDS?   2

4. WHAT IS THE TAROT?   2

5. TAROT CARDS AND THE OCCULT   3

6. WHAT IS THE ORIGIN OF TAROT CARDS?   3

7. SYMBOLS AND SYMBOLISM   8

8. ARCHETYPES   8

9. COLLECTIVE UNCONSCIOUS   9

10. NUMEROLOGY   9

11. ASTROLOGY   11

12. CHAKRAS   12

13. HOW TAROT CARDS ARE ORGANIZED   13

14. WHAT MAKES TAROT CARDS WORK?   13

15. HOW IS IT DETERMINED WHICH TAROT CARD WILL BE READ?   14

16. IS IT PURE LUCK WHICH CARD IS SELECTED?   15

17. WHY THE RIDER-WAITE (SMITH) DECK AND NOT
    OTHER ONES?   15

18. SHUFFLING TAROT CARDS   16

19. WHERE TO BEGIN?   16

PART II
THE MAJOR ARCANA CARDS

20. WHAT DOES MAJOR ARCANA MEAN?   21

21. AFFIRMATIONS   21

22. REVERSED MEANINGS OF CARDS   22

    CARD 0 - THE FOOL   25

    CARD 1 – THE MAGICIAN   31

    CARD 2 – THE HIGH PRIESTESS   37

    CARD 3 – THE EMPRESS   45

    CARD 4 – THE EMPEROR   51

    CARD 5 – THE HIEROPHANT   57

    CARD 6 – THE LOVERS   65

    CARD 7 – THE CHARIOT   71

    CARD 8 – STRENGTH   77

    CARD 9 – THE HERMIT   83

    CARD 10 – THE WHEEL OF FORTUNE   89

    CARD 11 – JUSTICE   95

    CARD 12 – THE HANGED MAN   101

    CARD 13 – DEATH   107

    CARD 14 – TEMPERANCE   113

    CARD 15 – THE DEVIL   119

    CARD 16 – THE TOWER   125

    CARD 17 – THE STAR   131

    CARD 18 – THE MOON   137

    CARD 19 – THE SUN   143

    CARD 20 - JUDGEMENT   149

    CARD 21 – THE WORLD   155

PART III
THE MINOR ARCANA CARDS

23. WHAT DOES MINOR ARCANA MEAN?   163

24. COURT CARDS   164

25. THE SUIT OF WANDS   167

    ACE OF WANDS   169

    TWO OF WANDS   173

    THREE OF WANDS   177

    FOUR OF WANDS   181

    FIVE OF WANDS   185

    SIX OF WANDS   189

    SEVEN OF WANDS   193

    EIGHT OF WANDS   197

    NINE OF WANDS   201

    TEN OF WANDS   205

    PAGE OF WANDS   209

    KNIGHT OF WANDS   213

    QUEEN OF WANDS   219

    KING OF WANDS   225

26. THE SUIT OF CUPS   231

    ACE OF CUPS   233

    TWO OF CUPS   237

    THREE OF CUPS   241

    FOUR OF CUPS   245

    FIVE OF CUPS   249

    SIX OF CUPS   253

    SEVEN OF CUPS   257

    EIGHT OF CUPS   261

    NINE OF CUPS   265

    TEN OF CUPS   269

    PAGE OF CUPS   273

    KNIGHT OF CUPS   277

    QUEEN OF CUPS   281

    KING OF CUPS   287

27. THE SUIT OF SWORDS   293

    ACE OF SWORDS   297

    TWO OF SWORDS   301

    THREE OF SWORDS   305

FOUR OF SWORDS   309

FIVE OF SWORDS   313

SIX OF SWORDS   317

SEVEN OF SWORDS   321

EIGHT OF SWORDS   325

NINE OF SWORDS   329

TEN OF SWORDS   333

PAGE OF SWORDS   337

KNIGHT OF SWORDS   341

QUEEN OF SWORDS   345

KING OF SWORDS   349

28. THE SUIT OF PENTACLES   355

ACE OF PENTACLES   357

TWO OF PENTACLES   361

THREE OF PENTACLES   365

FOUR OF PENTACLES   369

FIVE OF PENTACLES   373

SIX OF PENTACLES   377

SEVEN OF PENTACLES   381

EIGHT OF PENTACLES   385

NINE OF PENTACLES   389

TEN OF PENTACLES   393

PAGE OF PENTACLES   397

KNIGHT OF PENTACLES   401

QUEEN OF PENTACLES   407

KING OF PENTACLES   411

PART IV
SPREADS

29. HOW ARE SPREADS USED?   417

30. SPREAD EXAMPLES   417

31. A READING EXAMPLE   427

INDEX   431

PART I

Introduction

1. What is divagating?

Divagating means to wander around somewhere and often refers to straying off the subject under discussion. This happens frequently to me when I consult the Tarot. A variety of possibilities present themselves and one thought can lead to another often resulting in a search for other associated information.

2. What to expect from this book

- Tarot capitalized throughout as a sign of respect.
- A wealth of information describing each card.
- Information presented in a concise well organized and easy to follow format.
- Pictures of every card.
- SYMBOLIC EXPLANATIONS regarding colours, patterns on clothing, the position of the people and background items on each card.
- NUMEROLOGICAL EXPLANATIONS for the digits 0 through 9.
- ASTROLOGICAL CONNECTIONS including the zodiac sign, ruling planet, gender, element and quality.
- Major Arcana cards include the archetype represented, personal considerations, affirmations and unifying themes between cards.
- Explanations regarding the four suits in the Minor Arcana.
- Court card explanations.
- Traditional and reversed meanings listed on each card.
- A Tarot reading example.
- A number of Tarot card spread examples.
- An Index.
- And more, check the Contents for a full list.

3. Why another book on Tarot cards?

This book materialized over time. I started out wanting to understand the Tarot, what it was based on, how it worked and why it worked. It intrigued me as it fell into a somewhat enigmatic and murky realm. Within the circles I worked and socialized Tarot cards were a topic rarely if ever discussed. For some the card's association with New Age dynamics placed them in a silly and somewhat frivolous sphere. For others it was fear of association as the Tarot cards were historically connected to the occult. However the Tarot's obscure history and the extensive information contained in the cards grabbed hold of my imagination and wouldn't let go. In order to grasp its meaning I purchased a number of books and started writing notes. After a year of compiling information I realized symbolism and archetypes, the influence of myths, as well as the role of the collective unconscious were essential features in understanding the Tarot's meaning. I began studying and learning more about these subjects. Numerology, astrology, and chakra connections with the Tarot also kept cropping up so I began exploring those topics as well. Following more than three years of additions to my notes my friends began saying "you have created a book." And so I have.

Tarot card books are something like cook books. There is always some extra ingredient to be considered or a different aspect an author believes is important to include. This book attempts to answer the questions previously mentioned that sprang to my mind while I was trying to comprehend and utilize the Tarot cards. I have attempted to include the salient facts on each card so less time is spent hunting for information when learning about the Tarot. It is my hope that those who purchase this book find it a valuable resource in understanding the Tarot and perhaps in embracing it as I have.

4. What is the Tarot?

Usually illustrated with symbolism and archetypes to create meanings, Tarot decks include seventy eight cards. Originally used for playing games, Tarot cards are now more commonly used for divination, meditation, and for reflection purposes. For many individuals the information embedded in these cards leads to spiritual transformation and personal growth towards a sense of greater wholeness.

Studying the Tarot is an intriguing undertaking. Absorbing the information contained in the cards for the pure satisfaction of expanding personal knowledge is gratifying. Reflecting upon the information in a Major Arcana message is rewarding while using the cards to answer questions is both pleasurable and insightful. I am truly amazed at how the cards activate new understanding about situations. Reading the Tarot is thought provoking, inspiring and continually enlightening.

5. Tarot cards and the occult

Occult means hidden, however the word "occult" conjures up different meanings in different people. The occult typically refers to magical and divinatory beliefs and practices some of which include astrology, Tarot, palmistry, numerology, spirit contact, spiritualism, channelling, magic and witchcraft. As well the occult includes exploring past lives (*reincarnation*), casting spells and psycho kinesis (*mind over matter*). Surrounded by superstition many of these practices are feared. Established traditional religions sometimes use the word occult to describe something they don't understand, that alarms them, or they wish to condemn; they use it as an offensive label against a variety of ideas and practices.

Many people interested in paranormal activities have taken great pains to isolate certain disciplines such as astrology, numerology and the Tarot from the realm of the "occult." These three have been seen as different from other divinatory practices as they are based upon structured rules and principles and using them doesn't require psychic abilities or membership into a group or cult. Certainly the wide acceptance of astrology and daily horoscopes has shed many stigmas they once had due to their connections with the occult.

Casting nothing but bright light upon the occult would be naive and faulty. However rejecting everything that lies within a larger unit, because some parts of the larger unit are seriously flawed or even dangerous, is akin to never logging onto the internet because harm has befallen some who have. This type of thinking leads to narrow mindedness and extremism. With the wide spectrum of activities under the occult umbrella people need to discern what to explore, ignore, reject, and ultimately to leave alone.

Philosopher and psychologist, William James (1842-1910), has been quoted as saying "Contempt prior to investigation is a sure barrier against understanding." This book invites those who have avoided the Tarot for whatever reason to take a look and perhaps open up a whole new realm never yet explored.

6. What is the origin of Tarot cards?

There appears to be an abundance of misleading and false information surrounding the Tarot. It does not seem that any serious historian has investigated this topic which has allowed individuals to publish information that is not based on sound research. Misinformation picked up as fact is quoted again and again with additional information being blended into the mix making it difficult to sort truth from fabrication. After sifting through a great deal of information I have tried to capture various salient points that look as if they are based on some supportive evidence.

The authors and originators of the Tarot are unknown. The Tarot deck's Minor Arcana cards share many similarities with playing cards which showed up in France and Italy, via Muslim Spain, around thirteen hundred and seventy-five (1375). Contrary to some beliefs, the Romany (*gypsies*) did not either invent the Tarot or start the trend of divining with the deck. By the time the Romany appeared in Europe in the fifteenth century Tarot card decks and the game of trumps (*tarrochi*) were in widespread use both in Italy and France. Tarrochi included fifty-six minor cards which resembled playing cards along with a number of the Major Arcana "trump" cards. This game was not used for any type of divination.

Prior to fifteen hundred (1500) it is difficult to find any substantial information that relates to Tarot cards. From approximately twelve hundred (1200) to fourteen hundred (1400) during the medieval inquisition, the church documented in considerable detail what was considered as evidence of heresy. Playing cards were included in the list of evidence as being subject to censor. However Tarot cards were never mentioned suggesting they were too obscure to be noticed or they didn't exist. It is very likely that Tarot information, embedded with myths and symbolism, was being orally passed down from generation to generation and had yet to be captured on paper. For example early poets are known to have used the titles of the Major Arcana trump cards to create flattering verses called *tarocchi appropriati*, describing ladies of the court or famous people. One of the oldest known Tarot decks are hand painted cards from the late fifteenth century, of the northern Italian type likely coming from Venice or France, and are in the Biblioteque Nationale of France.

The Tarot was significantly influenced throughout the Italian renaissance especially in the latter years of the fourteenth century. This was a time of great intellectual diversity and activity. Hermeticism (*ideas or beliefs set forth in the writing of Hermes Trismegistus*), astrology, Neo-Platonism (*a thought form rooted in the philosophy of Plato c. 428-347 BC*), Pythagorean philosophy (*based on reason and numbers*) with roots in Alexandrian Egypt, study of the Kabbalah (*ancient Jewish mystical tradition*), and heterodox (*opinions or doctrines at variance with an official or orthodox position*), as well as Christian thought all thrived. Any or all of these may have influenced the intention as well as the design of the Tarot.

Drawn from medieval and renaissance Europe the symbolism on original Tarot cards is distinctive to European Christendom. Illustrations nearly identical to each of the earlier Tarot subjects can be found in European art and such detail on the cards is not found in other cultures. Prior to seventeen hundred and fifty (1750) most if not all known Tarot cards bore Italian labels and suit-marks which suggest an Italian origin, however they had French names.

The ties to Egypt many Tarot cards have did not occur until the late seventeen hundreds. Information and knowledge about pictographs found in the pyramids during the Napoleonic invasion could be related to the meanings of the Tarot cards. An Egyptian hieroglyphic book of seventy eight tablets was utilized by some to find overlapping meanings in the seventy eight Tarot cards. No one knows the origin of this book and it seems to have just mysteriously appeared. In the late seventeen hundreds Court de Gebelin, a Freemason, was shown a pack of Tarot cards and he was so impressed with how they reflected the ancient Egyptian religion that he wrote a treatise on the subject. In seventeen eighty one (1781) the Comte de Mellet published a short article on the Tarot which identified connections between the Hebrew letters and the cards. Many of the connections between the earliest established Tarot interpretations and Egyptology flow but a number of them are forced resulting in substantially altered or lost meanings. Following these publications Tarot cards began being used more for divination and less for playing and interest in the Tarot became an integral part of occult philosophy.

Though Egyptian influence cannot be substantiated prior to the late seventeen hundreds information in Tarot cards reflect ideas and beliefs found in both Egyptology and in the Kabbalah. Variations of these ideas are also reflected in many cultures dating back four thousand or more years BC. Druids, the knowledgeable sect of the Celts, shared many of the same beliefs as Egyptians and Kabbalists. The Druids who greatly influenced British culture trace their roots back to the beginnings of mankind. Knowledge about astrology, measurements, and numerology were all well known and utilized to construct standing stones, such as Stonehenge, found in Britain and other parts of the world. There is overlap in the myths and traditions in many early cultures. The essence of this ancient knowledge is what has been captured and embedded in the symbolism on Tarot cards.

Arthur E. Waite was a prominent member of the magical Hermetic Order of the Golden Dawn founded in eighteen hundred and eighty eight (1888) by Dr. W.W. Westcott, S.L. Macgregor-Matthews, and Dr. W.R. Woodman. The Golden Dawn, active during the late nineteenth and early twentieth century's, focused on and practiced theurgy (*the effect of supernatural or divine intervention in human affairs*) and spiritual development.

Waite created the Rider-Waite (Smith) deck in nineteen hundred and nine (1909) over four hundred years into the history of the Tarot. Waite's deck owes much of its symbolism to the Golden Dawn group and represents a departure from the earlier Italian - French Tarot card tradition. Rider was the publishing company and Pamela Coleman Smith, an American artist, contributed her own vision especially with the colours and creation of the pictures upon the fifty-six Minor Arcana cards. Originally these cards were like playing cards showing only the numbers of the suit they represented. Waite found many relationships between the Tarot and the Kabbalah. He related the twenty two trump cards (*the Major Arcana cards*) to the twenty two paths along the Kabbalah's Tree of Life. In order to make his theory fit he changed the accepted order of some of the cards. Since the trumps did not have numbers or any recorded order for the first hundred or more years of their existence his ordering method remains as viable as any other. Today Waite's ordering of the Major Arcana cards has become the standard for most Tarot decks.

Aleister Crowley, also a member of the Golden Dawn, wrote the *Book of Thoth*, which is based on Egyptian ideology. Considered another classic Tarot deck, Lady Frieda Harris began painting Crowley's cards according to his instruction in nineteen hundred and thirty eight (1938) and it was completed in nineteen hundred and forty three (1943). Crowley renamed several of the trumps and also re-arranged the astrological and Hebrew alphabet correspondences of some cards, in accordance with his earlier book, *Liber Al vel Legis* (*The Book of Law*).

In ancient Egyptian mythology, Thoth, is god of wisdom and technology. In art he was often depicted as a man with the head of an ibis (*bird*) or with the head of a baboon. The ibis and baboon were considered to be reincarnations of Thoth. Thoth was revered as the inventor of mathematics, engineering, astronomy, and botany. According to Plato's *Phaedrus*, Thoth also invented writing and he is often depicted as a scribe. Thoth was the measurer of time and devised the solar year. The curved beak of his ibis mask was associated with the moon and it was Thoth to which the ancient Egyptians ascribed their knowledge of the stars.

Both Waite and Crowley were deeply influenced by the occultist, Madame Blavatsky. Helena Blavatsky's master work, the *Secret Doctrine*, published in eighteen hundred and eighty eight (1888) will remain seminal for centuries. This fifteen hundred page book is a massive study of man, of nature, of spiritual evolution, and of the essence of reality. Blavatsky addresses questions such as the continuity of life after death, purpose of existence, good and evil, consciousness and substance, sexuality, karma, evolution, and human and planetary transformation. One of Blavatsky's theories is that everything, every theology, from the earliest and the oldest down to the latest has sprung from one universal esoteric or Mystery language. One of the topics Madame Blavatsky explores is the role of symbolism in the Tarot. Her book has remained in print for over one hundred years.

The Tarot terms Major Arcana, Minor Arcana, High Priestess, and Hierophant originated from the Golden Dawn influences. Historically the terms were the trumps, the suit cards, Papess and Pope. Likewise pentacles were referred to as coins, and wands were called staves or batons.

The original Italian titles of the cards were in some cases different from the later French titles popularized by the Tarot of Marseille decks. English translations from this deck have now become familiar to most that use the Tarot. The trumps originating in Italy varied considerably, they were not numbered, their ordering is not known and the number of trumps differed from deck to deck. The intention of the original designers of the Tarot in selecting the symbols for the trump cards is unknown, although there are many conjectures, some more plausible than others.

Arthur Waite's and Aleister Crowley's interest and research into the Tarot has been a spring board in the western world for the wide popularity of Tarot cards. Hundreds of varieties of decks have been created, some continue with the older tradition with no drawings on the Minor Arcana cards. Most follow Waite's format and some are eclectic using elements from traditional cards but branching out into new areas. Tarot cards are sold in most of the larger cities in the world and are easily ordered off the internet. Many decks are collected due to their beautiful art designs.

Sources

Decker, Ronald, Michael Drummet, and Theirry Depaulis, *A Wicked Pack of Cards*

Drummet, Michael, *The Game of Tarot*

Giles, Cynthia, *The Tarot: History, Mystery, and Lore*

Kaplan, Stuart, *The Encyclopaedia of Tarot, Vol. I & II*

Moakley, Gertrude, *The Tarot Cards painted by Bonifacio Bembo*

O'Neill, Robert V, *Tarot Symbolism*

Williams, Brian, *A Renaissance Tarot*

Williams, Brian, *The Minchiate Tarot*

Gomes, Michael, the abridged and annotated version of *The Secret Doctrine*, by H.P. Blavatsky

Websites
The Tarot History Sheet – http://www.tarothermit.com/infosheet.htm

7. Symbols and symbolism

Symbols and symbolism is the essence of Tarot cards. The pictures on these cards stir the unconscious and meaning is realized. Symbolism is a language. It is ubiquitous in myths, legends, art, literature, slang, jokes, obscenities, etc. The capacity for humans to perceive meaning from symbols is innate and evolves spontaneously during human development. Based on metaphors by way of association symbolism is a way of conveying meaning through the use of imagery, ideas or sound. We associate meaning immediately without thinking when encountering symbols. For example, holly and mistletoe together cause most people in western societies to think about Christmas and things associated with that time of year.

Using holly and mistletoe as an example of symbolism demonstrates the ancientness of symbols. According to Ross Nichols, author of *The Book of Druidry*, Druids trace their beginnings back to perhaps four thousand years B.C. Wise in astrological matters, the Celts, mentored by their Druids, celebrated the winter solstice on December twenty first. This celebration was referred to as the Yule and marked both the shortest day of the year and the rebirth of the sun. A log was burned on the twenty first using remains of the previous year's log and remained lit for twenty four hours. Holly and mistletoe cut from oak trees by the Druid priests was tied along with shapes representing the sun, moon and stars onto evergreen trees such as the pine. Gifts would also be hung from the Yule (*evergreen*) tree as offerings to the pagan gods and goddesses.

In ancient times before the written word symbols were used to pass on knowledge because the information contained within a single image could hold an entire story. Pictures on Tarot cards are embedded with symbolic meanings, the colours, the shapes and placement of objects are all symbols invoking meaning when viewed.

8. Archetypes

Archetypes, another characteristic of symbolism, refer to the original model of something that serves as a pattern for other things of the same type.

Easily recognizable archetypes are the hero – Superman or Spiderman; ill-fated lovers – Romeo and Juliet. Utilized to create meaning some Tarot card archetypes are the child (*Card 0 The Fool*) representing innocence and wonder; the mother (*Card 3 The Empress*) symbolizing nature and fertility; the father (*Card 4 The Emperor*) symbolizing masculine authority, the provider and protector; the wise old man (*Card 10 The Hermit*) representing wisdom; the trickster (*Card 1 The Magician*) symbolizing magic and power.

9. Collective unconscious

Coined by Carl Jung, collective unconscious is a term of analytical psychology. It is part of the unconscious mind, expressed in humanity as well as all life forms with nervous systems and describes how we organize experiences. Jung distinguishes the collective unconscious from the personal unconscious, in that the personal unconscious is a personal reservoir of experience unique to each individual, while the collective unconscious collects and organizes those personal experiences in a similar way with each member of a particular species.

The collective unconscious, believed to be inherited at birth, holds universal and impersonal information that is identical in all individuals. Religious, spiritual and mythological symbols and experiences, as well as the myths that explained how the world and humankind came to be in their present form are all stored in the collective unconscious. Archetypes present in the collective unconscious are explained as pre-existing spiritual entities, which are recognized by the mind when certain circumstances are encountered by the individual. This is where many of our instinctual tendencies are stored, for example our flight or fight responses, or perhaps praying when faced with overwhelming fears when this is not a normal practice. The shared memories stored in our collective unconscious are the basis of a culture.

10. Numerology

Existing for five thousand or more years numerology has various methods and versions but generally it can be described as a belief in a mystical or esoteric (*obscure, highly specialized information understood only by select groups*) relationship between numbers and physical objects or living things. All words, names and numbers may be reduced to single digits which correspond to certain arcane (*secret, mysterious*) characteristics that influence our lives. For example the number twenty two (22) is reduced to four (4) by adding 2+2 = 4. Nine a magical number can be cast out as it does not impact the final reduction. For example 1951 is 1 + 9 + 5 + 1 = 16 and 1 + 6 = 7. 1951 = 7. Casting out the 9 leaves 1 + 5 + 1 = 7. 1951 = 7 even with the 9 cast out.

The meanings of the digits 0 through 9 are included in the information on each card in this book.

One of the three qualities cardinal, fixed or mutable is included on every card's information in this book. Cardinal sign people begin things, fixed sign people are determined and maintain things, and mutable sign people are changeable and end things. Cardinal signs are Aries, Cancer, Libra and Capricorn. Fixed signs are Taurus, Leo, Scorpio and Aquarius. Mutable signs are Gemini, Virgo, Sagittarius, and Pisces. Although an astrological concept it also falls in the realm of numerology as the numbers one (1) through nine (9) have ruling planets which correspond to one of the qualities. Here is how they are assigned.

NUMBER	NUMBER'S RULING PLANET	QUALITY	CONSTELLATION	QUALITY
1	Sun	Cardinal	Aries	Cardinal
2	Moon	Fixed	Taurus	Fixed
3	Jupiter	Mutable	Gemini	Mutable
4	Uranus	Cardinal	Cancer	Cardinal
5	Mercury	Fixed	Leo	Fixed
6	Venus	Mutable	Virgo	Mutable
7	Neptune	Cardinal	Libra	Cardinal
8	Saturn	Fixed	Scorpio	Fixed
9	Mars	Mutable	Sagittarius	Mutable

- Note the ruling planets shown above are the single digit's ruling planet **not** the constellation's ruling planet. The constellation's ruling planets appear under the Astrology section.
- The constellations and associated quality were listed above to demonstrate how the single digit qualities match the constellation qualities.
- Utilizing numerological information is an important component to ensuring a comprehensive Tarot card reading.

11. Astrology

The study of stars and planets predates recorded history. Astrology is based on the belief that the movement of the stars and other celestial bodies affects our lives here on earth.

Used by eastern astrologers sidereal astrology is based on where the constellations are physically located when viewed from earth and this is continually changing. Tropical astrology, the one used by western astrologers, is based on where the constellations were when it was first developed. There is currently about twenty four (24) degrees difference between them. It takes approximately twenty five thousand (25,000) years for the zodiac to repeat its full cycle.

Twelve constellations make up the zodiac on which astrological information originates. These divide the year up into twelve equal sections. The astrological year always starts with Aries and ends with Pisces. Astrologers also use the Moon, Sun and eight planets, Mercury, Venus, Mars, Jupiter, Saturn, Uranus, Neptune and Pluto, in their studies. Explanations regarding the unique aspects of the constellation, ruling planet, gender, element, and quality and how they affect each card is included on every card.

CONSTELLATION	DATES	RULING PLANET	GENDER	ELEMENT	QUALITY
1. Aries	03-21 to 04-19	Mars	Masculine	Fire	Cardinal
2. Taurus	04-20 to 05-20	Venus	Feminine	Earth	Fixed
3. Gemini	05-21 to 06-21	Mercury	Masculine	Air	Mutable
4. Cancer	06-22 to 07-22	the Moon	Feminine	Water	Cardinal
5. Leo	07-23 to 08-22	the Sun	Masculine	Fire	Fixed
6. Virgo	08-23 to 09-22	Mercury	Feminine	Earth	Mutable
7. Libra	09-23 to 10-23	Venus	Masculine	Air	Cardinal
8. Scorpio	10-24 to 11-21	Pluto	Feminine	Water	Fixed

9. Sagittarius	11-22 to 12-21	Jupiter	Masculine	Fire	Mutable
10. Capricorn	12-22 to 01-19	Saturn	Feminine	Earth	Cardinal
11. Aquarius	01-20 to 02-18	Uranus	Masculine	Air	Fixed
12. Pisces	02-19 to 03-20	Neptune	Feminine	Water	Mutable

Like utilizing numerology it is important to consider the astrological affects of each card in order to ensure a more comprehensive Tarot reading.

12. Chakras

Chakra, a Sanskirt word, means wheel or turning. Chakras are energy centres of the body, each one is related to different areas of our physical, emotional, and mental body and it's functioning. There are seven chakras in the body.

1. **Root chakra** – located at the base of the spine. Associated to our sense of security in the world.

2. **Sacral chakra** – located in the bone plate curve above the cleft of the buttocks. Associated with vitality and enjoyment of life. This is where the energy of our ancestors exists.

3. **Solar plexus** – located in the upper stomach area just below the rib cage and behind the navel. Associated with our sense of personal power. This is where our energy comes from when we compete, protect, control, transform and make choices.

4. **Heart** – located in the centre of the upper chest behind the breast bone. Associated with emotions, love for self and others, peace, empathy, forgiveness, spiritual development, unconditional love, and unity with all living things.

5. **Throat** – located in the middle of the lower neck, below the larynx (*voice box*) and just above your clavicles (*collarbones*). Associated with creative energy, communication, sense of responsibility, and self-expression.

6. **Third eye** – located above and between your eyebrows. Associated with intuition, deep wisdom and spirituality, clairvoyance, telepathy, self-directedness, clarity of vision, inner understanding and inspiration, mental and spiritual processes.

7. **Crown** – located just above the top of your head. Associated with feeling and embracing love, it is the gateway and our direct connection to the Spirit World.

Information on chakras appears in the symbolism on some of the cards in this book.

13. How Tarot cards are organized

A Tarot deck consists of seventy eight (78) cards that are divided into two sections, the Major Arcana and the Minor Arcana. Arcanum means secrets or mysteries. The Major Arcana consists of twenty two (22) "trump" cards. The Minor Arcana include the other fifty six (56) cards which are organized into four suits each including fourteen (14) cards.

Minor Arcana cards numbered one through ten are referred to as "pip" cards. The other four cards in the suit called "court cards" include a Page, a Knight, a Queen and a King. The four suits are most commonly referred to as wands, cups, swords and pentacles. There are numerous creators of Tarot cards and the names they have assigned their cards can differ quite significantly.

Part II of this book explains Major Arcana cards in detail and Part III deals with the Minor Arcana cards.

14. What makes Tarot cards work?

Pictures filled with symbolic meanings on the seventy eight cards of the Tarot deck churn and swirl in our unconscious and create meaning for us. Through using a combination of innate understanding and intuitiveness insight is provided and this casts meaning upon the information being internally processed which then allows us to verbalize it.

Serving as symbolic codes to be interpreted the pictures on the Tarot cards provide meaning. Read as a whole the meanings can vary somewhat depending upon the order in which the cards appear however the essence of the card's meaning will still be present. The reading must have coherence with the question under consideration.

There are Tarot card readers that possess psychic abilities and use the Tarot as a framework to channel their thoughts and energies through. They could use many different vehicles as well such as tea leaves, palm reading, or psychometry (*holding an item of jewellery or clothing*) etc. The Tarot cards themselves do not possess any supernatural powers.

Because the messages embedded in Tarot cards are universal the Tarot speaks to each of us. Ancient information found in Egypt, in the writings of Hermes Trismegistus, contributions from Plato, knowledge contained in Hebrew texts and in the Kabbalah, as well as the Christian symbolism found on the early Italian and French Major Arcana cards have many overlaps and they all combine to create a collection of life's very essence. These messages speak to the individual as each of us have personally experienced something referred to in the Tarot cards or will likely experience one of these life lessons in the future.

I do not personally believe Tarot cards can foretell one's future as every human has free will and choices. The best Tarot cards can do is provide an insight into what may happen if you do not change any thoughts or behaviours you are currently engaged in. This should not be under estimated as this is in itself a wonderful and insightful endeavour. Through predicting an outcome you have the opportunity to change current beliefs and behaviours and generate a different outcome if the original one is troublesome or not desired.

Symbolism in Tarot cards provide a myriad of information. Casting a new way of thinking about a situation, or gaining a new perspective, which the Tarot does beautifully, can alter our faulty behaviours or thought processes leading to our personal growth.

15. How is it determined which Tarot card will be read?

There are various methods of dealing and reading cards, these are based on the personal preferences of the card reader. Some card readers pass their cards to the Querent (*person who is being read for*) and have her (*him*) shuffle the cards, thereby allowing some of her (*his*) personal energies to enter the cards. However most Tarot card readers are very particular about their cards and do not want anyone else touching them. If others handle Tarot cards the owner will often undertake a clearing session whereby the Tarot cards are freed of energies other than their own.

Following shuffling, either by the Tarot card reader or the Querent, various methods of choosing cards to be read are available. Sometimes the reader will have the Querent cut the deck generally using his (*her*) left hand and then read the number of cards they have predetermined in the order in which they were laid down. My personal preference is to shuffle the cards and then spread them out and have the Querent select the predetermined number of cards that will be read. I usually have them select an extra three or four cards which I set aside in case we need to clarify some information.

A common practice is using "spreads" to read from. A spread refers to a pattern in which the cards will be placed with each position in the pattern having a predetermined meaning. For example the spread may contain four cards which will be laid out next to one another. The first card describes the situation, the second card the obstacle, the third card the recommended action and the fourth card the expected outcome. There are numerous spreads and they all provide a format and structure to read from. There are some spreads appearing in the back of this book. Individuals are also encouraged to create their own spreads.

16. Is it pure luck which card is selected?

I don't have a solid answer for this. I am always truly amazed at how certain cards come up and how significant their messages are to the Querent. I think a great deal depends on the mindset of the Querent, if they believe the cards will present answers their own personal energies seem to select the cards they need to have the answers they are seeking. For very sceptical Querents this does not seem as likely. Sceptics can find issue with anything that is presented to them. I don't choose to read for people who see the Tarot as a hoax or a joke. I place great value on my Tarot cards, always approaching and handling them with the utmost respect.

I personally believe there is interconnectedness with all things in the universe. I also believe people have vibrational energies and that their personal vibrational energy may be at play when they select the specific cards they do for a reading.

There are times that some of the cards don't seem to fit with the overall theme or message that is being revealed. Usually when this happens it is the card reader that is misinterpreting the symbolism and the underlying meaning that may be salient to the Querent. I sometimes have the Querent help with this and ask them to study the card and see what it is telling them. I also have the Querent choose another three or four cards at the beginning of the reading which I set aside for clarification purposes should we need them.

17. Why the Rider-Waite (Smith) deck and not other ones?

There are hundreds of different decks on the market. Handling the cards and seeing if the symbolism speaks to you is a key feature to purchasing the deck you want to work with. I chose the Rider-Waite (*Smith*) Tarot cards as not coming from a background that understood Tarot I wanted a deck that many authors had discussed. The Rider-Waite symbolism seemed to speak to me and the brighter colours and clearer pictures in the radiant deck were more pleasing that some of the plainer Rider-Waite decks. In writing this book I utilized many author's definitions and sought those with similarities and those that seemed to match the symbolic meanings portrayed on the cards. Whichever deck a person selects should speak to them and the meanings of the cards should be readily accessible.

18. Shuffling Tarot cards

Shuffling Tarot cards is different than shuffling playing cards, as the latter does not have an upright position. To begin ensure all the cards are in the upright position, placing the deck on a table split the deck, squeezing the top left hand corner move the cards in the right hand pile into the left hand pile. Alternatively hold the cards in your left hand and move cards randomly into the deck using your right hand. If you pass the deck to the Querent to shuffle advise her (*him*) about upright positions. Otherwise the Querent may pass you back the deck shuffled in their normal manner and it would include so many reversed cards that the reading would be void of meaning. As well when the Querent hands the deck back to you ensure you begin the reading with the cards in their upright position. Some readers refuse to begin a reading with the first card in a reversed position; they place this card to the side and use one of the extra cards drawn to begin with.

19. Where to begin?

Using a deck of Rider-Waite (*Smith*) cards is advisable so the symbolism that is explained in this book can be viewed and understood. For the most part the card meanings in this book should be transferrable to other decks but all Tarot deck creators have a particular twist on certain cards. For example in Waite's and Crowley's decks the Strength and Justice cards are in reversed order (*this changes the associated numerological information*). As well some of Crowley's and Waite's meanings differ one example is the Devil card interpretations. With the vast variety of Tarot decks on the market today it would be nearly impossible to identify all the changes from the traditional meanings which have occurred. There is no absolute correct answer in reading Tarot cards, it is always a matter of interpretation.

Keeping your cards in a container and treating them with respect is very important.

A good starting point is holding the cards, gazing at them, then writing down what the card seems to be portraying to you. After you have attempted to gain a meaning look that card up in the book and see if your feelings and interpretations match. It is extremely difficult to memorize the meanings of each card, let the symbolism, numerological, and astrological information create meaning for you.

Like anything new the more you use your cards the more you will understand and gain meaning from them. There are numerous Tarot books for beginners that explain a number of ways to get to know your cards better and these books also include various exercises to follow. I never learned everything from one source and I encourage readers to find a variety of books on the subject of Tarot as every author has something to say and you can gain more by hearing information from different perspectives.

Containing a myriad of information Tarot cards are fascinating and the more you begin to understand the more you realize how much you have only tapped the surface. I hope you have a gratifying experience divagating through the Tarot.

PART II

The Major
Arcana Cards

20. What does Major Arcana mean?

Arcana is a variation on the word arcane and means secrets or mysteries. The Major Arcana cards represent your life. Embedded with symbolism each card indicates a significant life issue. The card's messages are symbolic of physical, intellectual, emotional and spiritual aspects of humankind. The cards illustrate the strengths, hopes and fears, weaknesses, and the most worthy as well as the darkest parts of an individual.

Referred to as trumps, the Major Arcana cards messages take priority over the Minor Arcana suit (pip) cards. Depending on where a Major Arcana card is placed in a spread, it can be considered a "central theme" striving to be recognized.

Some people take the Major Arcana cards out of their Tarot packs and spend time reflecting upon the messages embedded in them. Sometimes beginning with the Fool card and working their way through to the World card. The Major Arcana cards have been described as a personal journey with each card providing a new lesson to be learned. The Fool can be regarded as the beginning point of one's life and understanding and embracing the lessons found in the next twenty one cards lead to one's maturity and enlightenment.

21. Affirmations

Affirmations are a declaration that something is true. Used to develop a positive mindset, affirmations focus on beneficial outcomes and are worded to express a positive belief in oneself. Using affirmations regularly can improve one's health, abundance, love, romance, weight loss, and self esteem. They can also facilitate peace and harmony, and increase one's joy and happiness. Declaring affirmative statements establishes an optimistic mindset and uplifts one's spirit.

Examples of affirmations are "I am unique, special, creative and wonderful." "Every cell in my body vibrates with energy and health." "I give out love and it is returned to me multiplied." "My body heals quickly and easily." "The more grateful I am the more I have to be grateful for."

When formulating affirmations only positive statements should be used, avoid statements such as "I will have more friends if I stop criticizing others." A positive affirmation would be "I have many friends and I value their uniqueness."

22. Reversed meanings of cards

Sometimes cards are upside down when they are chosen. Readers all have preferences as to interpreting the meanings of cards in this position. Some readers simply turn the cards right side up and do not deal with reversed meanings. I have listed some reversed meanings and also provided some other options that a reader can use. However it is ultimately up to you as a reader to determine which reversed meaning fits best. Good advice is to choose one method and faithfully follow it unless the circumstances of the reading dictate differently.

0

THE FOOL

Card 0 - The Fool

REPRESENTS
- unlimited potential and spontaneity inherent in every moment

NUMBER ZERO
- 0 denoting everything represents the ultimate mystery, the incomprehensible absolute.
- 0 is pure potential, the point from which all other numbers spring.
- 0 is sometimes defined as the "void" that which was before the "One" (*God*) began to create.

ASTROLOGICALLY
- ZODIAC SIGN: AQUARIUS
  RULING PLANET: URANUS
  ELEMENT: AIR
  GENDER: MASCULINE
  QUALITY: FIXED

- AQUARIUS, which represents the Fool, is about the future and all that is new, fresh and promising. Idealistic Aquarius, ruled by URANUS, indicates freedom, independence, originality and innovation. Destroying old ideologies concepts and structures Uranus rules upheaval and revolution signifying sudden drastic change for good or evil. The advanced thinker, modern scientist and esoteric occultist, as well as nonconformists such as the hippie, revolutionaries, anarchists, rebels, and radical humanitarians are all represented by Uranus. Symbolizing intellectual genius and inventiveness, Uranus influences humanity's great forward leaps.

- Representing thinking, AIR SIGNS are intellectual, good at conceptualizing and great communicators who are intuitive, inquisitive, and constantly coming up with new ideas.

- Air signs MASCULINE ENERGY is protective, outward looking, action-oriented and primarily motivated by external concerns. Seeking to dominate the outside world this energy is hard, firm, logical, strong, rational, rough and loud.
- Aquarius, a FIXED SIGN, represents faithful, persevering people who are resistant to change and see projects through to the end. Attempting to adapt the environment to themselves they above all want to maintain things.

ARCHETYPE BEING REPRESENTED
- **Symbolic message** - Innocence and wonder.
- **Archetype** - The child representing each of us who like naive travellers are off on a great adventure to experience whatever life can teach us.

SYMBOLISM INCLUDES
- **Man (*the Fool*) is standing on the edge of a cliff gazing upward** - he is in a precarious position but does not appear to realize it; either he has enormous faith that nothing can happen to him, or he is extremely distracted.
- **Outer garment (*mandala*)** – the garment's pattern referred to as a mandala represents the whirling motion of the universe.
- **Wallet** – purse like bag on the end of his stick believed to contain unused or unavailable knowledge. Some suggest it holds memories of past experiences, information from the unconscious, or from past lives (*karma*).
- **Decoration on the wallet** – possibly a shell, eagle or bird. Eagles and birds are air signs (*thinking elements*); the shell was carried for good luck by medieval pilgrims.
- **White undergarment** – indicates purity.
- **Eight wheels appearing on the Fool's garment** – represent the Golden Dawn's symbol for spirit.
- **Belt** – symbolizes the seven planets and possibly the entire zodiac (*if the unseen portions of the belt were included*).
- **Laurel wreath on his head** – symbolizes his victorious spirit.
- **Red feather plumb** – feathers are associated with air and thinking. Red symbolizes passion.
- **Holding a white rose** – purity and a sense of love.

- **Yellow footwear** - optimism and enthusiasm. Yellow, the colour for air signs, signifies mental processing (*thinking*).
- **Facing left** – denotes feminine (*yin*) signifying the unconscious and the need to delve into it.
- **White dog trying to get the Fool's attention** – white represents purity; the dog is considered man's best friend and his animal instinct is to warn others of danger.
- **A cliff** –symbolizes the threshold of a new phase.
- **Abyss** – what lies below the cliff symbolizes the unknown and the depths awaiting each of us.
- **Mountains** – symbolize challenge, vision and achievement; being snow-capped indicates great height which could mean that esoteric thought and wisdom can be sought there.
- **Sun** – symbolizes clarity and optimism.
- **A lot of yellow** – represents a great deal of optimism and enthusiasm.

UPRIGHT MEANING

- Using spontaneity, trusting your feelings and following your hunches this card is about beginning a quest or search especially into the unknown.
- About an adventuress spirit willing to take risks and an impulse to change.
- Optimism coupled with such a belief in what you are beginning leads you to tempt fate by taking a step that common sense predicts would spell disaster. Your conviction in this venture is so strong you believe the universe will protect you from any negative fallout.
- No longer satisfied with the old way you willingly take a risk to facilitate change.
- Could mean deliberately refusing to acknowledge that you are being foolish.
- Could mean look before you leap; is your head up in the clouds?
- There is still time to avoid disaster if you pay attention.
- About naiveté and a place of innocence.

REVERSED MEANING

- This is not a good time for independent action. Disaster is assured.
- The situation is surrounded with carelessness, negligence, apathy, hesitation, and instability.
- *The meaning of the card is delayed or extended into the future.*
- *An aspect of the upright meaning of the card needs to be released so you can move forward.*
- *This is not about the upright meaning, place another card on top of the reversed one and read it.*

PERSONAL GROWTH CONSIDERATIONS

- Representing spontaneity, trust and curiosity the Fool symbolizes that part of us that goes forward to experience life regardless of the circumstances. Teaching us how to make appropriate and meaningful decisions he advises it is good to be focused on spiritual matters, but at the same time to stay grounded in the physical world.

VERBAL AFFIRMATION

- "I trust the Universe to support my endeavours."

THE MAGICIAN

Card 1 – The Magician

REPRESENTS
* acting with awareness and concentration

NUMBER ONE
* Ruled by the Sun one's quality is cardinal.
* One's energy is individual, solitary and self-contained.
* Representing the beginning of form number one relates to the active principle of creation.
* One represents mystery, secret information, hidden knowledge, and the mystic centre.
* One is about self-development, creativity, action, progress, a new chance, and rebirth.

ASTROLOGICALLY
* ZODIAC SIGNS: GEMINI AND VIRGO
  RULING PLANET: MERCURY
  ELEMENT: AIR (GEMINI) AND EARTH (VIRGO)
  GENDER: MASCULINE (GEMINI) AND FEMININE (VIRGO)
  QUALITY: MUTABLE

* The Magician Card is represented by GEMINI (*creative ideas*) and VIRGO (*the manifestation of ideas*). Both ruled by MERCURY, the planet of intellect, cleverness and changeability, they are associated with communication. Known for its reasoning power and quickness Mercury rules speaking, language, mathematics and logic.
* Intellectual and good at conceptualizing, AIR SIGN Gemini represents great communicators who are intuitive, inquisitive and constantly come up with new ideas.
* Protective, outward looking, action-oriented and primarily motivated by external concerns MASCULINE ENERGY seeks to dominate the outside world. This energy can be hard, firm, logical, strong, rational, rough and loud.

- EARTH SIGNS (*Virgo*) are about the manifestation of ideas and projects. Grounded and oriented towards what is real they bring form to ideas. Creating structure, demonstrating practicality, persistence, patience and reasonableness they are useful and productive.
- Receptive, intuitive, inward looking and sensitive FEMININE ENERGY works towards co-existence and consensus.
- Adaptable and versatile by nature MUTABLE SIGN people (*Gemini and Virgo*) see both sides of a situation and adjust to most circumstances. Rather than shape their environment they change their attitude and adapt to it. By accepting change mutable sign people thereby end what was.

ARCHETYPE BEING REPRESENTED
- **Symbolic message** - Magic and power.
- **Archetype** - The Trickster, moving things from their normal context he performs tasks to test illusions and create new realities.

SYMBOLISM INCLUDES
- **Dressed in a white gown** - symbolizes purity.
- **Orange robe** – represents enthusiasm, energy, optimism, and opportunity.
- **His belt is a snake swallowing its tail** – the snake forms a circle by swallowing its tail, which symbolizes unity, protection, continuity and includes notions of totality and wholeness.
- **Snake** – means hidden knowledge and kundalini energy. (*Kundalini, an unconscious and instinctive spiritual knowledge, coiled at the foot of the spine is awakened through meditation and moves up the spine to the crown chakra resulting in feelings of mental clarity, understanding and greater awareness of universal truths, creating a sense of bliss and joy*).
- **Band around his forehead** - shows he expects to be working hard.
- **Infinity sign above his head** – (*lemniscate*) the sign of infinity. It represents the Magician's connection with universal principles and his infinite spiritual potential.
- **Holding a wand** – symbolizes the ability to perform magic (*transformation*).

- **Right hand in the air** – denotes rational, conscious, logical thinking as well as aggressiveness and anxiousness.
- **Left hand pointing down** – this denotes weakness and decay; they are being pushed away, as they have no place in this operation.
- **Wooden table** – wood represents a carpenter or builder and this table is symbolizing something that is to be created.
- **The four Tarot suits** – a cup, pentacle, sword, and wand appear on the table implying each of them will be used symbolizing the Magicians' mastery over all that he surveys.
- **Flower garden** – represents earth energies, fertility and new things (*ideas*) sprouting.
- **Yellow** – symbolizes optimism and enthusiasm.

UPRIGHT MEANING

- You need to consider how your choices regarding your current situation are affected by your own illusions or fantasies.
- About creative energy being available to you.
- Using initiative and being thorough while making decisions.
- About your ability to shape or direct your future.
- About using wilful action.
- It is about grounding ideas into reality.
- About communication and inspired original thinking.
- A situation representing new beginnings, new relationships, and new choices.
- About your willingness and ability to fully utilize the situation to achieve your desired outcome.
- About leadership potential.
- Can mean that you possess the necessary skills and knowledge to effectively create any outcome you desire.

REVERSED MEANING

- You may be sending out pessimistic thoughts and thereby attracting negativity into your life.
- Use patience and don't make any changes until your internal and external situations improve.
- *The meaning of the card is delayed or extended into the future.*

- *An aspect of the upright meaning of the card needs to be released so you can move forward.*
- *This is not about the upright meaning, place another card on top of the reversed one and read it.*

PERSONAL GROWTH CONSIDERATIONS

- Representing intellectual awareness and conscious thought the Magician demonstrates you possess the ability to create and shape your destiny. Through using your mind constructively you become aware of how your abilities, beliefs, and emotions manifest as events in your life.

VERBAL AFFIRMATION

- "I am knowledgeable; I possess the necessary skills for success."

UNIFYING THEMES

- Card 10 - WHEEL OF FORTUNE and Card 19 -THE SUN both reduce to the number one and have unifying themes with Card 1 -THE MAGICIAN.
- One is a masculine number and these three cards are about masculine energies, although the Magician also encompasses feminine energy.
- These three cards are about active principles, the Magician is utilizing his knowledge to make things happen, the Wheel of Fortune is indicative of an action that has started and change is coming, and the Sun is about the action of starting something new.

II

THE HIGH PRIESTESS

Card 2 – The High Priestess

REPRESENTS
* guardian of the unconscious
* seeker of the concealed

NUMBER TWO
* Ruled by the Moon two's quality is fixed.
* Two represents some type of union or partnership with another person, a spiritual entity, or two parts of you.
* Associated with the balance of polarities such as yin/yang, male/female and public/separate.
* Two builds on the opportunity presented by one (*the ace*).
* Two can represent sensitivity to others sometimes to the point of considering their wellbeing over your own.
* Representative of immersing yourself into another person, an idea, or a project.
* Two is associated with choices and decisions.

ASTROLOGICALLY
* ZODIAC SIGN: CANCER
  RULING PLANET: THE MOON
  ELEMENT: WATER
  GENDER: FEMININE
  QUALITY: CARDINAL

* CANCER, which is ruled by the MOON, represents the High Priestess. Governing emotions and intuition the Moon is a metaphor for all that is instinctive. Cyclical and constantly changing, the Moon is called the soul of life, mediator between the planes of the spiritual (*Sun*) and the material (*Earth*). As a lunar figure the High Priestess speaks to your deepest inner needs, your memories, feelings, moods, and internal rhythms.

- WATER SIGN people are emotional, intuitive and attuned to subtle vibrations. Capable of great compassion and sensitivity they are quick to sum up others often at first meeting,
- Intuitive, inward looking, internally driven and emotional FEMININE ENERGY seeks to create co-existence and consensus while demonstrating introspection and nurturance.
- Cancer, a CARDINAL sign, is associated with new beginnings, enterprise and getting things started. Aries for spring, Cancer for summer, Libra for autumn and Capricorn for winter.

ARCHETYPE BEING REPRESENTED
- **Symbolic message** - Intuition.
- **Archetype** - The anima (*the unconscious female element of the male*) - the mysterious or unfathomable keeper of spiritual secrets. Secretive and guarded, she knows the secrets life holds but she shares them only with the wise.

SYMBOLISM INCLUDES
- **Light blue clothing** – symbolizes purity, serenity, mental clarity, and compassion.
- **Cross on front of gown** – crosses depict the union and integration between heaven and earth. Crosses can also represent the four elements, air, water, fire, and earth.
- **Headdress** - symbolically connected to the moon and moon deities; the horns on the headdress represent Taurus an earth energy which is about manifesting knowledge. They also represent the waxing and waning of the moon.
- **Solar disc (sphere) between the horns** - represents the full moon. The sphere is related to the Egyptian goddesses Nut and Hathor - these goddesses, connected to the cow, symbolize maternal fertility and nourishment, its horns link it to the crescent moon.
- **Moon phases** – a WAXING MOON symbolizes growth, manifestation, attainment and gravidity (*heavy with child both philosophical and literal*); a WANING MOON symbolizes letting go, surrender, release, quiet time, contemplation and a time of incubation; a NEW MOON symbolizes new beginnings, a fresh start, and rebirth; FULL MOON symbolizes our height of power, peak of clarity, fullness and obtainment of our desires -

the full moon can also symbolize our instincts out of control; a DARK MOON (*the stage when we don't see the moon*) symbolizes the void that which was before there was light.

- **Crescent moon at her feet** – crescent moons symbolize sacred ceremonies; on this card the crescent moon is warning of the danger of releasing higher knowledge to those unprepared to handle it; it also represents the beginning of mysterious or arcane cycles.

- **Priestess's right hand is hidden from view** - the right hand signifies rational, conscious thought; by having her right hand out of sight this type of thought is hidden.

- **Priestess's left hand is holding a half concealed book called Tora** – depicts knowledge that is being hidden; the left hand signifies hidden secrets of the consciousness; Tora means "law."

- **Seated in front of veil** (*screen behind her*) – veils symbolize hidden knowledge, secrecy and illusion – the veils connect the pillars and invite you to discover the hidden knowledge behind them which in turn is associated with the unveiling of your own mysteries.

- **Open pomegranates on the veil** – always denoting the feminine and used throughout history in almost every religion the pomegranate symbolizes human's beliefs and desires, including life, death, rebirth, eternal life, fertility, marriage, abundance and prosperity. Appearing in paintings and statues of the Virgin Mary and the baby Jesus pomegranates can denote resurrection and everlasting life. Pomegranate derives from the Latin pomum (*apple*) and grantus (*seeded*) and in Christianity pomegranates have sometimes been given the same meaning as the apple that Eve offered Adam in the Garden of Eden. Pomegranates are a Jewish ceremonial food used at New Years. Pomegranates are associated with the Greek goddess Persephone who returns to earth each year at spring time after spending her winters in Hades.

- **Palm trees on the veil** – the palm is an esoteric symbol for the fanning of the power of the pituitary gland and the third eye chakra – it signifies masculine or assertive energy, which is the ability to create through action.

- **Two pillars** – pillars denote opposites, heaven/earth, good/evil – the pillar is the bridge between heaven and earth so usually depicts a connection to a higher being and to spirituality.
- **Pillar bearing letter B** – (*on left side of card*) Boaz (*negative life force*) represents the left hand of God and means strength, it alludes to the great-grandfather of David who was the husband of Ruth. These two pillars refer to the Temple of Solomon – the priestess sitting between them refers to the gateway of their ancient wisdom.
- **Pillar bearing letter J** – (*on right side of card*) Jachin (*positive life force*) represents the right hand of God and means force, mercy, justice or love. The letter J is often translated to mean wisdom.
- **Lotus topping the two pillars** – an Egyptian symbol for the watery origins of the world and human life.
- **Body of water behind the High Priestess** – traditionally this is the source of all the waters shown in subsequent cards. Esoterically (*mysterious or obscure meanings*) water represents hidden or secret doctrines, which the High Priestess shields from the view of the uninitiated. This is a "mysterious card" hinting at the revelation and understanding of life's hidden secrets through the feminine guardian.
- **Indigo blue in background** – symbolizes intuition, focus and stability.

UPRIGHT MEANING
- About trusting yourself, using your intuition and independence.
- Something buried and hidden is gestating in the depths of your unconscious and is about to come forth, so you need to pay more attention to your inner world of dreams, imagination and intuition in order for it become known to your consciousness.
- This card tells us that universal wisdom is present in each of us we just need to tap into it.
- This card is about the realization of your hidden self or hidden aspects about you.
- About your need to trust unconscious wisdom.
- It's about listening to your inner voice by being emotionally sensitive.

- For a male it is about trusting his feminine aspects. For a female it is learning to tune into lunar cycles and listen to her intuitions.
- It's about beginning to recognize and to work with your opposite tendencies.
- This card urges us to be unafraid to work with information from both the conscious (*known*) and the unconscious.
- About the patience required to capture the unconscious meanings of things around us.
- Can indicate you are seeking clarity, this information is available to you but you must seek if from the person who possesses it.
- About following with your instincts (*gut feelings*).

REVERSED MEANING
- To others you seem withdrawn, vague, not yourself.
- Superficial knowledge or conceit influences a major decision.
- *The meaning of the card is delayed or extended into the future.*
- *An aspect of the upright meaning of the card needs to be released so you can move forward.*
- *The upright meaning is not what this is about, place another card on top of the reversed one and read it.*

PERSONAL GROWTH CONSIDERATIONS
- Representing intuition the High Priestess teaches you that your intellect is only part of the mind. She encourages you to begin reaching into the instinctual, psychic, and quintessential feminine part of yourself. You comprehend the duality of existence and the depths of your mind.

VERBAL AFFIRMATIONS
- "I am intuitive and perceptive; I trust myself."

UNIFYING THEMES
- Card 11 – Justice and Card 20 – Judgement reduce to the number two and share unifying themes with Card 2 - The High Priestess.

- Justice, Judgement and the High Priestess cards are about possessing information and how we consider it. The High Priestess protects her information, Justice considers information and Judgement provides information.

III

THE EMPRESS

Card 3 – The Empress

REPRESENTS
- fertility
- the life giving Mother reigning over nature and the rhythms of the earth

NUMBER THREE
- Ruled by Jupiter three's quality is mutable.
- Cosmic energy is embedded in threes.
- Three, a mystic number, represents Spirit.
- Threes possess celestial power – the sun stands still for three days at the solstices before resuming its motion; threes encompass past, present and future; the moon looks full for three days and disappears as dark for three days. Threes make up the trinity of mind, body and spirit.
- Group activities, movement, action, growth and development are expressed by threes.
- Sometimes expansion occurs too quickly with threes causing you to feel spread too thin or for your energies to become scattered.
- Paying attention to what you are doing results in threes vibration being cheerful, optimistic and pleasant, representing a period of happiness and benefits.

ASTROLOGICALLY
- ZODIAC SIGNS: TAURUS AND LIBRA
  RULING PLANET: VENUS
  ELEMENT: EARTH (TAURUS) AND AIR (LIBRA)
  GENDER: FEMININE (TAURUS) MASCULINE (LIBRA)
  QUALITY: FIXED (TAURUS) CARDINAL (LIBRA)

- The Empress is represented by TAURUS and LIBRA which are both ruled by VENUS, the planet of women, love, beauty, desire, pleasure, and relationships. Symbolizing the deeply feminine part of all people, male as well as female, Venus represents the capacity to reach out to others in a loving way, not just sexually or erotically.

- EARTH SIGNS (*Taurus*) are "grounded" and oriented towards what is real. Here to bring form to ideas earth signs are practical and useful, they create structure and are productive, tactile, dependable, persistent, patient and reasonable.

- FEMININE ENERGY earth signs are receptive, intuitive, inward looking, internally driven, sensitive, delicate and emotional. Seeking co-existence and consensus they are introspective and nurturing.

- Resistant to change FIXED SIGNS (*Taurus*) are faithful and preserving seeing projects through to the end. Attempting to adapt the environment to themselves they above all want to maintain things.

- Intellectual, good at conceptualizing and great communicators, AIR SIGNS (*Libra*) are intuitive, inquisitive and constantly coming up with new ideas.

- Outward looking and primarily motivated by external concerns, MASCULINE ENERGY (*air signs*) is action-oriented and protective. Seeking to dominate the outside world it can be hard, firm, logical, strong, rational, rough and loud.

- Libra, a CARDINAL SIGN, is associated with new beginnings, enterprise and getting things started. Aries for spring, Cancer for summer, Libra for autumn, and Capricorn for winter.

ARCHETYPE BEING REPRESENTED
- **Symbolic message** - Nature and fertility.
- **Archetype** - The Mother - the woman who nurtures and protects all of her creation, including humankind.

SYMBOLISM INCLUDES
- **White dress decorated with red roses** – white signifies her purity and the red roses her love.
- **Crown of twelve stars** – the headdress starts with braided green material (*a Venusians' plant called myrtle*) and is topped with stars. The braided green represents using nature. Myrtle sacred to Venus symbolizes female fertility and immortality. Stars represent hope, promise and constancy and the twelve

stars link the Empress to the heavens and to the archetypal principles reflected through astrology. In Revelations 12:1 (*the Bible*) a woman appears with twelve stars in her crown.

- **Pearl necklace** – pearls representing perfection, incorruptibility, long life and beauty are connected to the Moon due to their lustre; buried inside the oyster, pearls represent hidden knowledge and are highly feminine.

- **Right hand raised** – represents rational and logical thought and actions.

- **Holding a royal orb** – symbolizes human domination of the physical world as well as the soul of the world which the Empress holds in her hand.

- **Seated on an elaborate, lush couch** – the Empress symbolizes physical comfort and this couch being outdoors also represents her closeness to nature.

- **White heart shaped pillow with symbol** – white signifies purity, the heart shape love, the symbol represents Venus. This symbol depicts the sun and denotes the centre of being and intuition; it represents knowledge and warmth, glory and splendour.

- **Wheat** – growing at her feet represents nurturing, fertility and abundance.

- **Forest** – lots of evergreen trees and an oak tree which together signify closeness with nature. Forests symbolize mysterious places and emphasize the Empress's association with nature and feminine development.

- **Water** – feminine energy, flowing water symbolizes the Empress being wrapped in Mother Nature.

- **Waterfall** – represents the stream of consciousness and the prolific creativity of the flow of the unconscious.

- **Grain-near-a-waterfall motif** - this was a Gnostic (*Gnostic meaning knowledge refers to a mystical religious and philosophical doctrine of early Christian times. Gnostic's claimed that spiritual knowledge, rather than faith, was essential to salvation*) symbol of fertility later adopted by freemasonry to symbolize earth-sea fertility. The sea can represent the boundless mystery from whence we all originated and can be a symbol of birth. The sea is linked with the earth, which also represents the passive, feminine principle of mysterious "impregnation," of Creation.

The symbol "Mother Earth" is in contrast to the symbol "Father Spirit."

- **Orange and yellow colours** – orange is the colour of fertility, it means warmth, energy, activity, drive and confidence, it can also mean luxury – yellow stands for intellect and the sun's rays signifying faith and goodness.

UPRIGHT MEANING

- About love, wisdom and beauty.
- This card signifies a time of abundance, fertility and domestic stability.
- It represents a deep awareness of comfort with one's physical existence.
- It is about the sense of security and contentment that can be achieved through physical comfort.
- It's about possessing or exhibiting creative ability.
- It is about a time of renewal filled with fertility and productivity.
- It suggests the satisfaction that is gained from bringing something to fruition.
- This card is about motherhood and the boundless unconditional love that goes along with this.
- This card can be about facing and resolving your issues with your own sense of mothering, or even with your own mother.
- If the Empress represents you, this means you are the one who can make things work smoothly and well for others – if you can get them to listen and understand.
- Everything is being done according to your plan, be patient the harvest is about to begin.

REVERSED MEANING

- This is a call to take time for yourself; you may be worn out meeting other's needs.
- *The meaning of the card is delayed or extended into the future.*
- *An aspect of the upright meaning of the card needs to be released so you can move forward.*

- *This is not about the upright meaning, place another card on top of the reversed one and read it.*

PERSONAL GROWTH CONSIDERATIONS
- Representing the Divine Mother and nurturance the Empress symbolizes the fertile power behind all creative forms. She epitomizes the feminine archetype, one that is present in nature, abundance, harvest, love and beauty.

VERBAL AFFIRMATION
- "I am nurturing and supportive, I enjoy beauty, harmony, comfort and order."

UNIFYING THEMES
- Card 12 - The HANGED MAN and Card 21 - THE WORLD reduce to three and have unifying themes with Card 3 - THE EMPRESS.
- Three symbolizes cosmic energy. All three of these cards are about connecting with cosmic consciousness, the concept that the universe exists as an interconnected network of consciousness, with each conscious being linked to every other. When cosmic consciousness is realized in the individual this person experiences a euphoric feeling that includes a sense of wonder, a sense of being in the presence of the "One," and a sense of greater understanding of the universe as a whole.
- The Empress symbolizes "the mother archetype," she is about love and contentment and can be viewed as connected with cosmic consciousness. The Hanged Man is affected by Neptune's influences which are about the desire to connect with cosmic consciousness. The World is about cosmic order and the sense of fulfilment; it is the realization of cosmic consciousness.

IV

THE EMPEROR

Card 4 – The Emperor

REPRESENTS
- the Father
- worldly power
- provision and protection of those for whom he is responsible

NUMBER FOUR
- Ruled by Uranus, four's quality is cardinal.
- Four is the number associated to "matter."
- Four is a time to build a foundation that will support your ideas and projects.
- Hard work and self discipline are required with fours.
- A stabilizing time for creating structures and order.
- Representing manifestation of your ideas, fours represent prosperity, peace, happiness, abundance and even triumph.
- Sometimes fours represent a stage in personal development when a stalemate has been reached, a period that often seems necessary for unacknowledged emotions or dilemmas to come into consciousness so we can experience them and get on with growth or healing.

ASTROLOGICALLY
- Zodiac sign: Aries
  Ruling Planet: Mars
  Element: Fire
  Gender: Masculine
  Quality: Cardinal

- Aries ruled by the planet Mars represents the Emperor. Exemplar of all the traditional aspects we esteem in the male, Mars is related to sexual prowess, courage, energy, action, the protector and provider.

- FIRE SIGNS (*Aries*) symbolize leadership, initiative, action, energy, and new ideas. Self-starters people under this sign are leaders not followers.

- Outward looking and primarily motivated by external concerns MASCULINE ENERGY is action-oriented and protective. Seeking to dominate the outside world it can be hard, firm, logical, strong, rational, rough and loud.

- CARDINAL SIGNS are associated with new beginnings, enterprise and getting things started. Aries for spring, Cancer for summer, Libra for autumn, and Capricorn for winter.

ARCHETYPE BEING REPRESENTED

- **Symbolic message** - Masculine authority and power.

- **Archetype** - The Father and the Hero – the authoritative protector and provider who rules the known world; he brings order out of chaos so that civilization can prosper.

SYMBOLISM INCLUDES

- **Red robe with a heart on it** – red symbolizes action and passion, the heart shows compassion and love.

- **Jewelled crown** – depicts him as a King who is in complete charge, he has earned the right to wear this crown and others recognize this.

- **White hair and beard** - represents maturity, experience and wisdom.

- **Ankh in his right hand** – a tau or T-cross topped with a loop, it is the Egyptian symbol of life, the universe, and immortality. Formed from the combined male (*Osiris*) and female (*Isis*) symbols, it represents the reconciliation, or union, of opposites. Its shape links it to the symbolism of a key (*for unlocking the mysteries of life and death*). The ankh being held in his right hand represents yang, masculine energy, signifying he is a rational and logical ruler.

- **Orb in his left hand** – represents human domination of the physical world as well as the soul of the world which the Emperor holds in his hand; as this is in his left hand it represents yin, feminine energy.

- **Wearing armour** – symbolizes a readiness to fight or defend as well as possessing the necessary skills, tools, and traits to succeed.
- **Throne** - depicts royalty, he is a King and is in complete charge. The throne's shape which is box and square like epitomizes the number four as a square and thus symbolizes all the attributes of the number four.
- **Throne's grey colour** – symbolizes wisdom.
- **Ram heads on throne** – symbols of Mars, Aries and war it is also a fire sign and represents masculine energy. All combined these symbolize the Emperor's leadership and assertive powers.
- **Mountains** – symbolize challenge, vision and achievement.
- **Water at the foot of the mountains** – symbolizes feminine energy, intuitiveness, compassion and hidden knowledge.
- **Orange and yellow background** - orange means warmth, energy, activity, drive and confidence, it can also mean luxury – yellow stands for intellect and the sun's rays signifying faith and goodness – attributes of the Emperor.

UPRIGHT MEANING
- About leadership and being a visionary or pioneer.
- This card is about worldly achievements, success and stability.
- It is about any endeavour that takes energy, decisiveness, or the ability to raise the necessary resources to accomplish the task.
- It is about having or holding onto structured and logical beliefs.
- It is about using logic and linear thinking to resolve issues and make decisions (*not relying on intuition*).
- This card signifies you are willing to fight for and to defend your beliefs and family; however you must ensure you are fully aware of what you are fighting for.
- This card indicates you should trust someone in power who is an authority figure, someone who is able to look after you or at least point you in the right direction.

- This card can be about facing and resolving your issues with your sense of fathering or even with your own father.

REVERSED MEANING
- You may be in conflict with the established order – perhaps at your job or with your family, religion, or ethnic group.
- Perhaps you feel pressured to accept responsibilities you don't want or don't feel capable of handling.
- You may have recently experienced a loss of power, perhaps through down-sizing.
- You may lack the energy required to reach your goals.
- A need for more experience, drive, or improved health could be indicated.
- *The meaning of the card is delayed or extended into the future.*
- *An aspect of the upright meaning of the card needs to be released so you can move forward.*
- *This is not about the upright meaning, place another card on top of the reversed one and read it.*

PERSONAL GROWTH CONSIDERATIONS
- A male archetype the Emperor embodies the energy of leadership, strength, responsibility and organization. He is the Great Father, Divine Order, the form that materializes out of the creative forces operating in the universe. The Emperor teaches you how to direct your life, use your talents, and structure your world according to your own vision.

VERBAL AFFIRMATION
- "I value my leadership ability."

UNIFYING THEMES
- Card 13 – DEATH reduces to four and shares a common theme with Card 4 - THE EMPEROR
- The Number four is the number of balance and is distinctly feminine (2 x 2 = 4 or 2 + 2 = 4). Four also represents the square. Symbolically the square is the earth opposed to the heavens, it is geometric perfection, static, and denotes honesty and straightforwardness, morality and integrity.

- By Kabbalah astrological reckoning four is the number of the creative father-mother Jupiter.
- Balance is the unifying themes of these two cards, male and female balance each other. The Emperor is masculine energy realized and the Death card is feminine energy realized. They are opposites but required in order to create balance. The Emperor protects and traditionally maintains things; the Death card is about inescapable change and transition.

V

THE HIEROPHANT

Card 5 – The Hierophant

REPRESENTS
- adherence to conventional social behaviours, belief systems, roles, structure, and ritual
- traditional institutions and values
- conforming to fixed situations

NUMBER FIVE
- Ruled by Mercury five's quality is fixed.
- Fives always represent some type of difficulty, tension or crisis.
- Challenges often resulting in a winner or loser appear with fives.
- Fives suggest a sense of being on a roller coaster ride or being caught up in a whirlwind.
- Fluctuation, unrest and sometimes clashes create a sense of instability and can cause stress.
- Impulsive and impatient behaviours occur but resourcefulness and curiosity are also present.
- Fives indicate we have the quality of mind, but lack the maturity and knowledge to transform old ways into new patterns of being.
- We may be forced to make a choice in order to end the anxiety that is associated with fives.

ASTROLOGICALLY
- ZODIAC SIGN: TAURUS
  RULING PLANET: VENUS
  ELEMENT: EARTH
  GENDER: FEMININE
  QUALITY: FIXED

- The Hierophant is related to TAURUS which is ruled by VENUS. Venus symbolizes attraction, unity, beauty, balance, valuation and assets. It represents that rare and elusive harmony and radiance that is true beauty. Venus indicates refinement, grace, delicacy, sensitivity, charm and the aesthetic sense. Venus rules the love of nature and pleasure, luck and wealth.
- Taurus (EARTH ENERGY) is about the manifestation of knowledge, ideas and projects. Associated with constancy, patience, accumulating and preserving it relates to both material items and to institutions that have stood the test of time.
- Representing FEMININE ENERGY, earth signs are receptive, intuitive, inward looking, internally driven, sensitive, delicate and emotional. Seeking to create co-existence and consensus they are introspective and nurturing.
- Taurus, a FIXED SIGN, represents people resistant to change who are faithful and persevering, seeing projects through to the end. Attempting to adapt the environment to themselves they above all want to maintain things.

ARCHETYPE BEING REPRESENTED
- **Symbolic message** - Tradition and Spiritual Teacher.
- **Archetype** - Spiritual Leader – a traditional authority and influence. He's the head of a hierarchy determined to maintain his religious and cultural traditions.

SYMBOLISM INCLUDES
- **Red garment with crosses down the front** – denotes a religious garment, red depicts passion and energy, and the crosses depict the union between heaven and earth and are about integration they can also represent the four elements, air, water, fire and earth.
- **Blue clothing under the red garment** - symbolizes purity, serenity, mental clarity and compassion.
- **White on clothing and parts of his head dress** - symbolizes purity.
- **Crown with three levels** – symbolizes his ruler-ship over the three worlds of body, mind and spirit.

- **Right hand** – held in a position that symbolizes a blessing; right signifies conscious thought so he is depicting known knowledge not concealed or esoteric information.

- **Left hand** – holding a sceptre which symbolizes three worlds, the physical, astral (*that of the heavens*), and etheric (*the substance that is believed to join and flow through all things*).

- **Throne** – symbolizes an authority figure, someone who possesses power and the resources to use it.

- **Throne has a circle with a dot in the middle** - this is an alchemical symbol that represents the end of the quest and thus perfection. (*Alchemy, studied and practiced in the middle ages, sought to find a magical or mysterious power or process of transforming one thing into another*).

- **Pillars** – indicate a connection between heaven and earth (*spirituality*) and both being white they symbolize pureness. Two pillars are always symbolic of duality and in terms of religion can represent matter and spirit.

- **Decoration near top of pillars** – its shape is thought to represent an acorn or pinecone. Acorns symbolizing fertility, bountifulness and spiritual growth are sacred to the god Thor, ruler of fire and fertility. When carried on a person acorns are believed to preserve youthfulness. As the seed of the oak tree acorns symbolize strength and resiliency. Christian symbolism links the oak to Christ. The acorn like decoration on this card is also said to resemble a woman's uterus, suggesting that the Hierophant protects the feminine secrets of the High Priestess.

- **Two crossed keys** – symbolize intellect and intuition and the need to use them in tandem.

- **Acolytes** – the Hierophant is a teacher and he is providing instruction to two initiates (*the acolytes*).

- **Two acolytes** – they represent a twin motive which indicates information that is not yet fully conscious but about to emerge from the unconscious. Two symbols together represent an emerging awareness in our spiritual journey.

- **Roses and lilies motif on acolyte's garments** – the red roses symbolize the occult way (*hidden information only available to initiates*) and the lilies symbolize the mystic way. (*Mystic refers to the pursuit of conscious awareness of God through direct* *experience and a living realization over the mere acceptance of doctrine. Mysticism is about practice over theory and often includes breathing exercises, prayer, contemplation, meditation, chanting and other activities to heighten spiritual awareness).*

- **Vertical crosses on the acolyte's garments** - these garments worn by the Golden Dawn initiates are also worn in freemason rituals and indicate completion of the three basic initiations. These initiations include 1. Entered apprentice – the degree of an initiate which makes one a freemason, 2. Fellow craft – an intermediate degree involved with learning, and 3. Master mason the third degree, a necessity for participation in most aspects of masonry.

- **Checkerboard pattern on parts of the floor** – symbolizes duality, positive/negative, good/evil, light/darkness, or spirit/matter. Together the blacks and whites represent the beginnings and endings of a stage or a process. This also suggests life cycles.

- **Hierophant** – the name of the high priest of the Greek Elusian mysteries, an ancient cult originating about eighteen hundred (1800 BC) that held initiation ceremonies each year in Eleusis. This cult involved a celebration of the ancient Greek mythology figures of Zeus, Demeter, and Persephone. Waite's choice of this term may be a hint that he meant this card to depict the notion of "the hidden way," as these initiations were secret in nature. Hierophant was the name of a Golden Dawn official in initiation ceremonies so the use of this term may also indicate initiation into something.

- **Hierophant and the Emperor** – the Emperor represents the worldly father. The Hierophant represents the spiritual father and the religious process whereby we create a certain type of order so that we may cope with the unfathomable.

UPRIGHT MEANING
- About teaching, learning, family and community.
- About examining traditional thought whether it is religious or otherwise.
- About situations or actions that require you to seek counsel from a traditional establishment or setting.

- It could be a time to consider the problems or benefits related to organized religion or other traditional organizations with which you are involved.
- It is a time when you consider whether you are being true to your spiritual self.
- This card speaks to tradition and commitment so anything associated to that especially with a religious bent, perhaps a marriage or a baptism.
- It may mean you are to be initiated into something.
- Expect help to come from traditional means.
- Perhaps you need to seek counsel on a matter.
- A traditional factor is active in your life, whether it is a religion, a philosophy, a social organization, or another authoritative group. You feel a great deal of loyalty to this tradition or group and find it supportive. You choose to live in accordance with its beliefs. You may aspire to be a leader within the group or you may have a close relationship with someone who is a leader within the group.

REVERSED MEANING
- You may wish to overthrow an old tradition – religious, ideological, intellectual, or cultural – that you feel is suffocating you or simply no longer serves your needs.
- You want to live by whatever philosophy or belief structure resonates with your true nature.
- You want to direct your interests and life even if this puts you in direct conflict with some established traditions.
- Perhaps your faith is being challenged in some way and you must re-evaluate ideologies you previously took for granted.
- You want to be accountable to yourself alone.
- *The meaning of the card is delayed or extended into the future.*
- *An aspect of the upright meaning of the card needs to be released so you can move forward.*
- *This is not about the upright meaning, place another card on top of the reversed one and read it.*

PERSONAL GROWTH CONSIDERATIONS

- Representing social order, hierarchy, authority, rules, structure, belief systems and values the Hierophant oversees both spiritual and cultural laws. The Hierophant teaches you to accept limits as necessary for your growth and you come to understand your place in the greater whole, the society in which you live and the universe whose laws govern earthly existence.

VERBAL AFFIRMATION

- "I honour what is sacred within me; I am inspired by learning and teaching situations."

UNIFYING THEMES

- Card 14 – TEMPERANCE when reduced to five shares a common theme with Card 5 - THE HIEROPHANT.
- Number five represents intelligent energy and possesses masculine qualities.
- The unifying theme between the Temperance card and the Hierophant is one of religious and intellectual institutions.

VI

THE LOVERS

Card 6 – The Lovers

REPRESENTS
- relationships, personal beliefs, values, commitment, union of opposites, and wise decisions
- harmony between one's inner and outer life
- harmony achieved through the presence of another individual

NUMBER SIX
- Ruled by Venus six's quality is mutable.
- Sixes are always favourable.
- Sixes vibration is cooperative.
- Six's ability to transcend difficulties creates stability and provides a sense of peace and quiet after the storm.
- Six is a time of balance and respite that creates a base and a pivot for new experiences.
- Six, an important ceremonial number, refers to Spirit's connection to life in all directions (*north, south, east and west, above and below*).
- Because three (3) is a cosmic number its attributes are amplified by six (6).

ASTROLOGICALLY
- ZODIAC SIGN: GEMINI
  RULING PLANET: MERCURY
  ELEMENT: AIR
  GENDER: MASCULINE
  QUALITY: MUTABLE

- The Lovers card represented by GEMINI, symbolizes the dualistic character of humanity (*yin/yang, male/female etc*). Ruled by MERCURY, Gemini represents communication, intellect, reasoning power and discernment. Mercury rules speaking, language, mathematics and logic.

- Intellectual and good at conceptualizing AIR SIGNS are great communicators, intuitive, inquisitive and constantly come up with new ideas.
- Outward looking and primarily motivated by external concerns MASCULINE ENERGY is action-oriented and protective. Seeking to dominate the outside world it is hard, firm, logical, strong, rational, rough and loud.
- Through their versatility MUTABLE PEOPLE see both sides of a situation and can adapt to most circumstances. Rather than shape their environment they change their attitude and adjust to it. Through accepting change mutable sign people thereby end what was.

ARCHETYPE BEING REPRESENTED

- **Symbolic message** - Love and union of opposites.
- **Archetype** - The Soul or both anima and animus (*the anima is the female element of the male; the animus is the masculine element of the female*) embodies the twin principles of opposition and attraction. This card signifies a choice to be made between two equally strong desires.

SYMBOLISM INCLUDES

- **An angel** - symbolizes a messenger of God.
- **Angel's arms outstretched** - represents a blessing from Spirit.
- **Violet robe of the angel** - symbolizes truth and healing.
- **Red wings and flaming hair of angel** – symbolizes the element of fire, which represents strength, will, courage, sensuality, desire and passion.
- **Sun** - symbolizes absolute cosmic power, clarity, vitality, optimism, wisdom, intuition, knowledge, warmth and glory.
- **Cloud** – represents spirituality.
- **Tree of Life** - symbolizes wisdom.
- **Twelve triple flames on the Tree of Life behind the man** - symbolize the twelve signs of the zodiac and the three qualities (*cardinal, fixed and mutable*) into which each zodiac sign is divided. Cardinal signs include Aries, Cancer, Libra and Capricorn, fixed signs include Taurus, Leo, Scorpio and

Aquarius and mutable signs include Gemini, Virgo, Sagittarius and Pisces.

- **Tree of Knowledge of good and evil behind the woman** – links the woman to Adam and Eve and the time in paradise before the fall (*when Eve ate the apple and offered it to Adam who then also ate it*). Psychologists relate this to our time in the womb, prior to our fall (*birth*) into mortality and consciousness.
- **Serpent twisted on the tree** - represents good and can be associated with healing and rebirth.
- **Mountain** – symbolizes wisdom, eternity, stability, and a connection to spirituality.
- **Naked man and woman** – they symbolize the state of innocence, unconcealed reality and pure truth; masculine (*protection and logicalness*) trying to join with female energy (*intuitiveness and secrecy*). The man looks to the woman and the woman looks up, she realizes that to be whole one must incorporate spirituality into oneself.
- **Green grass** –symbolizes earth energy, which represents a high possibility for the manifestation of our ideas or projects.

UPRIGHT MEANING
- About relationships and the union of opposites.
- About life cycles of attraction and repulsion and the choices we make associated with these.
- It is about a time when you are required to make a wise decision, often regarding love.
- It is a time to consider the values and or implications that are reflected in the choices you make.
- About personally significant situations requiring a partner or another person to join with you. Making decisions and considering choices is required so cooperation and commitment is necessary for things to work out.
- About considering the opportunities available to you in order to make the correct choice between two equally worthy goals.
- Implicit in this card is the expectation of a happy outcome following the struggles you experience while making choices.

- About partnerships or marriages where harmony is created within each individual's inner and outer lives.
- About the insight, mutual respect, commitment, common goals and ongoing honest communication required for harmonious relationships to exist.

REVERSED MEANING
- May indicate you are trying to force cooperation among basically incompatible elements.
- *The meaning of the card is delayed or extended into the future.*
- *An aspect of the upright meaning of the card needs to be released so you can move forward.*
- *This is not about the upright meaning, place another card on top of the reversed one and read it.*

PERSONAL GROWTH CONSIDERATIONS
- Representing the merger of male and female energies the Lover's card reveals the urge to find a partner and unite with another human being. Symbolized as well is harmony between one's inner and outer life. The Lover's teach us to blend emotions and intellect in order for us to become whole.

VERBAL AFFIRMATION
- "I am loving and caring and relate well with others."

UNIFYING THEMES
- Card 15 – THE DEVIL when reduced is six and shares a common theme with Card 6 - THE LOVERS.
- Six represents a double triangle or two threes (3 + 3). The usual symbol is the interlaced triangle which creates the Star of David and signifies unity, integration and manifestation.
- The union of male and female and the need to make choices is the unifying theme between these two cards. Similar as well is the scene depicted, an angel above the male and female on the Lover's card and the devil above the male and female on the Devil card.

VII

THE CHARIOT

Card 7 – The Chariot

REPRESENTS
- resolving opposing forces
- asserting yourself
- using your will
- achieving victory
- mastering your emotions

NUMBER SEVEN
- Ruled by Neptune seven's quality is cardinal.
- Sevens are sacred numbers made up of three, the number of Spirit and cosmic energy and four the number of matter, that which is necessary for the manifestation of ideas or projects.
- Relating to the development of the soul, sevens deal with wisdom, completeness and perfection.
- Indicating a need to deal with your inner life, seven is a time of introspection and soul searching that requires solitude.
- A reflective time, seven indicates a period when you will find it necessary to seriously consider how and why specific events occur.
- Sevens represent a turning point as they begin a new cycle of threes. One, two and three were followed by four, five and six, and now we have seven, eight and nine.
- Sevens bring about a new restlessness possibly indicating a breakthrough in awareness which causes us to re-evaluate and willingly try new things, which may result in a changed understanding or perspective.

ASTROLOGICALLY
- ZODIAC SIGN: CANCER
  RULING PLANET: THE MOON
  ELEMENT: WATER
  GENDER: FEMININE

QUALITY: CARDINAL

- The Chariot is related to CANCER, which symbolizes the sheer tenacity of the life force. The Crab is known to hold on; if it has something in its claw the only way to get it loose is to cut off the claw. Cancer is ruled by the MOON which represents response, fluctuation, sensitivity and sympathy. Ruling our feelings, customs, habits and moods, the moon's position is an indicator of rapidly changing phases of behaviour and personality. The Moon rules the feminine element in both women and men.

- Emotional, intuitive and attuned to subtle vibrations WATER SIGN people are capable of great compassion and sensitivity and are often quick to sum up others at a first meeting.

- FEMININE ENERGY is intuitive, inward looking, internally driven, sensitive, and emotional. Seeking to create co-existence and consensus it is introspective and nurturing.

- CARDINAL signs represent new beginnings, enterprise and getting things started. People born under this sign are instigators and leaders. Aries for spring, Cancer for summer, Libra for autumn and Capricorn for winter.

ARCHETYPE BEING REPRESENTED

- **Symbolic message** - Hard work and victory.
- **Archetype** - The Warrior, an agent for forward motion and change. Represents being in command of your physical and emotional drives, even when they seem to oppose each other.

SYMBOLISM INCLUDES

- **Man dressed in armour** – denoting a readiness for battle he possesses the necessary skills and tools to succeed.
- **Crescent moons on man's shoulders** – symbolizes a hesitancy to reveal more than can be coped with; or unconscious habits that need to be changed.
- **Man's belt** – displaying planetary and alchemical symbols they represent his preparedness for a journey of enhanced consciousness and personal development.
- **Six sided star around his neck** - called the Star of David, it symbolizes unity, integration and manifestation.

- **Crown** - symbolizes authority, also denotes this man has the skills and abilities needed to wear the crown and the respect and recognition of other's that he is deserving of wearing it.

- **Eight sided star on crown** - symbolizes the great mother goddess linked to creativity and fertility.

- **Laurel wreath on his head** – symbolizes his victorious spirit; he is able to claim victory and success via his intellect.

- **Indigo blue canopy covered in stars** – symbolizes mysticism and wisdom, they represent cycles, the passage of time, a map of consciousness or the combination of personality traits in general.

- **Winged solar disc** – (*Egyptian*) it represents heavenly power, sometimes heavenly healing power. This disc was taken into battle by the falcon-headed son-god, Horus of Edifu, to slay Seth, the god of evil.

- **Yoni** – the Sanskirt symbol on the shield representing the womb, it is typically associated with the lingam (*phallic symbol*) and shown as a circle or sometimes as a pool of water. Together the two constitute the fundamental principle of duality, the feminine and the masculine as in the yin-yang symbol. The lingam expresses the notion of continuous fertilization.

- **Two sphinx** – sphinx symbolize arcane wisdom. In mythology the sphinx would ask traveler's a three part question and if they got it wrong she would strangle them. The sphinx has also been related to the Oedipus myth. These two sphinx also represent twin motives (*two*) symbolizing information that is not yet fully conscious but about to emerge from the unconscious creating an awareness within us which is necessary in our spiritual journey.

- **Black and white sphinx** - symbolizing complete opposites they represent the competing forces within each individual.

- **Standing in front of water** – symbolizes feminine energy, emotional aspects of life, intuition, and hidden knowledge.

- **Golden pillars in the water** – the gold colour symbolizes wealth, abundance, immortality and is an amulet for the wounded. The pillars are related to structure and upholding, supporting or the encompassing of some concept.

- **Castles in the background** – symbolize stability, warmth, and the possession of adequate resources.

- **Yellow background** – represents enthusiasm, optimism, energy, and opportunity.
- **Green grass** - this is an earth energy which symbolizes manifestation of one's ideas or projects.

UPRIGHT MEANING
- About the hard work involved in change and transformation.
- About opposing forces and your internal strengths to control these so you can make progress towards a goal.
- It is about any situation which requires your inner skill to control opposing ideas, feelings or thoughts, enough so that progress is being made.
- You are uniting opposing energies to stay on track.
- This card indicates that success is assured; you are up to the task and very much engaged even though things are moving quicker than average.
- It's about a great deal of focus, willpower and a sense that you are achieving your goal despite lots of internal energy to do so.

REVERSED MEANING
- It feels as though you are being pulled in two directions at once and you are stressed out with the pressure.
- It is time for inner reflection and to process the feelings of transition that are occurring within you.
- *The meaning of the card is delayed or extended into the future.*
- *An aspect of the upright meaning of the card needs to be released so you can move forward.*
- *This is not about the upright meaning, place another card on top of the reversed one and read it.*

PERSONAL GROWTH CONSIDERATIONS
- Representing victory and vision through harnessing our opposing energies, mastering our emotions, and directing our thoughts, the Chariot teaches us we can make progress and achieve our purpose. From the Chariot card we also learn that mastery is accomplished through aligning personal will with Divine Will.

VERBAL AFFIRMATION

- "I focus my energies to attain my goals."

UNIFYING THEMES

- Card 16 - THE TOWER when reduced to seven shares a common theme with Card 7 - THE CHARIOT.
- Number seven is 4 + 3, which means basis (*earth*) plus creation (*cosmos*).
- Energy is the theme that unifies these two cards. The Chariot teaches us to harness our energy and align it with divine will. The Tower teaches us about the energy of release, how to let things go or cease to be so new thoughts and behaviours can begin.

STRENGTH

Card 8 – Strength

REPRESENTS
- *(Strength - one of the four cardinal virtues, the others being Prudence, Justice and Temperance).*
- strength represents courage, fortitude, forbearance, endurance and the ability to confront fear and uncertainty, or intimidation
- inner courage
- spiritual connection to a higher power
- expressing compassion
- achieving self control
- applying love and consideration when handling situations

NUMBER EIGHT
- Ruled by Saturn eight's quality is fixed.
- Eight, the sign of infinity represents death and regeneration.
- The number of cosmic balance, eight's beneficial qualities are rarely diluted, they represent two times greater the benefits of four, the number of manifestation.
- Placed on its side eight becomes the lemniscate, the symbol of infinity representing the eternal spiralling movement of the heavens.
- The hour glass shape of eight symbolizes the passage of time and cycles by representing the four seasons the two solstices and two equinoxes.
- Eights vibration is linked with abundance, material prosperity, worldly power, influence, leadership, authority, possibility, options and potential.

ASTROLOGICALLY
- Zodiac sign: Leo
  Ruling Planet: the Sun
  Element: Fire

Gender: Masculine
Quality: Fixed

- Leo representing the card Strength symbolizes the personal ego with strong needs for self-expression and admiration. Ruled by the Sun Leo's are natural leaders who are not easily discouraged and who pursue goals with great determination. Symbol of strength, vigour, ardour, generosity and the ability to function as a mature individual the Sun represents creative force. The Sun indicates the complete potential of every human being.
- A fire sign, Leo displays vital energy, action, and creative talent.
- Outward looking and primarily motivated by external concerns, masculine energy is action-oriented and protective. Seeking to dominate the outside world it can be hard, firm, logical, strong, rational, rough and loud.
- Leo, a fixed sign, represents faithful and preserving people who see projects through to the end. Resistant to change people under this sign attempt to adapt the environment to themselves and above all they want to maintain things.

ARCHETYPE BEING REPRESENTED
- **Symbolic message** - Determination.
- **Archetype** - Endurance – with the heart of a lion she is able through her own inner strength to patiently control a force that could otherwise "eat her alive."

SYMBOLISM INCLUDES
- **White dress** – represents purity.
- **Lemniscate (*infinity sign*) above her head** – embedded with the beneficial qualities of the number eight it represents a strong spiritual connection.
- **Wreath like flowers on head dress and around her waist** - symbolize victory plus a connection to nature and instinctual life.
- **Woman's right hand closing lion's mouth** – representing will power and demonstrating how love can be stronger than physical power it indicates no struggle. Right signifies

conscious awareness of facing the future. Symbolically it illustrates the power of the female principle.

- **Woman's left hand petting the lion** – the left signifies the unconscious, the higher self and the place of intuition or knowing without reason.
- **Lion** – represents a savage beast, symbolizing the fiery life-force or energy that is the basis of all our actions.
- **Lion is licking the woman's hand** – the strength depicted here is one of trust and love. In return for the maiden's instinctual love the lion responds with a lick rather than an attack.
- **Woman and lion's interaction** – represents Strength, one of the four cardinal virtues, the others being Prudence better understood as Wisdom (*The Hermit card*), Justice and Temperance. The term "cardinal" comes from the Latin *cardo* or hinge; cardinal also means foundational and pivotal so all other morals spring from these four. Found in different forms and terms within the Old Testament of the Bible they are also mentioned by Socrates (469 – 399 BC). Plato is believed to be the first to enumerate the system. Most notably St. Ambrose, St. Augustine, and later St. Thomas Aquinas, further referred, supported and expounded upon these within Christianity helping to make these four virtues cornerstones of Western Philosophy. (*Strength represents courage, fortitude, forbearance, endurance and the ability to confront fear and uncertainty, or intimidation*). (*Prudence represents wisdom and therefore the ability to judge between actions especially regarding appropriate actions at a given time*). (*Temperance represents restraint, practising self-control, abstention and moderation*). (*Justice represents proper moderation between self-interest and the rights and needs of others*).
- **Mountain** – symbolizes wisdom, connection to higher power, stability and eternity.
- **Lots of yellow** – indicates the sun's energy – intellect, faith, goodness, cosmic power, knowledge and warmth, glory and splendour.
- **Green trees and grass** – symbolizes earth energy - the manifestation of one's ideas or projects.

UPRIGHT MEANING

- About passion, lustre, brilliance, radiance and luminosity.
- About balance and integration between instinct, passion, and intellect.
- It is about mastery, especially self-mastery which often requires personal strength and courage to achieve.
- It is about a time to use gentle force through your inner fortitude.
- It's about your ability to use your spiritual inner strength to navigate through trying times or upsetting situations.
- It's about your ability to control urges without repressing them.
- This card is about both inner courage and self discipline.
- It's about overcoming obstacles through spiritual strength and force of will.
- This card is about your victory over overwhelming odds.
- This card can represent facing a test of your own determination and will; if this is the case you can win if you persevere.

REVERSED MEANING

- Signifies someone or a situation in which there is an abuse of power occurring.
- Discord and disharmony.
- Giving into basic harsh instincts.
- *The meaning of the card is delayed or extended into the future.*
- *An aspect of the upright meaning of the card needs to be released so you can move forward.*
- *This is not about the upright meaning, place another card on top of the reversed one and read it.*

PERSONAL GROWTH CONSIDERATIONS

- Representing inner courage and a spiritual connection to a higher power the Strength card symbolizes self control through applying love and consideration when handling situations. We learn to overcome our self-absorption and impulsive animal instincts through using patience, gentleness, and compassion, and in so doing ultimately live in a place of faith, not fear.

VERBAL AFFIRMATION
- "I possess inner courage and compassion."

UNIFYING THEMES
- Card 17 – THE STAR reduces to eight and shares qualities with Card 8 - STRENGTH.
- 8 is 4 + 4. Four symbolizing earth represents manifestation. Eight is four amplified or twice as much, so the manifestations of our ideas or projects are fully realized with eight. In the astrological Kabbalistic (*Jewish mysticism*) scheme eight stands for intelligence.
- Both the Star and Strength cards represent goodness realized through demonstrating intellect, faith, goodness, cosmic power, knowledge and warmth, glory and splendour.

IX

THE HERMIT

Card 9 – The Hermit

REPRESENTS

- *(Prudence - one of the four cardinal virtues, the others being Strength, Justice and Temperance).*
- prudence represents wisdom and therefore the ability to judge between actions especially regarding appropriate actions at a given time
- being introspective
- seeking greater understanding
- accepting and offering wise counsel
- focusing on the inner world
- times of quiet and solitude

NUMBER NINE

- Ruled by Mars nine's quality is mutable.
- Nine's vibrations let you see beyond the physical into the limitlessness of the universe.
- Nine is the number of fulfillment, it triples the effect of three the number of cosmic power.
- Representing the end of a cycle nine indicates it is time to tie up loose ends.
- Generally nine depicts completion, wholeness and the sense of satisfaction that comes from reaching a hard worked for goal.
- Sometimes nine can demonstrate regrets as it's the end of a cycle and things may not have gone well, when this is the case you may experience anxiety about not knowing what to expect next.

ASTROLOGICALLY

- ZODIAC SIGN: VIRGO
  RULING PLANET: MERCURY
  ELEMENT: EARTH

GENDER: FEMININE
QUALITY: MUTABLE

- The Hermit is related to VIRGO, the sign symbolizing the quest for perfection through blending ideals with experience. Ruled by MERCURY Virgo is able to sort information and analyze it. Associated with intellect, reasoning power and discernment Mercury as the planet of the mind and the power of communication rules speech, language, mathematics and logic.
- Grounded and oriented towards what is real EARTH SIGNS bring form to ideas. Practical and creating structures, they are useful, productive, tactile and dependable while demonstrating persistence, patience and reasonableness.
- Receptive and intuitive FEMININE ENERGY is inward looking, internally driven, sensitive, delicate, and emotional, seeking to create co-existence and consensus it remains introspective and nurturing.
- Seeing both sides of a situation versatile MUTABLE SIGN people can adjust to almost any circumstance. Rather than shape their environment they change their attitude and adapt to it. By accepting change mutable sign people thereby end what was.

ARCHETYPE BEING REPRESENTED
- **Symbolic message** - Wisdom.
- **Archetype** - Wise Old Man – a recluse, far removed from the hustle and bustle of everyday life, he reflects on spiritual concerns and carries the light of wisdom as a beacon for others to follow.

SYMBOLISM INCLUDES
- **Bearded man** – symbolizes maturity and knowledge.
- **Hooded grey cloak** - grey depicts wisdom – hoods and cloaks can be symbolic of spirituality and denote that which is unknown.
- **Bowed head** – he is ready to receive higher spiritual impressions.
- **Holding a staff** – related to all the magic wands of mythology as in Merlin's wand and to Moses' powerful staff as well as to

the healing rod of Asclepius. The rod of Asclepius represents the constellation Ophiuchus, considered by some to be thirteenth sign of the sidereal zodiac (*see Astrology section*). Hippocrates worshipped Asclepius.

- **The Hermit's staff** - holding his staff the Hermit implies that he has acquired special knowledge and training. His staff, an emblem of elevated ability and spiritual clarity, is indirectly a statement of his power.

- **Closed eyes** - this denotes he is turning inward.

- **In Jungian terms** - the Hermit represents the "wise old man archetype," considered to represent the inner spirit and the notion that spiritual wisdom takes experience and effort and does not come about early. The Hermit also represents the energy required to bring unconscious knowledge to awareness through dreams and other experiences.

- **A recluse** – the Hermit represents the contemplative silence that occurs before creation. He is the union of personal consciousness and cosmic will.

- **Lantern** – symbolizes the archetype of the light-bearer who is the way-shower, for developing spirituality and for opening to unconscious knowledge. It represents sharing information and shedding light (*understanding*) onto questions.

- **Lantern held level with the heart chakra** – the heart chakra mediates between the body and the spirit and its energy allows us to accept our place as part of a divine plan. It is the chakra of compassion and forgiveness making the Hermit card one of inner or self-healing.

- **Six-pointed star shining out of the lantern** - called the Star of David or the Seal of Solomon this star is comprised of interlaced equilateral triangles, one with its point facing upward and one that is inverted. It represents the harmonic rhythm of active and passive, masculine and feminine as well as spirit and earthly principles. It also represents the union of male and female and of earth and sky, integration and manifestation. As a hexagram the six-pointed star can represent dominion over the laws of the greater world.

- **Indigo blue background** – symbolizes intuition, focus and stability.

- **Snow capped mountain top** – symbolizes the place where wisdom is and where it can be acquired.

UPRIGHT MEANING
- About completion, contemplation and reflection.
- About a time for soul-searching (*introspection*) for the purpose of seeking inner or higher knowledge.
- It is about the pursuit of achieving wisdom.
- It is about searching for truth, generally regarding your inner spiritual knowledge.
- It is about the perceptiveness that you gain from a time of solitude and detachment.
- It is about taking time to delve into the unconscious and learn its ways and in so doing shed light upon the shadow aspects of yourself.
- This card is suggesting you may need to withdraw by getting away on your own for awhile so you can gain a new perspective.
- Can represent a shift in perspective for you, an acknowledging and deep acceptance that life does not remain the same and that youth does not last forever.
- You may need to seek out assistance from a wise person, possibly a teacher, a psychologist, or a minister.
- Can indicate that a grandfatherly figure, an ancestor, or someone from the spirit world is looking out for you right now.
- Can indicate it is a time to hide out, retreat and lie low; inaction may be the best thing right now.

REVERSED MEANING
- Refusing to see available options by burying your head in the sand.
- You have little faith and feel spiritually isolated or unaware of the spiritual side of life.
- Misguided ideals.
- *The meaning of the card is delayed or extended into the future.*
- *An aspect of the upright meaning of the card needs to be released so you can move forward.*

- *This is not about the upright meaning, place another card on top of the reversed one and read it.*

PERSONAL GROWTH CONSIDERATIONS
- Representing your inner essence the Hermit teaches us that the quest for truth and greater understanding often leads to solitude. By retreating from the activity and distractions of the world you can turn inward and explore personal values and morals. Once you identify these you can begin behaving in a manner that reflects them and in so doing raise your spiritual awareness and set positive examples for others to follow.

VERBAL AFFIRMATION
- "I value solitude and contemplating what is meaningful and significant."

UNIFYING THEMES
- Card 18 - THE MOON reduces to nine and shares similar aspects to Card 9 - THE HERMIT.
- 9 is 3 x 3, energy by energy multiplied, hence power, often reckoned magical, identified with witchcraft and above all with the moon. Nine usually represents completion of creation, the last number as ten reduces to one.
- Demonstrating determined feminine energy at work the Moon card and the Hermit deal with inner thoughts, intuitions and deeper knowledge. The night skies shown in both cards indicate introspection and an absence of complete information.

X

WHEEL OF FORTUNE

Card 10 – The Wheel of Fortune

REPRESENTS
- destiny
- changes
- using what chance offers
- finding opportunities
- uncovering patterns and cycles
- having no control over some of life's circumstances

NUMBER TEN
- Ten reduces to number 1. (1+0=1)
- Ruled by the Sun one's quality is cardinal.
- One's energy is individual, solitary and self-contained.
- Representing the beginning of form number one relates to the active principle of creation.
- The mystic centre core of mysterious, inscrutable, symbolic, secretive and hidden knowing is represented by one.
- One represents self-development, creativity, action, progress, a new chance, and rebirth.

ASTROLOGICALLY
- Zodiac sign: Sagittarius
  Ruling Planet: Jupiter
  Element: Fire
  Gender: Masculine
  Quality: Mutable

- Sagittarius ruled by the planet Jupiter represents the Wheel of Fortune card. Jupiter symbolizes expansion, optimism, foresight and fortune. Ruling good luck and good cheer, health, wealth, happiness, success and joy Jupiter is the symbol of opportunity and is associated with gambling and games of chance. Jupiter rules acting, publishing, philosophy, religion, sports and travel.

- A FIRE SIGN, Sagittarius, displays vital energy, action, and creative talent.
- MASCULINE ENERGY fire signs are outward looking, primarily motivated by external concerns action-oriented and protective. Seeking to dominate the outside world this energy can be hard, firm, logical, strong, rational, rough and loud.
- Adaptable by nature MUTABLE SIGN people see both sides of a situation and can adapt to almost any circumstance. Rather than shape their environment these versatile people change their attitude and adjust to it. By accepting change mutable sign people end what was.

ARCHETYPE BEING REPRESENTED

- **Symbolic message** - Change, moving in circles.
- **Archetype** - Fate and Destiny – the spinning wheel of deeds and consequences demonstrating that nothing is certain but change itself.

SYMBOLISM INCLUDES

- **Large orange disc with directions on it** – the round shape and colour denote movement and energy, enthusiasm, optimism, promise and opportunity.
- **Eight spokes on the disc wheel** – symbolize the passage of time and cycles; the four seasons plus the two equinoxes and two solstices.
- **Symbol under the T on the inner wheel** – this is the alchemical symbol for mercury. Mercury represents consciousness and the source of all opposites. (*Mercury was one of two primal alchemical essences, the other being sulphur, salt was later added as a third reactive element. The female mercurial essence symbolized the fluid principle or force, the changeability of metals, and the personality and power of transmission*).
- **Triangular shaped symbol next to letter A on the inner circle of the wheel** – this is the alchemical symbol for sulphur. Sulphur refers to passion, activity, will, motivation and to the soul.

- **Two wavy lines above the letter R on the inner circle of the wheel** – the sign for the element of water it represents dissolution (*breaking up or ending of an association of any kind*), a fundamental process of alchemy.
- **Symbol to the right of the letter O on the inner circle of the wheel** - the alchemical symbol for salt it reflects the ignorance and inertia that leads to human suffering. (*Salt, as a preservative of food, has many cultural meanings and was often used in religious and purification rituals. Corresponding to the body, "alchemical salt" was the catalyst that typically worked in tandem with alchemical sulphur, the soul. It was at the centre of Hermetic mysticism, as the "secret central fire," the "salt of wisdom"*).
- **Four symbols on the outer circle between the T A R and O** – these are the tetragrammaton letters, they represent the fourfold division of the divine name (*God*) and the universal creative process, expressed in the four Hebrew letters Yod, Heh, Vav, and Heh (*Heh appears twice*). In Jewish tradition the name can be spelled YHVH but not pronounced, substituting the word Adonai (*Lord*). As a condensation of the three forms of the verb "to be" it signifies the timeless, unknowable source and context of all being.
- **Letters T A R O** – these can be interpreted as ROTA which means wheel in Latin.
- **Letters TARO interspersed with the Hebrew letters** – by interspersing the Hebrew letters with TARO this is showing that spiritual reality is unchanging, though the wheel (*ROTA*) of your personal life keeps turning.
- **Egyptian jackal-headed man floating in space holding the disc** – known for his keen eyesight, he symbolizes a visionary, fate and destiny.
- **Blue sphinx on top of disc** – she represents equilibrium and stability amidst movement. Alluding to the mystery of all things and therefore to the collective unconscious the sphinx is guardian and holder of secrets. This sphinx is holding a sword so that would imply she is actively guarding these secrets.
- **Snake** - the snake on this card is considered to be Typhon, the child of Hera's rage (*some say of Gaia or Mother Earth*). In Greek mythology Hera was Zeus's wife and her chief function was as the goddess of women and marriage. In mythology her son, Typhon, is considered the foe of Spirit. He is the power of

"aberrant instinct," which rejects sublimation (*the highest stage or purest form of things*) and surrenders to earthly drives.

- **Winged icons in all four corners holding books** – these icons represent all the wisdom of the ages. They are also the four fixed signs of the Zodiac. The human represents Aquarius (*air sign*), the bull represents Taurus (*earth sign*), the lion represents Leo (*fire sign*) and the eagle represents Scorpio (*water sign*). These four figures appear in the Bible in Revelations 4:7. These same four icons appear on The World card but without the wings.

- **Wings on the icons** – the icons all bear wings and wings represent motion and action – the Wheel of Fortune is about motion, the ball has started rolling.

- **Blue sky** – place where the gods live, eternity and order in the universe. This is also symbolic of positive outcomes.

- **Clouds** – represent loftiness, closeness to heaven and signify spirituality.

UPRIGHT MEANING

- About prosperity and abundance.
- It is about good fortune and fulfillment.
- Your actions, for example, quitting or starting a job or relationship, or something along this line has set the ball rolling and now the Universe will unfold as you desired. You will get what you wanted.
- Circumstances in your life are changing right now, generally for the better.
- There may be a situation occurring over which you have no control.
- This card is about change but also about constancy, in the sense of repeating cycles.
- About universal, cyclical, and personal change. It represents your recognition of recurring patterns of events in your life and is therefore sometimes associated with the laws of karma (*the principle of cause-and-effect*).
- This card is about change as a result of your past choices and decisions.
- This is a time to recognize and understand the personal patterns and cycles occurring in your own life.

- As the Hermit card was about introspection, the Wheel of Fortune card calls upon us to reverse our inner focus (*introversion*) and to pay attention to the actions of our worldly or physical life (*extroversion*).

REVERSED MEANING
- Failing to make necessary changes your life feels somewhat frustrated and stagnant.
- *The meaning of the card is delayed or extended into the future.*
- *An aspect of the upright meaning of the card needs to be released so you can move forward.*
- *This is not about the upright meaning, place another card on top of the reversed one and read it.*

PERSONAL GROWTH CONSIDERATIONS
- Representing change the Wheel of Fortune is about finding opportunities, uncovering patterns, and recognizing cycles. This is about accepting that the only constant in our life is change and the necessity of adapting to current circumstances in order to find peace. We make our own good fortune by working with the times, rather than against them – if we want to reap a harvest in the fall we must plant seeds in the spring. Also in this message is the stability of spirituality that is ever present even in the face of change.

VERBAL AFFIRMATION
- "I pay attention to my actions and enjoy their outcomes."

UNIFYING THEMES
- Card 10 - WHEEL OF FORTUNE and Card 19 -THE SUN both reduce to one and have unifying themes with Card 1 - THE MAGICIAN.
- The masculine energy of number one is reflected in these three cards although the Magician also encompasses feminine energy. These cards are about active principles, the Magician is utilizing his knowledge to make things happen, the Wheel of Fortune is indicative of an action that has started and change is coming, and the Sun is about starting something new.

XI

JUSTICE

Card 11 – Justice

REPRESENTS

- *(Justice - one of the four cardinal virtues, the others being Strength, Prudence and Temperance).*
- justice represents proper moderation between self-interest and the rights and needs of others
- strict fairness
- impartial and unbiased justice
- decision making using ethical principles
- understanding the cause and effect of your choices
- balance achieved through logic

NUMBER ELEVEN

- The number eleven reduces to two. (1+1 = 2)
- Ruled by the Moon two's quality is fixed.
- Represents some type of union or partnership with another person, a spiritual entity, or two parts of you.
- Associated with the balance of polarities such as yin/yang, male/female and public/separate.
- Two builds on the opportunity presented by one *(the ace).*
- Two can represent sensitivity to others sometimes to the point of considering their wellbeing over your own.
- Representative of immersing yourself into another person, an idea, or a project.
- Two is associated with choices and decisions.

ASTROLOGICALLY

- ZODIAC SIGN: LIBRA
  RULING PLANET: VENUS
  ELEMENT: AIR
  GENDER: MASCULINE
  QUALITY: CARDINAL

- LIBRA ruled by the planet VENUS represents the Justice card. Venus symbolizes attraction, unity, balance, valuation and assets. Ruling the love of nature and pleasure, luck and wealth it represents that rare and elusive harmony and radiance that is true beauty.

- Libra, an AIR SIGN, is about thinking. Intellectual air signs are great communicators and good at conceptualizing. Intuitive and inquisitive they constantly come up with new ideas.

- Representing MASCULINE ENERGY air signs are outward looking, primarily motivated by external concerns, action-oriented and protective. Seeking to dominate the outside world masculine energy can be hard, firm, logical, strong, rational, rough and loud.

- A CARDINAL SIGN, Libra, represents new beginnings, enterprise and getting things started; people born under this sign are instigators and leaders.

ARCHETYPE BEING REPRESENTED

- **Symbolic message** - Balance and justice.
- **Archetype** - Justice – both the giver and enforcer of laws. As the ultimate arbiter, she holds a two-edged message – a reminder that fairness cuts both ways.

SYMBOLISM INCLUDES

- **Two grey pillars** – grey denotes wisdom. Two pillars are always symbolic of duality in terms of law this would be innocence and guilt.

- **Justice seated between the pillars** – pillars can indicate a connection between heaven and earth and Justice seated here is depicting a connection to higher thinking.

- **Red coloured robe** - red depicts passion, energy, and action.

- **Snakes sewn into the red robe** – snakes symbolize hidden knowledge that will be brought forth and used in decision making.

- **Green colour of the snakes** – green signifies the earth element which allows ideas to manifest.

- **Snakes extending below Justice's knees** - symbolizes kundalini energy. (*Kundalini is an energy wrapped around a person's spine that when awakened creates a vertical connection* *between the seven chakra's. A healing force it is experienced in the individual as an intense energy that undulates through the body starting at the spine and continuing up and through one's head).*

- **Sword** - swords in the Tarot represent logic and the pursuit of truth despite any outcome.

- **Circle with a dot in the middle on the sword** - an alchemical symbol representing the end of the quest and perfection.

- **Scales** – symbolic of balancing and getting an exact measurement, in this case it's about weighing the information and finding the truth of the situation.

- **Crown** – symbolizes someone with recognized authority; Justice is the ruler or administrator of the law.

- **Jewel in the crown over her third eye** – represents higher wisdom and insight. (*The third eye is the sixth chakra in the body and is located in the forehead*).

- **Square broach on cape** – represents "squaring the circle" (*squaring the circle, or a circle shown within a square is a freemasonry concept, as well as an important Jungian idea*). Representing consolidation within the four elements, air, water, earth and fire it signifies a balance of four and unites sacred and profane, heaven and earth, the eternal and the now. In so doing this becomes a representation of the self.

- **Broach over the heart chakra** – by being over Justice's heart chakra it ensures her judgements are backed by higher wisdom coupled with compassion.

- **Colour purple** - purple symbolizes the authority bestowed by royalty, and implies Justice possesses ultimate decision making.

- **Purple cloth connected to the pillars** – called a veil this connects the pillars and invites you to discover the hidden knowledge behind them. Associated with the unveiling of one's own mysteries.

- **Yellow in the background** – symbolizes that intellect is in the background.

UPRIGHT MEANING
- About balance and objectivity.
- It is time to weigh our internal lives and refine them if necessary. We need to consider the actions we have taken and

their consequences, the values we actively live by, and how we justify our positions.

- This card is about impartial decision making, it is a call to balance objective and subjective thinking, feeling, and responding.
- This is a time to take care of legal matters.
- This may indicate involvement in an external situation such as a lawsuit. It is important to resolve this situation in a way that is fair to all parties involved.
- Could indicate a need for creating balance, not only of power but in terms of your emotional reactions to the situation in hand.
- If this card represents you then your perception of the situation or the people you are dealing with is absolutely accurate.
- You are capable of making the right decision and don't let anyone sway you from what you know is right.

REVERSED MEANING
- There could be delays in legal matters.
- Feeling disconnected from reality your thoughts are swinging from one extreme to another.
- Bias was at play in a decision that has affected you.
- Be careful who you trust; true intentions are not being revealed at this time.
- You may be around police or someone involved in criminal activities at this time.
- *The meaning of the card is delayed or extended into the future.*
- *An aspect of the upright meaning of the card needs to be released so you can move forward.*
- *This is not about the upright meaning, place another card on top of the reversed one and read it.*

PERSONAL GROWTH CONSIDERATIONS
- Representing the cause and effect of your choices Justice teaches us how actions are balanced by reactions. From Justice you learn you cannot escape the ramifications of your thoughts, words, and deeds. The lesson here is one of rectification and

adjustment. You reap what you have sown, according to Divine Law.

VERBAL AFFIRMATION
- "I am balanced and honour my word and commitment."

UNIFYING THEMES
- Card 11 – JUSTICE and Card 20 – JUDGEMENT both reduce to two and share similarities with Card 2 – THE HIGH PRIESTESS.
- The number two is about basic division, pillars of entry, male and female. It is feminine generally in contrast to one which represents masculine energy.
- All three of these cards are about the holding of information. The High Priestess protects her information, Justice considers information, and Judgement provides information.

XII

THE HANGED MAN

Card 12 – The Hanged Man

REPRESENTS
- letting go
- personal sacrifice to attain a goal
- seeing different perspectives

NUMBER TWELVE
- The number twelve reduces to three. (1+2=3)
- Ruled by Jupiter three's quality is mutable.
- Cosmic energy is embedded in threes.
- Three, a mystic number, represents Spirit.
- Threes possess celestial power – the sun stands still for three days at the solstices before resuming its motion; threes encompass past, present and future; the moon looks full for three days and disappears as dark for three days. Threes make up the trinity of mind, body and spirit.
- Group activities, movement, action, growth and development are expressed by threes.
- Sometimes with threes expansion occurs too quickly causing you to spread yourself too thin or for your energies to scatter.
- If you pay attention to what you are doing threes vibration is cheerful, optimistic and pleasant, representing a period of happiness and benefits.

ASTROLOGICALLY
- ZODIAC SIGN: PISCES
  RULING PLANET: NEPTUNE
  ELEMENT: WATER
  GENDER: FEMININE
  QUALITY: MUTABLE

- The Hanged Man is represented by PISCES; the zodiacal sign symbolizing humans' desire to connect with cosmic consciousness. Ruled by NEPTUNE it represents dreams, imagination, inspiration, spirituality and deception. Related to all that is unreal, ethereal, mystical, otherworldly, invisible, imaginative and creative Neptune is the planet of emotional genius and has dominance over many of the arts and inspirational thought. Neptune rules theatre, sensationalism, poetry, music, and transcendent modes of creativity. Neptune is also identified with escapism, drugs and alcohol, avoiding responsibilities, destructive self-indulgence, deception, fraud and delusions of all sorts, fascination with celebrities' lives and involvement in religious cults.

- Intuitive and attuned to subtle vibrations WATER SIGN people are quick to sum up others, often at a first meeting. Emotional and sensitive they are a capable of great compassion.
- Inward looking, internally driven, intuitive FEMININE ENERGY is sensitive and emotional. While seeking to create co-existence and consensus it is introspective and nurturing.
- MUTABLE SIGN Pisces represents versatile and adaptable people who willingly serve others often by working in service industries. Seeing both sides of a situation these people choose to adapt to an environment rather than to shape it. By accepting change mutable people end what was.

ARCHETYPE BEING REPRESENTED

- **Symbolic message** - Necessary sacrifice.
- **Archetype** - Sacrifice – the Hanged Man sacrifices his comforts and passions for a time knowing that better things will occur as a result. He is the visionary, often looking at things differently from others, who sacrifices one life to be rewarded with another.

SYMBOLISM INCLUDES

- **Man hanging upside down** – symbolizes looking at things from a different perspective.
- **Blue tunic** – represents purity and mental clarity.
- **Red tights** – red symbolizes passion and action.
- **Red belt** – symbolizes passion, action and instinctual vitality that creates a temporary separation so other interests may be pursued.

- **Arms and crossed legs form triangles** – a triangle often represents the divine trinity, movement and the three dimensional existence of the universe. Triangles the alchemical sign for sulphur refer to passion, action, will and motivation.
- **One leg unbound** – this person can become unbound whenever he wishes which means he has voluntarily placed himself in this upside down position.
- **Hands behind his back** – symbolizes he is hiding his thoughts; he is not ready yet to share what he is contemplating.
- **Halo around head** – symbolizes positive upright spiritual thoughts and further symbolizes his being "illuminated" as in gaining higher knowledge about a subject.
- **Relaxed facial expression** – indicates he is not feeling stressed, he is contemplating things.
- **Living tree** – denotes earth energies which relate to fertility and trying to get an idea to grow.
- **Purple background** – symbolizes authority, signifying the man has given his permission to be hung upside down.

UPRIGHT MEANING
- About surrender, sacrifice and breaking old patterns.
- Can signify a new direction for your life is in the making which will include some adjustments.
- Can mean it is time for a new perspective, you need to look at things from a different angle.
- Can signify you are going through a major transformation, perhaps caused by an illness or some loss. The result has shaken up your old way of life and made you realize that there is more to life than money, material goods, and physical reality.
- Can indicate you are willing to make some self-sacrifice for the objective of attaining wisdom, special insights, or personal growth.
- About giving something up for the sake of something better.

REVERSED MEANING
- You may be sacrificing some part of your life unnecessarily due to a martyr complex.

- You are feeling stagnated as you refuse to consider other options or to view things differently.
- *The meaning of the card is delayed or extended into the future.*
- *An aspect of the upright meaning of the card needs to be released so you can move forward.*
- *This is not about the upright meaning, place another card on top of the reversed one and read it.*

PERSONAL GROWTH CONSIDERATIONS
- Representing the release of attachments, rigidly held beliefs, and old patterns the Hanged Man teaches us to look at things from a different perspective. From the Hanged Man we learn to let go of our will and let a higher power (*God*) direct our journey. Surrender and even sacrifices are part of the lesson of the Hanged Man, though what you are required to sacrifice is usually something that has outgrown its usefulness and is now limiting your progress.

VERBAL AFFIRMATION
- "I value and embrace new and effective patterns."

UNIFYING THEMES
- Card 12 - The HANGED MAN and Card 21 - THE WORLD both reduce to three and share similarities with Card 3 - THE EMPRESS.
- Three is the product of one (*individuality*) and two (*duality*) and stands for creative energy. It is the beginning of the Apparent (*creation*) and identified with the first shapes of matter.
- All three of these cards are about connecting with cosmic consciousness, the concept that the universe exists as an interconnected network of consciousness, with each conscious being linked to every other. When cosmic consciousness is realized in the individual this person experiences a euphoric feeling that includes a sense of wonder, a sense of being in the presence of the "One" and a sense of greater understanding of the universe as a whole.
- The Empress symbolizes "the mother archetype," she is about love and contentment and can be viewed as connected with cosmic consciousness. The Hanged Man is influenced strongly

by Neptune's influences which are about the desire to connect with cosmic consciousness. The World is about cosmic order and the sense of fulfilment; it is the realization of cosmic consciousness.

XIII

DEATH

Card 13 – Death

REPRESENTS
- lasting change
- an end of things as they were
- off with the old and on with the new
- accepting the inevitable

NUMBER THIRTEEN
- The number thirteen reduces to four. (1+3=4)
- Ruled by Uranus four's quality is cardinal.
- Four is the number associated to "matter."
- Four is a time to build a foundation that will support your ideas and projects.
- Four a stabilizing time for creating structures and order requires hard work and self discipline.
- Representing manifestation of your ideas, fours represent prosperity, peace, happiness, abundance and even triumph.
- Sometimes four represents a stage in personal development when a stalemate has been reached, a period that often seems necessary for unacknowledged emotions or dilemmas to come into consciousness so we can experience them and get on with growth or healing.

ASTROLOGICALLY
- ZODIAC SIGN: SCORPIO
  RULING PLANET: PLUTO
  ELEMENT: WATER
  GENDER: FEMININE
  QUALITY: FIXED

- The Death Card, represented by SCORPIO, symbolizes the transforming powers of life and death. Ruled by PLUTO, Scorpio represents resurrection, renewal, regeneration and resolution. Symbolizing the capacity to change totally and forever one's lifestyle, thought and behaviour, Pluto rules the forces of creation and destruction. As the planet of beginnings and endings, Pluto can effect total transformation. Pluto can also bring a lust for power with strong obsessions.

- Scorpio, a WATER SIGN, represents intuitive people attuned to subtle vibrations who are quick to sum up others, often at first meeting. They are emotional and capable of great compassion and sensitivity.
- Introspective and nurturing FEMININE ENERGY is receptive, intuitive, inward looking, internally driven, sensitive and emotional while it seeks to establish co-existence and consensus.
- FIXED SIGN Scorpio represents faithful and persevering people who see projects through to the end. Resisting change and attempting to adapt the environment to themselves above all they want to maintain things.

ARCHETYPE BEING REPRESENTED

- **Symbolic message** - Change and transition.
- **Archetype** - Rebirth – like the Grim Reaper, who clears away all that cannot survive, this card depicts the turning of a page, the completion of one chapter of life and the exciting start of a new story.

SYMBOLISM INCLUDES

- **Skeleton** – symbolizes what is common to us all.
- **Skeleton moves from left to right on the card** – denotes from the unconscious toward the conscious, from the imprisonment of the past toward the rising awareness of the future.
- **Armour** – symbolizes a readiness to fight or defend.
- **White horse** – symbolizes purity, justice and good things being delivered. Animals symbolize our instincts.
- **Black flag with a white flower** - called the Mystic Rose it symbolizes life and following the mystic path. Requiring extensive knowledge of the fundamental way that nature works the mystic becomes a partner with nature, not separate

from it. The mystic is able to merge intuition and intellect in a way that supports both earth and humanity.

- **Priest dressed in yellow** – symbolizes spiritual connectedness; he has crosses on his arm and hand signifying he has completed his initiation.

- **A lying down man dressed in royalty robes whose crown has fallen off** - symbolizes that some things must come to an end, even if you have possessed full authority over your life and others this someday must end.

- **Mother in white dress, head turned eyes closed** – represents not wanting to see and symbolizes fear of acknowledging what has changed.

- **A child holding onto parent's arm, holding flowers looking up**- symbolizes innocence, dependence and curiosity.

- **Green grass and trees** - earth energy which means the manifestation of our ideas and projects.

- **Light yellow crosses in the field** – symbolize eternity.

- **Flowing water** – symbolizes emotional turmoil or that change is occurring here.

- **Ships sailing** – this symbolizes promise and that something is being delivered.

- **Color purple in armour, saddle, and cliffs** – purple is the color of royalty and signifies permission is granted.

- **Two towers** – they represent a twin motive, in dreams these signify unconscious content attempting to become known by approaching the threshold of the consciousness. Usually two objects appear, not necessarily the same things. The two towers on this card are symbolizing a new or emerging awareness (*not yet consciously realized*) in our spiritual journey.

- **Sun rising** – symbolizes new beginnings, warmth and hope.

UPRIGHT MEANING
- About release, detachment and the act of letting go.
- Could mean a positive change for the better as the old way was no longer working.
- This is about new opportunities brought about by liberation from old and worn out concepts, beliefs or behaviours.

- This can be a time to examine and explore things, principles, and ideas to their true depths.
- This is about releasing outgrown ideas or attitudes.
- This is about bringing order back into your spiritual life.
- This card may signify a lasting, dramatic and profound change for you based on a decision you have made and the course of this change cannot be altered.
- If the reading is about a love relationship this card indicates that is it over, say your goodbyes.
- Something is passing away, could be old ideas and thoughts and making way for something new. Sometimes it is sad because it has to do with losing something, however the new being ushered in is usually an improvement.
- A death to someone around you **ONLY** if it appears with the Nine or Ten of Swords cards.

REVERSED MEANING
- Fear of change is holding you back from making necessary adjustments.
- *The meaning of the card is delayed or extended into the future.*
- *An aspect of the upright meaning of the card needs to be released so you can move forward.*
- *This is not about the upright meaning, place another card on top of the reversed one and read it.*

PERSONAL GROWTH CONSIDERATIONS
- Representing major adjustments and lasting change the Death card teaches you about facing your fears and recognizing the defences you have established to protect yourself. You learn how to strip away old coping mechanisms so that transformation can take place on many levels – mental, physical, emotional, and spiritual.

VERBAL AFFIRMATION
- "I am excited about growing and becoming more of who I am."

UNIFYING THEMES

- Card 13 – DEATH reduces to four and shares a common theme with Card 4 - THE EMPEROR
- Balance is the theme unifying these two cards. The Emperor is male energy realized and the Death card is feminine energy realized. The Emperor protects and traditionally maintains things; the Death card is about change and transition.

XIV

TEMPERANCE

Card 14 – Temperance

REPRESENTS

- (*Temperance - one of the four cardinal virtues, the others being Strength, Prudence and Justice*).
- temperance represents restraint, practising self-control, abstention and moderation
- cooperation
- sharing and balance
- bringing together opposites
- patience
- working in harmony with others
- moderation as the key to contentment

NUMBER FOURTEEN

- The number fourteen reduces to five. (1+4=5)
- Ruled by Mercury five's quality is fixed.
- Fives always represent some type of difficulty, tension or crisis.
- Challenges often result in a winner or loser with fives.
- Fives suggest a sense of being on a roller coaster ride or being caught up in a whirlwind.
- Fluctuation, unrest and sometimes clashes create a sense of instability and can cause stress.
- Impulsive and impatient behaviours occur but resourcefulness and curiosity are also present.
- Fives indicate we have the quality of mind, but lack the maturity and knowledge to transform old ways into new patterns of being.
- We may be forced to make a choice in order to end the anxiety that is associated with fives.

ASTROLOGICALLY

- ZODIAC SIGN: SAGITTARIUS
  RULING PLANET: JUPITER
  ELEMENT: FIRE
  GENDER: MASCULINE
  QUALITY: MUTABLE

- Ruled by the planet Jupiter, SAGITTARIUS represents the Temperance card. JUPITER, symbolizing expansion, represents good luck and good cheer, health, wealth, happiness, success and joy. The symbol of opportunity Jupiter is associated with gambling and games of chance. It rules acting, publishing, philosophy, religion, sports and travel.

- A FIRE SIGN Sagittarius displays vital energy, action, and creative talent.

- Outward looking and primarily motivated by external concerns MASCULINE ENERGY is action-oriented and protective. Seeking to dominate the outside world, it can be hard, firm, logical, strong, rational, rough and loud.

- Versatile by nature MUTABLE SIGN people see both sides of a situation and can adapt to most circumstances. Changing their attitudes they adjust to environments rather than shaping them and in so doing end what was.

ARCHETYPE BEING REPRESENTED

- **Symbolic message** - Moderation and balance.
- **Archetype** - The Union of Opposites – Temperance is the archangel of balance. With dexterity and grace she demonstrates that moderation can serve as a bridge to wholeness.

SYMBOLISM INCLUDES

- **Angel** – symbolizing the messengers of God, they are liaisons between heaven and earth. Signifying enlightenment angels were made of pure spirit whereas humans were made of spirit and matter. Sometimes angels symbolize the element of air.
- **Reddish orange wings** – wings symbolize spirituality and movement, red signifies action and passion. Orange represents warmth, energy, activity, drive and confidence.
- **White gown** – symbolizes purity.

- **Upright triangle on the gown** – symbolizes the divine masculine, either fire or air elements, or both.

- **Water being poured from one cup into another cup** – symbolically transferring or mixing different elements, the lower chalice in the left hand represents the unconscious and the higher chalice in the right hand represents consciousness.

- **Two chalices** – chalices within Christianity symbolize the last supper and Holy Communion. There are two chalices here so they represent twin motives (*two*) which denote information that is not yet fully conscious but about to emerge from the unconscious. Two symbols together represent the emerging awareness in our spiritual journey.

- **Angel with one foot in the water and one foot on land** – both water and earth represent feminine qualities, the water element symbolizes emotions, mystery and secrets and the earth element symbolizes practicality and manifestation.

- **Round disc in her hairline with a dot inside a circle** – the disc representing the sun's energy is radiating from her head; the circle with a dot is an alchemical symbol representing the end of the quest and thus perfection.

- **Halo** – symbolizes spiritual connectedness.

- **Crown in the middle of the sun** – represents glory; Jungian's consider this the highest goal of evolution – "he who conquers himself wins the crown of eternal life."

- **Mountains** – symbolize stability, endurance and loftiness in terms of spiritual connectedness.

- **Green field with road running through it** – represents earth energy, being grounded and the possibility of manifestation.

- **Iris's growing** - relating to a divine messenger they are symbolic of Iris the Greek goddess. (*Winged, swift and carrying a caduceus, Iris was the Greek messenger of the gods. She carried a pitcher which contained water for putting perjurers to sleep. The rainbow is considered both the essence of Iris and the pathway by which she traveled.*)

- **Lake** – symbolizes the connection between, or need to balance, the conscious and the unconscious. Water a feminine energy depicts intuitiveness and hidden knowledge.

UPRIGHT MEANING

- About integration and synthesis.
- This card is about blending different things like raw materials, resources, personnel or ideas into a harmonious whole.
- About the need for adaptation by utilizing self-control and working in harmony with others.
- This card speaks to the need for us to find the right mixture of inner certainty and outer expression. Our behaviours need to match our thoughts.
- Representing the higher self in action the Temperance card encourages us to develop a new sense of internal balance through raising our personal levels of consciousness.
- About situations that require adaptation and patience to succeed.
- Can indicate times when it appears nothing is happening or moving, when everything seems to be at a standstill and there is nothing you can do about it.

REVERSED MEANING

- Indicates bad management, poor judgement or competing inharmonious interests.
- The combinations of what you are trying to be put together may be unwise or even harmful to yourself or others (*intentionally or otherwise*).
- *The meaning of the card is delayed or extended into the future.*
- *An aspect of the upright meaning of the card needs to be released so you can move forward.*
- *This is not about the upright meaning, place another card on top of the reversed one and read it.*

PERSONAL GROWTH CONSIDERATIONS

- Representing rebirth and balance the Temperance card teaches you patience, moderation and about working in harmony with others. Teaching you about the sense of renewal coming from harmony and hope Temperance's lesson includes your learning the only way to experience this sense of peace is to merge your personal will with Divine Will.

VERBAL AFFIRMATION
- "I am well integrated and experience harmony."

UNIFYING THEMES
- Card 14 – TEMPERANCE when reduced to five shares a common theme with Card 5 - THE HIEROPHANT.
- Intelligent energy is embedded in fives.
- The Temperance and Hierophant cards are unified by connections to Spirituality and Divine Will.

XV

THE DEVIL

Card 15 – The Devil

REPRESENTS
- imprisoned power and energy
- feelings of entrapment, bondage and oppression
- a sense you cannot see the way out of a bad situation
- excessive focus on materialism
- over indulgences
- wilfully staying in ignorance

NUMBER FIFTEEN
- The number fifteen reduces to six. (1+5=6)
- Ruled by Venus six's quality is mutable.
- Sixes always favourable have a cooperative vibration.
- Six represents the ability to transcend difficulties and a sense of peace and quiet after the storm.
- Demonstrating the integration of newly learned skills and improved coping mechanisms challenges have been overcome resulting in six's stability.
- Six is a time of balance and respite that creates a base and a pivot for new experiences.
- Six, an important ceremonial number, refers to Spirit's connection to life in all directions (*north, south, east and west, above and below*).
- Because three (3) is a cosmic number its attributes are amplified by six (6).

ASTROLOGICALLY
- Zodiac sign: Capricorn
  Ruling Planet: Saturn
  Element: Earth
  Gender: Feminine
  Quality: Cardinal

- The Devil is represented by CAPRICORN, the world leader, which depicts social order, pragmatism, and the slow but sure ascent to the top of the heap. Regarded as a sacred sign due to the winter solstice taking place within its boundaries Capricorn brings an increase of daylight to the Northern Hemisphere. Associated with restriction, obstacles and discipline Capricorn's ruling planet SATURN creates limits and represents ambition, selfishness, depression, jealousy and greed. Sometimes a harsh task master Saturn's lessons once learned often lead to wisdom, understanding and the granting of lasting rewards.
- Grounded and oriented towards what is real EARTH SIGNS bring form to ideas. Practical and creating structures they are useful, productive, tactile and dependable while demonstrating persistence, patience and reasonableness.
- Receptive, intuitive and inward looking FEMININE ENERGY seeks consensus and co-existence while displaying nurturing qualities.
- Capricorn, a CARDINAL SIGN, represents new beginnings, enterprise and getting things started. People born under this sign are instigators and leaders.

ARCHETYPE BEING REPRESENTED

- **Symbolic message** - Being trapped, materialism and bondage.
- **Archetype** - The Trickster - about the shadowy side of our existence. The devil demonstrates how a selfish devotion to material possessions and ill-conceived passions can tie us down and keep us from true happiness.

SYMBOLISM INCLUDES

- **The Devil** – symbolizes primitive chaos, our lower instincts, obsessions, indulgences, greed, perversion, ignorance, irresponsibility, ability to hurt others, cruelty and addictions.
- **Horns, clawed feet, and bat type wings** – this depiction of the devil comes from European medieval art. The Bible never physically describes the devil as he is depicted here but he is easily recognizable. Much of the devil's depiction is based on various pagan horned gods, Pan being one. In Medieval times bat wings symbolized demons and evil spirits.

- **Five sided star on his head** – often referred to as a pentagram this star is a symbol of faith in many wiccans, it is akin to the cross in Christianity and the Star of David (*six sided star*) by the Jews. The pentagram has magical associations and is used by freemasons. When the pentagram is pointing upward it symbolizes spirituality's dominance over the material world. When pointing down (*as it is on the devil's head*) it represents the physical world ruling over the spiritual and thus is connected with dark magic.

- **Devil's right hand pointing up** – depicts a mockery of spiritual connectedness, the way he holds his fingers are not as if in a blessing. His right hand denotes rational, conscious, logic – but note the difference between how the devil's hand is up but his elbow is bent, not like the Magician who holds his whole arm up – this is indifference and mockery on the part of the devil.

- **Devil's left hand pointing down** – left hand denotes the unconscious, he holds a burning stick in his, it seems to be saying our hidden thoughts are possibly fiery, or full of rage.

- **Naked woman and man** –mockery of innocence and purity as they have grown horns and tails.

- **Loose chains around woman and man's necks and their hands are free** – as they could remove these chains they are representing self-imposed limitations.

- **Black in the background** – darkness and the absence of love.

UPRIGHT MEANING
- About recognizing our own follies, weaknesses and self harming behaviours.
- You need to recognize and acknowledge negative aspects within your life, e.g. gluttony, greed, self-indulgence or perhaps self-deception, then put these out in the open so you can begin to deal with them.
- This card can be about the pull of self-defeating patterns (*habits, dependency or addictions*) it is a call to acknowledge them and begin to deal with them.
- Sometimes there is a sexual component in your life that is having a harmful effect on you.

- We do have the personal ability to remove blocks and inhibitions within us that keep us from being healthy.
- Could signify you're being offered a quick fix to all of your problems, if you are impatient and take it you may see the destruction of all your dreams.
- You can succeed on your own, don't be tempted by however attractive the short cuts, nor dismayed by the hard work involved (*Saturn demands hard work*).
- You may feel helpless and oppressed and see no way out of your situation.
- Materialism has so financially overwhelmed you that you almost cannot see daylight.
- If this card lies close to a number of sword cards it may indicate violence in a relationship or at the very least verbal abuse.
- If this card lies close to the Lover's card or the Two of Cups it is doubtful that the relationship is a healthy one.

REVERSED MEANING
- A personal disaster which benefits others.
- Being around a person that is not nice.
- *The meaning of the card is delayed or extended into the future.*
- *An aspect of the upright meaning of the card needs to be released so you can move forward.*
- *This is not about the upright meaning, place another card on top of the reversed one and read it.*

PERSONAL GROWTH CONSIDERATIONS
- Representing personal fears and doubts the Devil symbolizes deep-seated issues from childhood that may show up as confusion, obsession, dependency, and the misuse of power. Sometimes materialism, over indulgences, and wilfully staying in ignorance enslave you. This card teaches you to acknowledge your dark side – your personal demons – and to do battle with them.

VERBAL AFFIRMATION
- "Recognizing my follies I work towards rectifying them."

UNIFYING THEMES

- Card 15 – THE DEVIL when reduced is six and shares a common theme with Card 6 - THE LOVERS.
- The union of male and female and the need to make choices unify these two cards. Even the depiction on the cards is similar. The Lovers card has a male and female with an angel above them and the Devil card has a male and female but with the Devil above them.

XVI

THE TOWER

Card 16 – The Tower

REPRESENTS

- demolishing the old to make way for the new
- release
- sudden realization of the truth
- momentous change

NUMBER SIXTEEN

- The number sixteen reduces to seven. (1+6=7)
- Ruled by Neptune seven's quality is cardinal.
- Sevens are sacred numbers made up of three, the number of Spirit and cosmic energy and four, the number of matter, that which is necessary for the manifestation of ideas or projects.
- Relating to the development of the soul, sevens deal with wisdom, completeness and perfection.
- Indicating a need to deal with your inner life, seven is a time of introspection and soul searching requiring solitude.
- A reflective time, seven indicates a period when you will find it necessary to seriously consider how and why specific events occur.
- Sevens represent a turning point as they begin a new cycle of threes. One, two and three were followed by four, five and six, and now we have seven, eight and nine.
- Sevens bring about a new restlessness possibly indicating a breakthrough in awareness which causes us to re-evaluate and willingly try new things, which may result in a changed understanding or perspective.

ASTROLOGICALLY

- ZODIAC SIGN: ARIES
  RULING PLANET: MARS
  ELEMENT: FIRE
  GENDER: MASCULINE
  QUALITY: CARDINAL

- ARIES ruled by the planet MARS represents the Tower. Exemplar of all the traditional aspects we esteem in the male, Mars is related to sexual prowess, courage, energy, action, the protector and provider.
- FIRE SIGNS (*Aries*) symbolize leadership, initiative, action, energy, and new ideas. Self-starters people under this sign are leaders not followers.
- Outward looking and primarily motivated by external concerns MASCULINE ENERGY is action-oriented and protective. Seeking to dominate the outside world it can be hard, firm, logical, strong, rational, rough and loud.
- CARDINAL SIGNS are associated with new beginnings, enterprise and getting things started. Aries for spring, Cancer for summer, Libra for autumn, and Capricorn for winter.

ARCHETYPE BEING REPRESENTED

- **Symbolic message** - Chaos, sometimes unexpected or unwanted change.
- **Archetype** - Chaos – forceful clearing of pent-up energy that strikes like lightning. It's a bolt from the blue and it can shake any over built structure to its foundation.

SYMBOLISM INCLUDES

- **Tower is on top of mountain** – this symbolizes something that was built "too lofty" and is now bringing about its own destruction as there is no alternative.
- **Tower** – is also symbolic of the Tower of Babel in the Bible that God demolished due to human's arrogance.
- **Black windows spurt fire** – black indicates devoid of light and goodness, the fire is active and cleansing.
- **Lightning bolts** – ultimate destruction, coming from the gods.
- **Flash of lightning** – in ancient mythologies from many cultures (*Norse, Roman, Greek, Native American, etc.*) the lightning bolt would be hurled by male sky gods to punish, provide water or to fertilize the earth. Here it could be an act of fertilizing so that new ideas can be brought to fruition.
- **Triangular shape at the end of the lightning** – this is the glyph for Mars, the planet of conflict.

- **Fire and smoke** – symbolize destruction.
- **The crown flung out of the top of the tower** – symbolizes the loss of authority, resources and prestige.
- **Man and woman falling to earth** – represents a sense of being totally out of control.
- **Twenty two yods falling from the sky** – the Yod a dew drop shaped symbol represents the primary Hebrew letter and all other Hebrew letters are a variation on it. Yods are associated with the astrological sign Virgo (*earth sign*). These twenty two yods represent the twenty two letters of the Hebrew alphabet, the twenty two paths of the Kabbalistic Tree of Life, and the archetypes of the twenty two "Major Arcana" cards. The ten yods above the female represent the ten elementary Hebrew letters or the ten sephiroth of the Kabbalistic Tree of Life. (TREE OF LIFE – *a symbol or concept of the mystical tradition of the Kabbalah. Perceived as the ten emanations of energy through which God created the world, the Kabbalistic Tree of Life serves as a model of creations and a blueprint for leading a more spiritual life. It consists of three pillars along with ten spheres, called sephiroth each representing an ideal necessary for human spiritual evolution; they are placed and connected by twenty two lines or paths. When so linked, the Tree represents the totality of the cosmos. Each path bears one of the twenty two Hebrew letters. Together the sephiroth and the paths comprise the "Thirty-two Paths of Wisdom." {Freemasonry uses many Kabbalah teachings hence the thirty two (32) degrees of a freemason}. The* three *pillars of the Tree of Life have several names. The left hand pillar is called the Left Hand of God, the pillar of form, severity, majesty, understanding, or judgement. The right pillar is called the Right Hand of God, the pillar of force, mercy, justice, or love. The middle pillar is called the pillar of equilibrium, or mildness*).
- **Black sky** – symbolizes darkness, absence and opposite of good and light.

UPRIGHT MEANING

- About awakening, healing and restoration.
- This card is about a change of your world view.
- This card teaches us about the energy of release, how to let things go or cease to be so new thoughts and behaviours can begin.

- It is intellectual destruction; those ideas and values you held as meaningful no longer are experienced or seen by you to be important.
- The Tower challenges us to examine our beliefs and our defences, to re-evaluate those things we may have developed to protect us but which no longer do as good a job as they, perhaps, once did. The foundation of the Tower is anchored in the past, rather than the present. Doubly so if this card falls into a position that represents the past in a reading.
- This card is about a breakthrough experience that causes us to sort out our ideas or values, especially those that have become conditioned or constricting.
- This card represents a renewal for us through the destruction of falseness that has surrounded us or an illusion of truth that we have been living with.
- This card is about a flash of illumination or insight.
- This card herald's sudden change, often unexpected.
- This card is about upheaval and destruction of significant thoughts we have held.
- About swift dramatic change that you may experience as shocking and upsetting.
- You may be well aware of a pressing need to make change but are steadfastly refusing to, then along comes a divorce, losing your job, having an accident, or a financial setback, and this forces you to face reality.
- Could mean it is time to deal with situations as your life is not running smoothly.
- Unless you think fast and make some adjustments a situation is about to explode in your face.
- Finding you cannot bear to continue with your current life you are ready for a call to take action.
- This could be a time of break ups in relationships and friendships; quarrels and arguments.

REVERSED MEANING
- At a deep level you are being prepared for the changes that need to take place, but you are resisting what your inner self already knows.

- *The meaning of the card is delayed or extended into the future.*
- *An aspect of the upright meaning of the card needs to be released so you can move forward.*
- *This is not about the upright meaning, place another card on top of the reversed one and read it.*

PERSONAL GROWTH CONSIDERATIONS

- Representing the breaking down and releasing of old patterns the Tower demonstrates how in response to fear you put walls up around yourself and hide behind old defences and self-limiting patterns. Many of these old beliefs are based on faulty thinking and illusions of reality. You learn that outlived coping mechanisms keep you separated from your true self and from others. Perhaps as a result of an unexpected event, you experience upset, insecurity and confusion, however the destruction ultimately brings freedom.

VERBAL AFFIRMATION

- "I restore my energy in a healthy manner."

UNIFYING THEMES

- Card 16 - THE TOWER when reduced to seven shares a common theme with Card 7 - THE CHARIOT.
- Number seven is four plus three which means basis (*earth*) plus creation (*cosmos*).
- Energy is the theme that unifies these two cards. The Chariot teaches us to harness our energy and align it with divine will. The Tower teaches us about the energy of release, how to let things go or cease to be so new thoughts and behaviours can begin.

XVII

THE STAR

Card 17 – The Star

REPRESENTS
* hope and inspiration
* faith in the future
* generosity
* peace of mind
* opportunities
* living up to your highest potential

NUMBER SEVENTEEN
* The number seventeen reduces to eight. (1+7=8)
* Ruled by Saturn eight's quality is fixed.
* Eight, the sign of infinity represents death and regeneration.
* The number of cosmic balance, eight's beneficial qualities are rarely diluted, they represent two times greater the benefits of four, the number of manifestation.
* Placed on its side eight becomes the lemniscate, the symbol of infinity representing the eternal spiralling movement of the heavens.
* The hour glass shape of eight symbolizes the passage of time and cycles by representing the four seasons the two solstices and two equinoxes.
* Eights vibration is linked with abundance, material prosperity, worldly power, influence, leadership, authority, possibility, options and potential.

ASTROLOGICALLY
* ZODIAC SIGN: AQUARIUS
  RULING PLANET: URANUS
  ELEMENT: AIR
  GENDER: MASCULINE
  QUALITY: FIXED

- AQUARIUS, which represents the Star, is about the future and all that is new, fresh and promising. Idealistic Aquarius, ruled by URANUS, indicates freedom, independence, originality and innovation. Destroying old ideologies concepts and structures Uranus rules upheaval and revolution signifying sudden drastic change for good or evil. The advanced thinker, modern scientist and esoteric occultist, as well as nonconformists such as the hippie, revolutionaries, anarchists, rebels and radical humanitarians are all represented by Uranus. Symbolizing intellectual genius and inventiveness, Uranus influences humanity's great forward leaps.

- Representing thinking, AIR SIGNS are intellectual, good at conceptualizing and great communicators who are intuitive, inquisitive and constantly come up with new ideas.

- Air signs MASCULINE ENERGY is protective, outward looking, action-oriented and primarily motivated by external concerns. Seeking to dominate the outside world this energy is hard, firm, logical, strong, rational, rough and loud.

- Aquarius, a FIXED SIGN, represents faithful, persevering people who are resistant to change and see projects through to the end. Attempting to adapt the environment to themselves they above all want to maintain things.

ARCHETYPE BEING REPRESENTED
- **Symbolic message** - Hope and the Spirit.
- **Archetype** - The Star – a shining light in the darkness. Like the goddess of the night, she symbolizes the carefree and amiable spirit that offers hope, inspiration and guidance.

SYMBOLISM INCLUDES
- **Naked woman** – symbolizes unveiled truth, innocence, purity, not covering up anything.
- **Water being poured into lake** –the lake means water energies, feelings, emotions, and pouring back into the water means giving water attributes back to others.
- **Water being poured onto land** – land means earth energies, abundance, structure, sharing, manifestation of ideas and projects and pouring water onto the land means giving this to others.

- **Left hand pouring water** – left signifies unconsciousness – from this pitcher water pours into a pond, rippling its water, i.e. stirring the unconscious or possibly the collective unconscious, from which we are called upon to retrieve ancient and universal knowledge.

- **Right hand pouring water** – right signifies conscious awareness of facing the future – from this pitcher five streams of water pour onto the earth, representing the physical consciousness (*the five senses – touch, feel, smell, sight, and hearing*) which are nourished by meditation. One of the steams runs back to the pool, symbolizing the connection between the information we take in with our senses and the processing of it in the unconscious.

- **Two pitchers** - Representing a twin motive (*two*) they signify information that is not yet fully conscious but about to emerge from the unconscious. Two symbols together represent an emerging awareness in our spiritual journey.

- **Left knee on the earth** – she helps support herself by receiving impressions (*ripples*) from the unconscious.

- **One foot in water and one foot on land** – earth and water energies are both at play here – she establishes her rule and authority over the material and the spiritual plane. In psychological terms she establishes these over the conscious and the unconscious.

- **Lake** – suggests the connection between or need to balance the conscious and the unconscious.

- **Ripples on the water** – the pond symbolizes the collective unconscious filled with archetypal knowledge. The ripples suggest that deep or profound work is required to provide meaning for us.

- **Large yellow eight pointed star** – symbolizes hope, optimism, radiance, infinity, abundance, enlightenment and spiritual connectedness. This star could either represent the North Star which symbolically is considered to be the centre of the universe or the Morning Star which is the light of the planet Venus. The Morning Star is a symbol of the life principle as it is the last star seen in the morning and the first and brightest evening star.

- **Seven smaller eight-pointed stars in the sky** – represent the seven stars/planets referred to in Revelation 1:16-20, 2:1 and 3:1 (*the Bible*) and therefore the star or birth planet unique to each of us.
- **Mountain in the background** - symbolizes stability, endurance and wisdom.
- **Tree** – denotes earth energies, fertility and the manifestation of ideas and projects.
- **Ibis bird in the tree** – oversees the transformation of unconscious material into consciousness. Also depicts the reincarnation of Thoth and all that he symbolizes. (*see Thoth*)
- **Flowers and green grass** – symbolizes abundance, good will, and growth.

UPRIGHT MEANING
- About self-esteem, confidence and self-realization.
- This card represents hope and a belief that the future will be a brighter, better place.
- Could mean you have integrated universal wisdoms into your thoughts and behaviours which have resulted in an increase in your conscious awareness.
- About experiencing a sense of renewal or regeneration through meditation and guidance from your higher consciousness.
- This is about good fortune and your wishes coming true. You will feel like you are receiving help from unseen forces or possibly guidance from above.
- About being well suited to your environment and living up to your potential.
- About feeling inspired, having great hopes and possessing the energy to realize your goals.
- Represents "putting back a part of ourselves." When we give to others through sharing knowledge, or teaching some aspect of our life to others, we gain a deep sense of satisfaction.

REVERSED MEANING
- A sense of frustration. Unfulfilled expectations.
- Perhaps theft.
- A sense of feeling abandoned.

- A lack of hope that things will be getting better.
- *The meaning of the card is delayed or extended into the future.*
- *An aspect of the upright meaning of the card needs to be released so you can move forward.*
- *This is not about the upright meaning, place another card on top of the reversed one and read it.*

PERSONAL GROWTH CONSIDERATIONS
- Representing hope, inspiration, faith in the future, and regeneration the Star teaches us that bad times won't last forever. As a result of having faced challenges along the way you now are better equipped to make the best of new opportunities and to live up to your highest potential.

VERBAL AFFIRMATION
- "I value who I am."

UNIFYING THEMES
- Card Number 17 – THE STAR when reduced is eight and shares qualities and aspects with Card 8 - STRENGTH.
- 8 is 4 + 4. Four symbolizes earth which represents manifestation. Eight is four amplified or twice as much, so the manifestations of our ideas or projects are fully realized with eight.
- In the astrological Kabbalistic scheme eight stands for intelligence.
- The Star and Strength cards representing goodness realized both demonstrate intellect, faith, goodness, cosmic power, knowledge and warmth, glory and splendour.

XVIII

THE MOON

Card 18 – The Moon

REPRESENTS
- fluctuation and confusion
- heightened intuitiveness
- vivid dreams or visions
- mystery
- deception

NUMBER EIGHTEEN
- The number eighteen reduces to nine. (1+8=9)
- Ruled by Mars nine's quality is mutable.
- Nine's vibrations let you see beyond the physical into the limitlessness of the universe.
- Nine is the number of fulfillment, it triples the effect of three the number of cosmic power.
- Representing the end of a cycle nine indicates it is time to tie up loose ends.
- Generally nine depicts completion, wholeness and the sense of satisfaction that comes from reaching a hard worked for goal.
- Sometimes nine can demonstrate regrets as it's the end of a cycle and things may not have gone well, when this is the case you may experience anxiety about not knowing what to expect next.

ASTROLOGICALLY
- ZODIAC SIGN: PISCES
  RULING PLANET: NEPTUNE
  ELEMENT: WATER
  GENDER: FEMININE
  QUALITY: MUTABLE

- The Moon is represented by PISCES the zodiacal sign symbolizing humans' desire to connect with cosmic consciousness. Ruled by NEPTUNE it represents dreams, imagination, inspiration, spirituality and deception. Related to all that is unreal, ethereal, mystical, otherworldly, invisible, imaginative and creative Neptune is the planet of emotional genius and has dominance over many of the arts. Neptune rules theatre, sensationalism, poetry, music and transcendent modes of creativity. Neptune is also identified with escapism, drugs and alcohol, avoiding responsibilities, destructive self-indulgence, deception, fraud and delusions of all sorts, fascination with celebrities' lives and involvement in religious cults.
- Intuitive and attuned to subtle vibrations WATER SIGN people are quick to sum up others, often at a first meeting. Emotional and sensitive they are a capable of great compassion.
- Inward looking, internally driven, intuitive FEMININE ENERGY is sensitive and emotional while seeking to create co-existence and consensus it is introspective and nurturing.
- MUTABLE SIGN Pisces represents versatile and adaptable people who willingly serve others often by working in service industries. Seeing both sides of a situation these people choose to adapt to an environment rather than to shape it. By accepting change mutable people end what was.

ARCHETYPE BEING REPRESENTED
- **Symbolic message** - Emotions.
- **Archetype** - The Moon – linked with dreams. A symbol of the unconscious mind and associated with the night sky the moon represents secrets and mysteries that may not be understood or even recognized.

SYMBOLISM INCLUDES
- **Night sky** – symbolizes darkness, secrets, mystery, the opposite of light and knowing.
- **Large yellow moon radiating energy** – symbolizes things are not as they appear, it is night but you can see the sun's rays.
- **Looks like the moon is an eclipse, right in front of the sun** – symbolizing that sometimes the same thing seems different when viewed in moonlight.

- **Yods** – the yod a dew drop shaped symbol represents the primary Hebrew letter. Yods are associated with the astrological sign Virgo. Symbolizing creative seeds yods represent divine grace and healing and the potency of activity, power and direction. Translated they mean "open hand" and represent the new possibility of divine energy coming through us manifesting in the material act of creation. The yods yellow colour denotes enthusiasm, opportunity and energy.

- **Two pillars (*as gateway towers*)** – symbolizing spirituality and a connection to the heavens they represent duality as in night and day and signify a portal to another realm.

- **Two pillars** –these same towers (*pillars*) appear on the Death card and represent a twin motive. In dreams twin motives or two things not necessarily the same often occur when some unconscious content is approaching the threshold of our consciousness as it is attempting to make itself known. On this card these pillars are symbolizing a new or emerging awareness in our spiritual journey.

- **Green grass** – denotes earth energy, fertility, being grounded in reality, manifestation and wisdom.

- **Mountain** – symbolizes an infinite object, stability, wisdom and denotes spiritual loftiness.

- **Twisting path** –symbolizes a treacherous, twisting, yet rising path between our animalistic (*wolf*) and our more civilized (*dog*) nature, between the realm of magic and the rational world, between inspirations and understanding, it is another example of the tension of opposites.

- **Dog** – represents the tame (*conscious*) aspects of personality.

- **Wolf** – represents the wild (*unconscious*) aspects of personality. The wolf was one of the creatures of Artemis, the maiden aspect of the Great Mother. A shadow aspect of this is the werewolf, which appears when the moon is full (*instincts out of control, or the dark side of our instincts*), and can only be destroyed by a weapon made of silver, the moon's traditional metal.

- **Crab** – the sign of Cancer (*water sign*) which represents caring and tenaciousness. The crab represents the dark and hidden process of regeneration and a need to plunge to the depths of inner emotions.

- **Water** - symbolizes feminine energy, hidden knowledge, secrets, and intuitiveness – it represents our watery origins.

UPRIGHT MEANING

- About choice, karma and authenticity versus dutifulness.
- This card represents the unconscious, the shadowy, hidden side of our natures and the complex, emotionally driven, murky situations in which we find ourselves, as well as the deep well of intuitive knowing that cannot be accessed through intellect alone.
- Pay attention to your hunches and dreams, this is a good time to develop your psychic skills.
- This is a time to examine emerging ideas and information, especially as they appear in imagination and dreams, in order to achieve a sense of inner integration.
- Do not surrender to your instincts as all the information surrounding this situation is not available to you.
- May represent a situation where all the information is not out in the open, secrets are being kept from you making it difficult or impossible to arrive at a correct conclusion.
- Nothing can be taken for granted. Sleep on any decisions, give them more time, this is not a good time to establish plans. Let events take their natural course, do not force a decision.
- Hidden forces are operating around you. You may not be able to control them but you can avoid being controlled by them. Watch your step.

REVERSED MEANING

- There are lies and deceit occurring around you.
- For a female you or someone close to you might experience gynaecological problems, for a male this could be stomach ulcers.
- *The meaning of the card is delayed or extended into the future.*
- *An aspect of the upright meaning of the card needs to be released so you can move forward.*
- *This is not about the upright meaning, place another card on top of the reversed one and read it.*

PERSONAL GROWTH CONSIDERATIONS

- Representing fluctuation, confusion, heightened intuitiveness, vivid dreams or visions, mystery, and deception, the Moon card symbolizes the deepest recesses of your inner being. From the Moon you learn to connect with the unconscious realm – both the personal and the collective. The lesson being taught in this mysterious and shadowy world is that you cannot rely on intellect alone; instead you must often follow your intuition, emotions and primal instincts.

VERBAL AFFIRMATION

- "I value intuitiveness when making important decisions."

UNIFYING THEMES

- Card 18 - THE MOON when reduced is 9 and shares similar aspects to Card 9 - THE HERMIT.
- The Moon and the Hermit cards both convey determinedly feminine energies at work. They deal with inner thoughts, intuitions, and deeper knowledge. Physically the cards both show night skies which indicate introspection and an absence of complete information.

XIX

THE SUN

Card 19 – The Sun

REPRESENTS
- optimism
- clarity of vision
- feeling energized
- confidence
- experiencing joy

NUMBER NINETEEN
- The number nineteen reduces to one. (1+9 = 10 / 1+0=1)
- Ruled by the Sun one's quality is cardinal.
- One's energy is individual, solitary and self-contained.
- Representing the beginning of form number one relates to the active principle of creation.
- The mystic centre and core of mysterious, inscrutable, symbolic, secretive and hidden knowing is represented by one.
- One represents self-development, creativity, action, progress, a new chance, and rebirth.

ASTROLOGICALLY
- Zodiac sign: Leo
  Ruling Planet: the Sun
  Element: Fire
  Gender: Masculine
  Quality: Fixed

- The Sun card is represented by the astrological sign Leo. Natural leaders who are not easily discouraged Leo's pursue goals with great determination. Ruled by the Sun Leo represents the personal ego with its strong need for self-expression and admiration. The Sun symbolizes creative force, strength, vigour, ardour, generosity and the ability to function as a mature individual. The Sun indicates the complete potential of every human being.

- A FIRE SIGN, Leo displays vital energy, action, and creative talent.
- Primarily motivated by external concerns MASCULINE ENERGY is outward looking, action-oriented and protective. Seeking to dominate the outside world, it can be hard, firm, logical, strong, rational, rough and loud.
- Leo, a FIXED SIGN, represents faithful and persevering people who see projects through to the end. Resisting change they attempt to adapt the environment to themselves and above all they want to maintain things.

ARCHETYPE BEING REPRESENTED

- **Symbolic message** - Joy.
- **Archetype** - The Sun – is a symbol of consciousness and action. It's the centre of the universe and the source of heat, illumination, and life on earth.

SYMBOLISM INCLUDES

- **Blue sky** – symbolizes the home of the gods, good times and no cares.
- **Huge yellow sun with extended rays** – represents absolute cosmic power, clarity, vitality, growth, goodness, and warmth. This is a masculine energy which is all about glory and splendour and getting things done. Symbolizing unlimited resources from the Divine the wavy and straight lines indicate directness versus indirectness and positive versus negative influences.
- **Four sunflowers growing** – symbolize happiness, vitality and good feelings. They also represent the four kingdoms of nature, mineral, vegetable, animal and human.
- **Red banner** – red signifies passion and action, this banner represents a fire sign so included here are warmth, energy, confidence and drive. The child holds this banner lightly (*no burden*) which suggests unfurling energy, action and vibration.
- **Naked child** – nakedness symbolizes complete and absolute innocence. The child symbolizes your plans bearing fruit (*a child*) – the child represents our psyche's urge to realize itself.

The child is riding with outstretched arms, using no reins and thus symbolizes the perfect balance between conscious and unconscious. Consciousness has no need to control unconscious forces and instincts (*the horse*) because they trust one another and can work together to bring information, knowledge and insight "into the light." This child is a divine child; it represents the inherent divinity and unity in us all from which we can create new forms.

- **Wreath of flowers on child's head** - they have bloomed and thus symbolize the near approach of the harvest of final realization and liberation; there are six flowers and these denote an emphasis on the development of the soul.
- **Red feather in child's hair** - the feather is associated with air signs and thinking and red signifies passion and action.
- **White horse** – white signifies purity and goodness; the horse symbolizes our instincts.
- **Sunflowers on the wall** - symbolize constancy.
- **Grey stone wall** – grey symbolizes wisdom and the wall symbolizes protection from danger. The wall represents being cut off from things you don't want right now and makes only forward motion possible. The wall also depicts the physical and natural world.

UPRIGHT MEANING
- About a cheerful time when things are going well.
- About feeling confident and experiencing a sense of accomplishment and overall contentment.
- A new beginning, perhaps starting a job, the birth of a child or a new project.
- About gaining an enlightened perspective through turning your focus toward knowledge.
- You can see clearly now, all that you have worked for is coming to be.
- You may receive unexpected gifts – don't analyze why they came or what they mean just enjoy them.
- Savour life, you don't live to work but work to live, enjoy yourself.

- This card indicates it's a good time to make the major purchase you have been thinking about.
- This card improves the ones that are near it in a reading.
- This card is about a comprehensive understanding of the components of a situation.
- It is about "casting light" on the complexities of the situation.
- It is about new confidence through transforming one's life.
- It is a time when greater clarity is present and practical inspiration occurs.
- It is about unconscious workings becoming conscious awareness.

REVERSED MEANING
- Always a positive card, it improves everything around it.
- *The meaning of the card is delayed or extended into the future.*
- *An aspect of the upright meaning of the card needs to be released so you can move forward.*
- *This is not about the upright meaning, place another card on top of the reversed one and read it.*

PERSONAL GROWTH CONSIDERATIONS
- Representing joy, optimism, confidence and energized feelings the Sun is about illumination and chases away doubts and fears. It teaches you how to move outward into the world after having journeyed inward to identify your dark side. The Sun represents the strengths and capabilities you now possess, from the lessons you have learned so far, thereby enabling you to demonstrate your sense of clarity and confidence.

VERBAL AFFIRMATION
- "I am confident and capable."

UNIFYING THEMES
- Card 19 - THE SUN and Card 10 - WHEEL OF FORTUNE both reduce to one and share commonalities with Card 1 - THE MAGICIAN.
- Masculine energy represented by number one is expressed in all three of these cards, although the Magician also encompasses

feminine energy. These cards are about active principles, The Magician is utilizing his knowledge to make things happen, the Wheel of Fortune is indicative of an action that has started and change is coming, and the Sun is about starting something new.

JUDGEMENT

Card 20 - Judgement

REPRESENTS

* change but always for the better
* making an honest appraisal
* reaching a final decision
* reflecting on past events

NUMBER TWENTY

* The number twenty reduces to two. (2+0=2)
* Ruled by the Moon two's quality is fixed.
* Two represents some type of union or partnership with another person, a spiritual entity, or two parts of you.
* Associated with the balance of polarities such as yin/yang, male/female and public/separate.
* Two builds on the opportunity presented by one (*the ace*).
* Two can represent sensitivity to others sometimes to the point of considering their wellbeing over your own.
* Representative of immersing yourself into another person, an idea, or a project.
* Two is associated with choices and decisions.

ASTROLOGICALLY

* ZODIAC SIGN: SCORPIO
  RULING PLANET: PLUTO
  ELEMENT: WATER
  GENDER: FEMININE
  QUALITY: FIXED

* Judgement is represented by SCORPIO, which symbolizes the transforming powers of life and death. Scorpio, ruled by PLUTO, represents resurrection, renewal, regeneration and resolution. Ruling the forces of creation and destruction Pluto symbolizes the capacity to change totally and forever one's

lifestyle, thought and behaviour. As the planet of beginnings and endings, Pluto can effect total transformation. Pluto can also bring a lust for power with strong obsessions.

- Scorpio, a WATER SIGN, represents intuitive people attuned to subtle vibrations who are quick to sum up others, often at first meeting. They are emotional and capable of great compassion and sensitivity.

- Inward looking and internally driven, intuitive FEMININE ENERGY is sensitive and emotional, while seeking to create co-existence and consensus it is introspective and nurturing.

- FIXED SIGNS represent faithful and persevering people who see projects through to the end. Resistant to change they attempt to adapt the environment to themselves and above all they want to maintain things.

ARCHETYPE BEING REPRESENTED

- **Symbolic message** - Judgement and completion. It can be considered the Last Judgement and the ramifications of that upon the individual.

- **Archetype** - Evaluation and reward – reveals all, heralds the dawn of a new world and stands as a reminder of the power of forgiveness.

SYMBOLISM INCLUDES

- **Angel blowing into a horn** - delivering a divine message that will clarify questions. This message will always be good news.

- **Angel** – is either Gabriel (*water*) the angel of completion, or Michael (*fire*) the leader of the forces of light.

- **Angel's wings are purple and red** - purple signifies authority and red indicates energy and passion, there is enough action here to deliver the message.

- **Flag attached to the angel's horn** – this is an equal armed Greek cross which is an ancient emblem of Hecate, goddess of the crossroads. The centre created by the crossroads represents the union of opposites, but in their crossing they represent ambivalence.

- **Seven streaks of sound emitted from the horn** - these are sound waves, vibrations, stimulating the seven chakras and awakening the grey figures, which all arise from floating coffins.

- **Opened coffins** – coffins represent the vessel of transmutation – here the coffins depict "awakened" figures casting off their mental restrictions thus they are ready for transmutation.
- **Mountains** - symbolize wisdom, loftiness and a connection to spirituality.
- **Water** – symbolizes feminine energy, emotions, caring, intuition and hidden knowledge.
- **People standing with arms upraised** – these people are asking for feedback, they consist of a male, female and child. The male represents masculine energy the female feminine energy and the child the inner aspects of us. The three people in the foreground represent a time of transition through the conscious choice of discarding deadened aspects of our self. They also symbolize spiritual growth through the reconciliation of opposites and with community (*the three people in the background represent community*). The people are also indicating that the reality of life has changed and our only choice is to follow.
- **Shape the centre child's arms are making** – represents the Hebrew letter *shin*; when shown graphically it resembles the three-pronged flame (*colour of child's hair*) representing the fiery spirit.
- **Shape the foreground figures are making** – form the Latin letters L (*the woman*), V (*the child*), and X (*the man*), which means "light."

UPRIGHT MEANING
- About good judgement.
- How we use power is one of the important lessons depicted in this card.
- About expecting positive results very soon, your actions have been correct all along even if you have received negative feedback or harboured your own doubts.
- Important questions will now be answered, assurances received and doubts resolved. You will be rewarded for your efforts.
- In some cases this may indicate a "wake up call," a time to ponder and reflect on what you believe and what you are doing. The energy in this card is positive so even if you have not

been pleased with your thoughts, deeds or beliefs you have the ability to change these and thereby experience a better future.

- This card is about re-evaluation, rethinking or altering our perceptions; these may even be radical in nature.
- This card can mean shedding our personal illusions by moving beyond our past experiences.
- It can be a time to rise to a higher calling by attending to a new message or a call.
- This card is about the ongoing changes that occur in life, the birthing and renewal process.

REVERSED MEANING
- Can indicate fear of failure which results in inaction.
- Can indicate confusion and a sense that you have lost your way.
- *The meaning of the card is delayed or extended into the future.*
- *An aspect of the upright meaning of the card needs to be released so you can move forward.*
- *This is not about the upright meaning, place another card on top of the reversed one and read it.*

PERSONAL GROWTH CONSIDERATIONS
- Representing how your thoughts and actions have led you to the place you are now the Judgement card promises change but always for the better. Even if you don't yet know what you are being called to do, you realize from all the lessons you have learned that you have developed the necessary skills and faith you need to succeed.

VERBAL AFFIRMATION
- "I make good judgements and expect positive results."

UNIFYING THEMES
- Card 20 – JUDGEMENT and Card 11 – JUSTICE both reduce to two and have unifying themes with Card 2 - THE HIGH PRIESTESS.
- Two is about basic division, pillars of entry, male and female.

- All three of these cards are about the holding of information. The High Priestess protects her information, Justice considers information and Judgement provides information.

XXI

THE WORLD

Card 21 - The World

REPRESENTS
- attainment
- achievement
- success
- completion
- integration
- savouring the present
- self fulfillment

NUMBER TWENTY ONE
- The number twenty one reduces to three. (2+1=3)
- Ruled by Jupiter three's quality is mutable.
- Cosmic energy is embedded in threes.
- Three, a mystic number, represents Spirit.
- Threes possess celestial power – the sun stands still for three days at the solstices before resuming its motion; threes encompass past, present and future; the moon looks full for three days and disappears as dark for three days. Threes make up the trinity of mind, body and spirit.
- Group activities, movement, action, growth and development are expressed by threes.
- Sometimes with threes expansion occurs too quickly causing you to spread yourself too thin or for your energies to scatter.
- If you pay attention to what you are doing threes vibration is cheerful, optimistic and pleasant, representing a period of happiness and benefits.

ASTROLOGICALLY
- ZODIAC SIGN: CAPRICORN
  RULING PLANET: SATURN
  ELEMENT: EARTH
  GENDER: FEMININE

QUALITY: CARDINAL

- The World is represented by CAPRICORN, the world leader, which depicts social order, pragmatism, and the slow but sure ascent to the top. Regarded as a sacred sign due to the winter solstice taking place within its boundaries Capricorn brings an increase of daylight to the Northern Hemisphere. Associated with restriction, obstacles and discipline Capricorn's ruling planet SATURN creates limits and represents ambition, selfishness, depression, jealousy and greed. Sometimes a harsh task master Saturn's lessons once learned often lead to wisdom, understanding and the granting of lasting rewards.
- Grounded and oriented towards what is real EARTH SIGNS bring form to ideas. Creating structures they are practical, productive, tactile and dependable while demonstrating persistence, patience and reasonableness.
- Receptive, intuitive and inward looking FEMININE ENERGY seeks consensus and co-existence while displaying nurturing qualities.
- Capricorn, a CARDINAL SIGN, represents new beginnings, enterprise and getting things started. People born under this sign are instigators and leaders.

ARCHETYPE BEING REPRESENTED
- **Symbolic message** - Fulfilment.
- **Archetype** - Satisfaction and wholeness – depicts the never-ending, spiral dance of life. It's a card of completion and success – as well as the chance to start another round.

SYMBOLISM INCLUDES
- **Naked woman with a purple cloth** – she is not an angel but appears to be the same as an angel as she can fly or remain suspended in air – purple grants her authority. She represents our divine essence.
- **Position of her legs and feet create a triangle** – the same as the Hanged Man's, the triangle is an alchemical sign for sulphur. Sulphur symbolizes passion, activity, will and motivation.

- **Woman appears to be perpetually dancing within the wreath** – represents movement which is the generator of all things.
- **Wands** – the woman holds a wand in each hand signifying balance. The wands also signify the ability to perform a transformation e.g. it is possible for your wishes to come to fruition. The wands have also been considered to be sacred scrolls of knowledge.
- **Green wreath** – symbolizes Christmas, giving, good will, new beginnings, and perpetuity – the red ribbon tying the wreath is done in an infinity knot or lemniscate. Green represents the earth which signifies that manifestation of ideas and projects is not only possible but highly likely.
- **Green wreath** – is also thought to represent a Tattvas *(also Tatwas)* which are East Indian geometrical symbols, often painted on separate cards, and sometimes worked into Tarot illustrations. They act as gateways into the astral world for purposes of divination, mediation and scrying.
- **Green wreath** – this wreath also forms a 0 which balances the beginning card the Fool.
- **Icons in the 4 corners** – these same symbols appear on the Wheel of Fortune card. These icons represent the four fixed signs of the Zodiac. The human is Aquarius *(air sign)*, the bull is Taurus *(earth sign)*, the lion is Leo *(fire sign)* and the eagle is Scorpio *(water sign)*. These four figures also appear in the Bible in Revelations 4:7.
- **Blue sky** – symbolizes happiness, good times and contentment.

UPRIGHT MEANING
- About self-actualization, individuation *(to form into a distinct entity)* and building new worlds.
- About the promise of success.
- The potential and the conditions are right to make just about anything happen.
- All is right with the world, whatever you do right now prospers, change of job, new residence, move to another place, new friendships, or a new relationship.
- If this card represents a situation you know that you have attained all you can and have done a great job. You are entitled to all the benefits that are coming your way from the hard work you accomplished. You can now go onto other things.

In fact you need to, as your talents have achieved all they can in this area.

- In terms of spirituality this card is about recognizing one's wholeness.
- It is about ordering one's life by higher or cosmic principles.
- The World represents the cosmic order depicted by the seasons and cyclic nature of life.
- A card of home, and promise, it also symbolizes light at the end of the tunnel, the sense of satisfaction and fulfillment that come from knowing you've done your best.
- This card reminds us that the highest value in life is the condition of our own soul.
- It may mean travel abroad.

REVERSED MEANING

- You have fallen into a rut but can make the necessary changes to start achieving your goals.
- If the situation you are in is wrong for you use it to gain experience and move forward.
- *The meaning of the card is delayed or extended into the future.*
- *An aspect of the upright meaning of the card needs to be released so you can move forward.*
- *This is not about the upright meaning, place another card on top of the reversed one and read it.*

PERSONAL GROWTH CONSIDERATIONS

- Representing attainment, fulfilment, wholeness and wisdom the World card symbolizes the state of contentment and inner peace that results from having united your personal will with Divine Will. You understand your place in the universe. Everything is as it should be, and all is right with the world.

VERBAL AFFIRMATION

- "I order my life by cosmic principles and recognize my wholeness."

UNIFYING THEMES

- Card 12 - The HANGED MAN and Card 21 - THE WORLD both reduce to three and share similarities with Card 3 - THE EMPRESS.

- All three of these cards are about connecting with cosmic consciousness, the concept that the universe exists as an interconnected network of consciousness, with each conscious being linked to every other. When cosmic consciousness is realized in the individual this person experiences a euphoric feeling that includes a sense of wonder, a sense of being in the presence of the "One" and a sense of greater understanding of the universe as a whole.

- The Empress symbolizes "the mother archetype," she is about love and contentment, and can be viewed as connected with cosmic consciousness. The Hanged Man is influenced strongly by Neptune's influences which are about the desire to connect with cosmic consciousness. The World is about cosmic order and the sense of fulfilment; it is the realization of cosmic consciousness.

PART III

The Minor Arcana Cards

23. What does Minor Arcana mean?

Arcana means secrets or mysteries. The numbered cards in the Minor Arcana called pip cards do not hold as much importance in a reading as Major Arcana trump cards. Of the seventy eight (78) cards in a Tarot deck, twenty two (22) belong to the Major Arcana and the remaining fifty six (56) to the Minor Arcana. The pip cards flesh out the information in a reading.

Similar to standard playing cards Minor Arcana cards are made up four suits commonly referred to as wands, cups, swords and pentacles. Some Tarot decks name these suits differently. In standard playing cards wands are associated with clubs, cups with hearts, swords with spades and pentacles with diamonds. Unlike playing cards which have thirteen cards per suit, the Major Arcana cards have fourteen. Suit cards are numbered one through ten and include four royalty cards, a Page, a Knight, a Queen and a King.

Like standard playing cards the original pip cards did not have pictures but were represented by the number of the symbols associated to that card. For example the two of wands was illustrated with two wands, the nine of swords with nine swords etc. This is a major reason why the numbers on Tarot cards are significant in a reading as prior to Waite's deck, created in nineteen hundred and nine (1909), the card's number is what would have been used to flesh out the meanings of the trump cards.

The first suit in the Minor Arcana is often seen as wands followed by cups, swords and then pentacles.

- Wands – idea stage, deals with concepts.
- Cups – emotional stage, the bridge between idea and action.
- Swords – action, movement, struggle and effort.
- Pentacles – results, fruition, realization and prosperity.

24. Court cards

Often considered the most difficult to read the court cards present certain challenges. The best advice is to choose a method to follow with the necessary flexibility to utilize other possible meanings given the circumstances found in a particular reading.

1. VIEWED AS INDICATING PEOPLE. The attributes of the particular royal figure are used to describe someone who is associated with the Querent. This can be someone from the past or in the present or someone who will be entering the Querent's life soon. The royal figure can also be representing the Querent. You need to get to know the royal figures well when using this method. Pages are seen as children, knights as young adults, queens and kings as mature adults. Create a personality profile for them and learn it.

2. COURT CARDS AS SYMBOLISM. The page always brings a message, the knight means movement, trips or change is coming.

3. VIEWED AS SITUATIONS. The zodiacal and numerological aspects associated to the card plus the personalities of the royal figures are used to describe a situation.

• My method is to consider Pages as messages and lay a card by the Page and interpret its meaning as the message.

• I read Knights as always meaning change is coming; the stance of the horse on the card indicates the speed in which the change will occur, for example the Knight of Swords is on a charging horse so this indicates that change is coming fast.

• I read the Queens and Kings in terms of situations or circumstances the Querent will be involved in.

• As mentioned earlier it is necessary to create a personality profile for each court card in case this interpretation seems to be the one that best fits the reading. Depending upon the reading I use different methods sometimes blending several of them together.

The Suit of Wands

25. The Suit of Wands

- The wand suit focuses on enterprise, work and career, destination (*travel*), and one's abilities and potentials.
- Wands, a fire sign, are represented by Aries, Leo and Sagittarius. Fire signs symbolize leadership, initiative, action, energy, and new ideas. Self-starters people under this sign are leaders not followers.
- Wands represent masculine energy. Outward looking, action-oriented and protective masculine energy is primarily motivated by external concerns. Seeking to dominate the outside world, it can be hard, firm, logical, strong, rational, rough and loud.
- In medieval times wands represented the peasants, people who had to work for anything they gained.
- Wands are associated with clubs in playing cards.
- In a reading the wand and sword suits are sometimes thought of representing the depths of tribulation while the cup and pentacle suits represent the heights of bliss.
- Often seen as the first suit in the Minor Arcana wands are the idea or concept stage.

Reversed Cards

Sometimes cards are upside down when they are chosen. Readers have preferences as to interpreting the meanings of cards in this position. I have listed some reversed meanings and also provided some other options. It is up to you as a reader to determine which meaning best fits. Some readers simply turn the cards right side up and do not deal with reversed meanings. It is good practice to choose a standard method of reading reversed cards and deviate only when circumstances in the reading make it sensible to do so.

WANDS

Ace of Wands

REPRESENTS
- beginnings
- possibly an inheritance
- an outburst of creativity
- opportunity comes knocking

NUMBER ONE
- One's energy is individual, solitary and self-contained.
- Representing the beginning of form number one relates to the active principle of creation.
- The mystic centre and core of mysterious, inscrutable, symbolic, secretive and hidden knowing is represented by one.
- One represents self-development, creativity, action, progress, a new chance, and rebirth.

ASTROLOGICALLY
- The Ace of Wands is the root of the power of fire.
- The Ace (1) ruled by the Sun is very egocentric quite often representing a person who is somewhat of a loner.
- One corresponds to CARDINAL SIGNS which are about new beginnings, enterprise and getting things started. Aries for spring, Cancer for summer, Libra for autumn, and Capricorn for winter.
- Wands are represented by FIRE SIGNS, Aries, Leo and Sagittarius. They display vital energy, action, and creative talent.
- Fire signs MASCULINE ENERGY primarily motivated by external concerns is outward looking, action-oriented and protective. Seeking to dominate the outside world, it can be hard, firm, logical, strong, rational, rough and loud.

SYMBOLISM INCLUDES

- **Thumb is pointing up** – a signal that things are ready to start. You're good to go on anything you want.
- **Hills** – due to being rounded they suggest age (*as opposed to mountains that have not yet worn down*) hence ancient wisdom.
- **Green** – denotes fertility, growth, potential for prosperity.
- **Trees** – symbolize the inexhaustible life process.
- **Castle** – as this castle is on the left side of the card it suggests that the innate security, refuge, place of protection and safety that castles always imply comes from one's past family of origin.
- **Purple mountains in the far distance** – denotes authority, divine inspiration, spiritual insight and knowledge.
- **Winding stream in the foreground** – suggests action, the passage of time, or the flow of life.
- **Grey cloud** – denotes wisdom.
- **Radiating light around the hand** – this is like a halo and it symbolizes divinity, an unusual holiness and the possession of higher powers.
- **Ten budding leaves attached to the wand** - they symbolize the potential for completion.
- **Eight leaves in the shape of the Hebrew letter yod** - (*leaves not attached to the wand*) symbolizing creative seeds and representing divine grace and healing yods can be translated to mean "open hand." A yod represents the new possibility of divine energy or intelligence coming through us and becoming manifest in the material act of creation.

UPRIGHT MEANING

- This is a gift from the universe.
- Whatever you are thinking about is possible, especially if this is to do with career or endeavours in creative areas.
- This card is about new beginnings, so it may indicate a new job starting, a promotion, or acceptance into a program or school.
- It could mean success with artistic endeavours such as writing, painting, pottery etc.

- This can mean a starting point of a whole new cycle.
- It may mean starting your own business.
- The time is right for you to choose to initiate something and there is a high likelihood of success.

REVERSED MEANING

- *The meaning of the card is delayed or extended into the future.*
- *An aspect of the upright meaning of the card needs to be released so you can move forward.*
- *This is not about the upright meaning, place another card on top of the reversed one and read it.*

TWO

WANDS

Two of Wands

REPRESENTS
* ambitions
* personal power
* work is underway

NUMBER TWO
* Two represents some type of union or partnership with another person, a spiritual entity, or two parts of you.
* Associated with the balance of polarities such as yin/yang, male/female and public/separate.
* Two builds on the opportunity presented by one (*the ace*).
* Two can represent sensitivity to others sometimes to the point of considering their wellbeing over your own.
* Representative of immersing yourself into another person, an idea, or a project.
* Two is associated with choices and decisions.

ASTROLOGICALLY
* Ruled by the Moon, two is associated with relationships, cooperation, emotions and feelings.
* Two corresponds to FIXED SIGNS Taurus, Leo, Scorpio and Aquarius. Resistant to change these people are faithful and persevering seeing projects through to the end. They attempt to adapt the environment to themselves and above all they want to maintain things.
* Wands are represented by FIRE SIGNS, Aries, Leo and Sagittarius. They display vital energy, action, and creative talent.
* Fire signs MASCULINE ENERGY primarily motivated by external concerns is outward looking, action-oriented and protective. Seeking to dominate the outside world, it can be hard, firm, logical, strong, rational, rough and loud.

SYMBOLISM INCLUDES

- **Man holding the globe** – suggests domination over nature or the process of unlimited manifestation of an idea or creation.
- **Orange clothing** – signifies warmth and good will.
- **Red hat** –symbolizes an active and passionate mind.
- **Standing between two wands** – can be like pillars denoting a connection to Spirit; they also represent a connection to "outside" rather than an internal experience; as a man made material they are representative of structure so symbolize "upholding," "supporting," or the "encompassing" of some concept.
- **Man is standing behind the wall of his house** – symbolizes a separation; it could mean he is not physically involved right now in an activity but he is mentally involved. It also symbolizes an orderly mind, someone who is practical, as the wand is anchored to the wall.
- **Cross of St. Andrew set into the white lilies and red roses** - this cross forms an X and is also known as the cross saltire. St. Andrew's cross acts as an amulet against danger, a weapon against monsters, even the Devil. As the union of male/female or earth/sky, it signifies integration and manifestation. The X also refers to decisions needing to be made, chances to take and the need for communication between the conscious and the unconscious. It can refer to information or material seeking to emerge from the unconscious.
- **White lilies and red roses together** – lilies represent mystic ways and red roses represent esoteric knowledge - on this card they represent choice.
- **Sea** - the sea, as opposed to the ocean, has known boundaries, it is not "limitless" as is the ocean. The sea is symbolic of the "known quantities of life."
- **Mountain** – represents challenge, vision, achievement, stability and loftiness in terms of spirituality.
- **Green grass** – denotes earth energy, new beginnings, manifestation of ideas.
- **Ploughed field** - symbolizes the readiness to accept something; it's the preliminary work that needs to occur before the "seeding" of an idea.

- **Road** – symbolizes the cyclic nature – the ups and downs that occur in life and in our spiritual journeys.

UPRIGHT MEANING
- About a time for making plans.
- A time to consider ideas on how to start something.
- The need to explore the "how to" of the opportunity presented by the ace.
- Expanding on an idea and determining how it will be made manifest.
- This is a time of making choices.
- The need for networking, finding financial backers, exploring partnerships, engaging in cooperative bargaining, and the forming of teams.
- About a relationship based on something other than love.
- Expectation that the idea launched from the ace can and will succeed.
- This can be about requiring patience.
- This is a time to allow intuition a dominate place.
- This is sometimes about issues using power, it could mean you or someone else has it or wants it. Carefully consider your goals and activities to ensure you are using power respectfully, wisely, and in positive ways.
- About allowing yourself free thought, this is not a time for subtlety rather it is a time for bold, innovative, and creative ideas.

REVERSED MEANING
- *The meaning of the card is delayed or extended into the future.*
- *An aspect of the upright meaning of the card needs to be released so you can move forward.*
- *This is not about the upright meaning, place another card on reversed one and read it.*

THREE

WANDS

Three of Wands

REPRESENTS
- distribution and productivity
- problems can be resolved if you remain calm, dignified and intelligent
- completion of the first stage
- demonstrating leadership

NUMBER THREE
- Cosmic energy is embedded in threes.
- Three, a mystic number, represents Spirit.
- Threes possess celestial power – the sun stands still for three days at the solstices before resuming its motion; threes encompass past, present and future; the moon looks full for three days and disappears as dark for three days. Threes make up the trinity of mind, body and spirit.
- Group activities, movement, action, growth and development are expressed by threes.
- Sometimes with threes expansion occurs too quickly causing you to spread yourself too thin or for your energies to scatter.
- If you pay attention to what you are doing threes vibration is cheerful, optimistic and pleasant, representing a period of happiness and benefits.

ASTROLOGICALLY
- JUPITER, considered a major benefit, rules three.
- With Jupiter's influence over the number three money often comes and goes easily.
- Three corresponds to MUTABLE SIGNS Gemini, Virgo, Sagittarius and Pisces. Seeing both sides of a situation they adjust their attitudes and adapt to almost any circumstances. Versatility allows mutable sign people to accept change and thereby end what was.

- Wands are represented by FIRE SIGNS, Aries, Leo and Sagittarius. Born leaders they display vital energy, action, and creative talent.
- Fire signs MASCULINE ENERGY primarily motivated by external concerns is outward looking, action-oriented and protective. Seeking to dominate the outside world, it can be hard, firm, logical, strong, rational, rough and loud.

SYMBOLISM INCLUDES

- **Yellow** – symbolizes creativity, optimism, and enthusiasm.
- **Two wands on right hand side of man** – the right side symbolizes masculine energy so lots of action.
- **Orange clothing** - represents warmth and energy.
- **Checkerboard pattern on man's sash** – represents the duality (*positive/negative, good/evil, light/darkness, and spirit/matter*) of destiny or wisdom. They also represent a sorting process that leads to transformation (*greater understanding and connectedness with the universe*).
- **Standing on high ground looking down** – symbolizes a need to gain perspective, to take the long view of something.
- **Green grass and green clothing** – denotes earth energy and the high likelihood of manifestation of ideas or projects.
- **Ships arriving** – "ships are coming in" it means the venture was successful.
- **Mountains** – symbolize challenge, vision, achievement, stability and loftiness in terms of spirituality.
- **Water** – represents feminine energy, feelings, emotion, and hidden information. This water is calm indicating how the person needs to be.
- **Body language** – he looks engaged, confident and calm, from his stance and clothing he seems to possess resources.

UPRIGHT MEANING

- About a time of beginning activity, the idea has taken shape and now the work is starting.
- Indicates a need to stay focused and not to scatter your energies.

- About looking into the future to understand how the choices you are currently making will impact the long term project.
- Lots of optimism and potential to succeed.
- It can indicate premonitions or other intuitions about what is to come.

REVERSED MEANING
- Scattering of one's energies. Careless mistakes.
- A strong competitor who has gained the edge.
- A caution against pride and arrogance.
- *The meaning of the card is delayed or extended into the future.*
- *An aspect of the upright meaning of the card needs to be released so you can move forward.*
- *This is not about the upright meaning, place another card on reversed one and read it.*

FOUR

WANDS

Four of Wands

REPRESENTS
- trouble is behind you
- relax and enjoy life for a while
- a time for celebrations
- a time to reap rewards

NUMBER FOUR
- Four is the number associated to "matter."
- Four is a time to build a foundation that will support your ideas and projects.
- Hard work and self discipline are required with fours.
- A stabilizing time for creating structures and order.
- Representing manifestation of your ideas, fours represent prosperity, peace, happiness, abundance and even triumph.
- Sometimes fours represent a stage in personal development when a stalemate has been reached, a period that often seems necessary for unacknowledged emotions or dilemmas to come into consciousness so we can experience them and get on with growth or healing.

ASTROLOGICALLY
- Eccentric and unusual URANUS rules the number four.
- Where four is prominent invention and ingenuity are very important elements to any given situation.
- Four corresponds to CARDINAL SIGNS which are associated with new beginnings, enterprise and getting things started. Aries for spring, Cancer for summer, Libra for autumn and Capricorn for winter.
- Wands are represented by FIRE SIGNS, Aries, Leo and Sagittarius. Born leaders they display vital energy, action, and creative talent.

- Fire signs MASCULINE ENERGY primarily motivated by external concerns is outward looking, action-oriented and protective. Seeking to dominate the outside world, it can be hard, firm, logical, strong, rational, rough and loud.

SYMBOLISM INCLUDES

- **Predominance of yellow** – symbolizes vibrancy, enthusiasm, creativity and optimism.
- **Wands as pillars** – represent portals to the sky and a connection to spirituality.
- **Swag of oak leaves and grapes** - oak leaves symbolize slow growth and progress, from the acorn to the tree; grapes represent abundance, fruitfulness, and the achievement that occurs from having successfully attended to one's "vines."
- **Large castle** – this represents resources, a home and sufficient income to maintain one's lifestyle.
- **Arched bridge in front of castle** - arches signify communication, rebirth, leaving the old behind and beginning anew; they can also signify a passage from one state into another.
- **People celebrating** - represents a joyous occasion.

UPRIGHT MEANING

- This is a time for celebration, you have come through the ace's idea, the two's choices, the three's planning and now you are into the manifestation stage.
- Things that you laid a foundation for are looking good; you are celebrating your early successes.
- This is only a four – so even though you are celebrating a great deal of hard work lies ahead of you to bring this venture to its completion.
- This is a time of prosperity, spending money on things you want, spending time with friends.
- A joyful time.
- If this reading is about a relationship then it implies that the couple has gone through some rough times, things are very positive right now but hard work lies ahead in order for them to succeed.
- Sometimes this signals a surprise or a spontaneous thrill.

- Sometimes this represents a planned celebration such as a wedding, anniversary, birthday or victory party.
- This can mean freedom and the exhilarating feeling associated with that.

REVERSED MEANING
- Could mean you are spending too much money.
- *The meaning of the card is delayed or extended into the future.*
- *An aspect of the upright meaning of the card needs to be released so you can move forward.*
- *This is not about the upright meaning, place another card on reversed one and read it.*

FIVE

WANDS

Five of Wands

REPRESENTS
- struggle and frustration
- stiff competition for financial gain
- experiencing hassles
- feeling at cross purposes with others

NUMBER FIVE
- Fives always represent some type of difficulty, tension or crisis.
- Challenges often result in a winner or loser with fives.
- Fives suggest a sense of being on a roller coaster ride or being caught up in a whirlwind.
- Fluctuation, unrest and sometimes clashes create a sense of instability and can cause stress.
- Impulsive and impatient behaviours occur but resourcefulness and curiosity are also present.
- Fives indicate we have the quality of mind, but lack the maturity and knowledge to transform old ways into new patterns of being.
- We may be forced to make a choice in order to end the anxiety that is associated with fives.

ASTROLOGICALLY
- MERCURY the planet associated with communication rules five.
- If five is significant in a reading it may mean this individual needs to make adjustments in order to fit in.
- Five corresponds to FIXED SIGNS Taurus, Leo, Scorpio and Aquarius. Resistant to change these people are faithful and persevering seeing projects through to the end. They attempt to adapt the environment to themselves and above all they want to maintain things.

- Wands are represented by FIRE SIGNS, Aries, Leo and Sagittarius. Born leaders they display vital energy, action, and creative talent.
- Fire signs MASCULINE ENERGY primarily motivated by external concerns is outward looking, action-oriented and protective. Seeking to dominate the outside world, it can be hard, firm, logical, strong, rational, rough and loud.

SYMBOLISM INCLUDES

- **People in the card are wearing different clothing** - symbolizes differing points of view.
- **Person in the middle has no twigs on his stick and is the only one wearing a hat** - depicts the differences amongst these people, even the tools differ; wearing a hat symbolizes the thoughts of the wearer.
- **People are batting their sticks at one another** - signifies tension but it could indicate debating differing opinions.
- **Green grass** – represents earth energy and a high likelihood for manifestation (*worth fighting for a belief or idea*).

UPRIGHT MEANING

- About anxiety, restlessness and strife.
- About being surrounded with tension and conflict and feeling somewhat out of control.
- Possibly you are experiencing a lot of back lash regarding your efforts.
- Could be about numerous differing points of view.
- About the feelings associated with taking a stand for or against a matter or an idea you believe in especially when peers or those in authority (*parents, employers*) see things differently and strongly oppose the position you have taken.
- Can indicate strong competition at work.
- Can be about quarrels with co-workers, neighbours or with others in the home.
- It might indicate writer's block, or a time an artist cannot seem to produce any work. Not a major block just many small irritating ones.

- This is a very trying and challenging time and you feel you might be in a crisis situation.
- There is no peace, calm or harmony.
- You feel as though you are in a dog eat dog environment.
- It is a time to sort out what you really believe compared to conflicting or provocative new beliefs being suggested by your peer group.
- About taking time to keep wrestling with new ideas as this fortifies your own beliefs and makes you stronger when you face new obstacles. The idea is not to end this struggle too soon.
- Facing a challenge that requires considerable effort.

REVERSED MEANING
- Staying in your present situation will require ongoing fighting to maintain the status quo.
- The competition is neither fair nor honest; expect trickery, deceits, and even legal problems and litigation.
- *The meaning of the card is delayed or extended into the future.*
- *An aspect of the upright meaning of the card needs to be released so you can move forward.*
- *This is not about the upright meaning, place another card on reversed one and read it.*

SIX

WANDS

Six of Wands

REPRESENTS
- public acclaim and success
- triumph and victory
- excellent news
- possibly gifts about to received
- feeling pride

NUMBER SIX
- Sixes are always favourable.
- Sixes vibration is cooperative.
- Six represents the ability to transcend difficulties and a sense of peace and quiet after the storm.
- Following the conflicts experienced with fives, sixes demonstrate the integration of new skills learned. Improved coping mechanisms and overcoming challenges has resulted in stability.
- Six is a time of balance and respite that creates a base and a pivot for new experiences.
- Six, an important ceremonial number, refers to Spirit's connection to life in all directions (*north, south, east and west, above and below*).
- Because three (3) is a cosmic number its attributes are amplified by six (6).

ASTROLOGICALLY
- Ruled by the planet Venus six is a pleasant, harmonious number that governs music and the arts. Relationships are of paramount importance with tact and diplomacy figuring prominently.
- When number six is significant money plays an important role.

- Enabling a free flow of energy six allows many opportunities for success.
- Six corresponds to MUTABLE SIGNS Gemini, Virgo, Sagittarius and Pisces. Seeing both sides of a situation they adjust their attitudes and adapt to almost any circumstances. Versatility allows mutable sign people to accept change and thereby end what was.
- Wands are represented by FIRE SIGNS, Aries, Leo and Sagittarius. Born leaders they display vital energy, action, and creative talent.
- Fire signs MASCULINE ENERGY primarily motivated by external concerns is outward looking, action-oriented and protective. Seeking to dominate the outside world, it can be hard, firm, logical, strong, rational, rough and loud.

SYMBOLISM INCLUDES
- **Green** - symbolizes earth energy which is the manifestation and forward movement of a plan.
- **Orange robe** - indicates warmth and a sense of wellbeing.
- **Riding a white horse** - symbolizes purity, justice and good things being delivered. Animals symbolize instincts at play.
- **One person riding others walking** - the rider is depicted as a winner especially as others are walking behind. In modern times this can symbolize a new way of getting around, perhaps a new vehicle.
- **Wreath on head and on top of wand** - these are sometimes referred to as "laurels of victory" so this means success through some action of your own.

UPRIGHT MEANING
- This is a time to keep it simple and attend to everyday needs. Any misunderstanding that occurred during an earlier period of upheaval can now be resolved harmoniously.
- Represents very good news, a message of hope and victory and may indicate gifts about to be received.
- This card indicates something you have hoped for will come to pass.
- This card could indicate you have received a promotion at work and your hard work has been recognized publically.

- This is really triumphing over some adversity, you have won.
- Can expect harmony, equilibrium and making progress toward your destination or goal.
- Can indicate changes in your thought processes or values.
- Can indicate you will be purchasing a new vehicle.

REVERSED MEANING
- There are delays.
- You lost the battle you were in and need to rethink your current position.
- If there are a number of swords around this card it may mean you will experience problems with your vehicle.
- *The meaning of the card is delayed or extended into the future.*
- *An aspect of the upright meaning of the card needs to be released so you can move forward.*
- *This is not about the upright meaning, place another card on reversed one and read it.*

SEVEN

WANDS

Seven of Wands

REPRESENTS
- stiff competition
- success achieved by courage and determination
- showing conviction
- defending yourself

NUMBER SEVEN
- Sevens are sacred numbers made up of three, the number of Spirit and cosmic energy, and four the number of matter, the necessary component for the manifestation of ideas or projects.
- Relating to the development of the soul, sevens deal with wisdom, completeness, and perfection.
- Indicating a need to deal with your inner life, seven is a time of introspection and soul searching that will require solitude.
- A reflective time, seven indicates a period when you will find it necessary to seriously consider how and why specific events occur.
- Sevens represent a turning point as they begin a new cycle of threes. One, two and three the first cycle was followed by four, five and six, and now we have seven, eight and nine.
- Sevens bring about a new restlessness indicating a breakthrough in awareness. Causing us to re-evaluate and willingly try new things sevens often contribute to changing our understanding or perspective.

ASTROLOGICALLY
- Ruled by the planet NEPTUNE, seven a spiritual number with surreal qualities, is connected to mystics, visionaries and seers. Associated with idealism the number seven can represent depression when our expectations of others and our personal goals are not met.

- Seven corresponds to CARDINAL SIGNS which are about new beginnings, enterprise and getting things started. Aries for spring, Cancer for summer, Libra for autumn, and Capricorn for winter.
- Wands are represented by FIRE SIGNS, Aries, Leo and Sagittarius. Born leaders they display vital energy, action, and creative talent.
- Fire signs MASCULINE ENERGY primarily motivated by external concerns is outward looking, action-oriented and protective. Seeking to dominate the outside world, it can be hard, firm, logical, strong, rational, rough and loud.

SYMBOLISM INCLUDES

- **Standing on a cliff** – represents decisions that need to be made; it symbolizes a time you are removed from others.
- **Body language** – looks like he is ready to defend himself, his face looks as if he is thinking and feeling very determined.
- **Green clothing** - signifies earth energy growth and prosperity.
- **Wearing two different shoes** – indicates either being too overwhelmed to notice things or feeling indecisive.
- **One foot in the water the other on land** - his foot in the water ties him to the feminine, i.e. intuitiveness, sensitivity and emotional things in the unconscious; one foot on land provides him with earth energy and a feeling of being grounded and the expectation of success regarding his ideas or projects.
- **Green hills** – earth energy but not mountains so this is not lofty spiritual thoughts, but it does represent potential for manifestation.
- **Water running through a field** – involves feminine energy, emotions, feelings, and a great deal of inward thinking.
- **Wands leaning against a cliff** – he might have to engage in conflict but definitely has the upper hand given he is standing over the others.
- **Six wands partially obscured** – can represent hidden aspects of yourself (*since they are not fully revealed in the card*) which you may have difficulty seeing or accepting.

UPRIGHT MEANING

- About a great deal of inner thoughts occurring at this time.
- This card is about defending yourself. You have the advantage, it deals with the ability to hold one's own against competition and adversaries.
- This card represents having the courage and stability of our convictions in the face of opposition. About those times when your ideas are pitted against the ideas of others and you have to hold your own moral ground.
- The card foretells success achieved by courage and determination.
- If this card comes in answer to a question it is a good time to take that gamble you likely will succeed.
- This card suggests healthy and creative conflict which can be very productive.
- This card can predict a change of job or promotion.
- About knowing you have the ability to succeed and all will be well so don't walk away from current difficulties.

REVERSED MEANING

- This can be a caution against indecision.
- A time of confusion but a warning that right now any decision is better than no decision at all.
- *The meaning of the card is delayed or extended into the future.*
- *An aspect of the upright meaning of the card needs to be released so you can move forward.*
- *This is not about the upright meaning, place another card on reversed one and read it.*

EIGHT

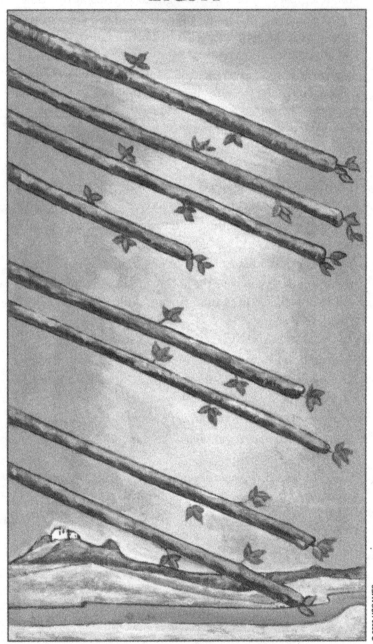

WANDS

Eight of Wands

REPRESENTS

- action and excitement
- time to be hopeful
- planning your next move
- forward motion
- setting goals and targets
- obtaining needed information

NUMBER EIGHT

- Eight, the sign of infinity represents death and regeneration.
- The number of cosmic balance, eight's beneficial qualities is rarely diluted, representing two times greater the benefits of four, it is the number of manifestation.
- Placed on its side eight becomes the lemniscate, the symbol of infinity representing the eternal spiralling movement of the heavens.
- The hour glass shape of eight symbolizes the passage of time and cycles by representing the four seasons the two solstices and two equinoxes.
- Eights vibration is linked with abundance, material prosperity, worldly power, influence, leadership, authority, possibility, options and potential.

ASTROLOGICALLY

- Ruled by the planet SATURN, the hard task master, eight is a solid and very stable number. When this number is prominent in an individual's life they often are presented with many harsh lessons and must learn by experience.
- Eight corresponds to FIXED SIGNS Taurus, Leo, Scorpio and Aquarius. Resistant to change these people are faithful and persevering seeing projects through to the end. They attempt

to adapt the environment to themselves and above all they want to maintain things.

- Wands are represented by FIRE SIGNS, Aries, Leo and Sagittarius. Born leaders they display vital energy, action, and creative talent.
- Fire signs MASCULINE ENERGY primarily motivated by external concerns is outward looking, action-oriented and protective. Seeking to dominate the outside world, it can be hard, firm, logical, strong, rational, rough and loud.

SYMBOLISM INCLUDES
- **Wands on a downward trajectory to earth** - represents ideas or plans that have been thrown out there, there is movement, but where they land is still up in the air.
- **Stream** - suggests action and the progression or flow of life. Water is always symbolic of feminine energy which focuses on feelings, emotion, intuitions, and hidden information.
- **Lots of green in landscape** – represents earth energy indicating there is potential for manifestation of ideas.
- **House on top of a hill** - represents security and stability.
- **Smoke in the middle of the card all the way up from the land to the top of the card** - smoke is a way to send messages; this card is sometimes about receiving information.

UPRIGHT MEANING
- This is a time to take action, it denotes movement, it is time to be hopeful and plan your next move.
- This card is about projects, goals, targets and forward motion.
- Could mean you have launched some plans or ideas and what transpires from them is still up the air but things appear positive.
- Could mean hearing the outcome about ideas or plans you have been engaged in.
- Some of your ideas will be accepted but others will not.
- Modern interpretations indicate this card represents a journey by air.

- This card can also mean you will be receiving news or information.
- About hopefulness and the high likelihood of abundance.

REVERSED MEANING

- Could represent unwanted movement, example transfer across the country. Stay positive this should lead to a good outcome.
- Could mean a time to stand back and observe rather than jump into action.
- Disappointment as an awaited for message has not arrived, or the news it brought was not expected.
- *The meaning of the card is delayed or extended into the future.*
- *An aspect of the upright meaning of the card needs to be released so you can move forward.*
- *This is not about the upright meaning, place another card on reversed one and read it.*

NINE

WANDS

Nine of Wands

REPRESENTS

- inner strength
- a job well done
- ability to plan wisely
- courage under fire
- perseverance and stamina
- duty to yourself or others
- taking your responsibilities seriously

NUMBER NINE

- Nine's vibrations let you see beyond the physical into the limitlessness of the universe.
- Nine the number of fulfillment triples the effect of three the number of cosmic power.
- Representing the end of a cycle nine indicates it is time to tie up loose ends.
- Generally nine depicts completion, wholeness and the sense of satisfaction that comes from reaching a hard worked for goal.
- Sometimes nine can demonstrate regrets as it's the end of a cycle and things may not have gone well, when this is the case you may experience anxiety about not knowing what to expect next.

ASTROLOGICALLY

- The planet MARS which is related to sexual prowess, courage, energy, action, protectiveness, valour and being an able provider rules nine. Forceful and dominating nine creates stability and is a good number when attempting to build foundations.
- When nine is prominent, quite often people will need to overcome obstacles before they will be able to reach their highest potential.

- Nine corresponds to MUTABLE SIGNS Gemini, Virgo, Sagittarius and Pisces. Seeing both sides of a situation they adjust their attitudes and adapt to almost any circumstances. Versatility allows mutable sign people to accept change and thereby end what was.
- Wands are represented by FIRE SIGNS, Aries, Leo and Sagittarius. Born leaders they display vital energy, action, and creative talent.
- Fire signs MASCULINE ENERGY primarily motivated by external concerns is outward looking, action-oriented and protective. Seeking to dominate the outside world, it can be hard, firm, logical, strong, rational, rough and loud.

SYMBOLISM INCLUDES
- **Wands are behind the man** - symbolizes that the fight is behind him.
- **Orderliness of the wands** - implies the man holds firmly onto his ideas.
- **Gap between some of the wands** - implies he could leave his post and walk down into the fertile valley.
- **Looking left** - implies his problem, attitude, or wounds have something to do with what he's carrying from his past, possibly an attitude he holds onto but he likely is unaware of doing so.
- **Body language** - signifies wariness, he senses a need to stay on alert.
- **Bandage on his head** - his head has been wounded, this could imply his feelings have been injured.
- **Facial expression** - implies he is hopeful there is no more trouble, but being cautious and on guard in case there is.
- **Green hills in the background** – represents earth energy which means manifestation is very likely and things are worth fighting for.
- **Orange clothing** - warmth but also the color of energy which implies action might be needed.

UPRIGHT MEANING
- Indicates a lot of hard work is behind you.

- Can mean you have or are experiencing some mental stresses.
- Can indicate feelings of uneasiness where you cannot identify a threat but you don't want to lose anything you have gained.
- This is a card about your duty to yourself or to others; you are expected to take your responsibilities seriously.
- This card suggests inner strength and determination; you possess an accumulation of strength and courage which can be drawn upon in critical times.
- This card speaks of internal resources rather than a reliance on the outside world to rescue you in times of trouble.
- This card suggests that you will be called upon to use your integrity and innate courage to free yourself from hardships and opposition.
- This card always indicates a struggle but as well it always carries the hope of victory, no matter how impossible this may appear at first glance.
- Never give up; you do have the strength you need to succeed.
- An experience has wounded you but has made you stronger.
- Could indicate a warning that small groups of people around you are working against you so you need to keep a watchful eye regarding this.

REVERSED MEANING
- Someone you know may be struggling with an internal problem.
- Cut your losses now, the venture did not succeed, and get on with your life.
- *The meaning of the card is delayed or extended into the future.*
- *An aspect of the upright meaning of the card needs to be released so you can move forward.*
- *This is not about the upright meaning, place another card on reversed one and read it.*

TEN

WANDS

Ten of Wands

REPRESENTS
- oppressive burdens and struggles
- a warning not to take things for granted
- over extending yourself

NUMBER TEN
- The number ten reduces to one. (1+0=1)
- One's energy is individual, solitary and self-contained.
- Representing the beginning of form it is the active principle of creation.
- Represents the mystic centre.
- Associated with self-development, creativity, action, progress, a new chance, and rebirth.

ASTROLOGICALLY
- Ruled by the SUN ten which reduces to one is egocentric often representing a person who is somewhat of a loner.
- One corresponds to CARDINAL SIGNS which are about new beginnings, enterprise and getting things started. Aries for spring, Cancer for summer, Libra for autumn, and Capricorn for winter.
- Wands are represented by FIRE SIGNS, Aries, Leo and Sagittarius. Born leaders they display vital energy, action, and creative talent.
- Fire signs MASCULINE ENERGY primarily motivated by external concerns is outward looking, action-oriented and protective. Seeking to dominate the outside world, it can be hard, firm, logical, strong, rational, rough and loud.

SYMBOLISM INCLUDES
- **Man carrying a heavy load** – implies being burdened by too much, the man might make it back to town but he is

wearing himself out in the process; if he laid down his load and reconsidered getting it there by another means he would not be so weary. As well the wands are so close to his face he can't see where he is going, he is feeling over burdened.

- **Body language** - slumped, tired, exhausted, the end in sight is still far away.
- **Orange clothing** – indicates activity, action and warmth.
- **Brown in foreground** – symbolizes drudgery.
- **A house in the distance** - prosperity is seen in the distance, so the goal is worth working for.
- **Greenery in distance** – indicates earth energy, fertility and the high likelihood for manifestation.
- **Ploughed field** – symbolizes fertility, waiting for something to come; fertile implies one is keen to learn; the ploughed field also implies the labour, work and commitment involved in making something come to fruition.

UPRIGHT MEANING
- This is about oppressive burdens.
- It could mean you are assuming too much responsibility.
- It could indicate you are under a lot of pressure.
- It indicates someone who has taken on more work than they can reasonably manage.
- It could mean your employer has assigned too much work for you to reasonably accomplish.
- This could indicate a workaholic.
- There is a strong work ethic here but focus and purpose has been lost due to the overwhelming workload currently being experienced.
- This card suggests that the joy, sparkle, and magic has gone out of the work and it is now a heavy burden.
- Working hard but not working smart.
- If the reading is focused on relationships it could mean your partner is pressuring you about something causing you to feel emotionally worn out.
- May indicate you are in a dead end job and it is time to find different work that you can enjoy.

REVERSED MEANING

- Work has been shifted to someone else.
- May mean an injury such as a broken bone.
- *The meaning of the card is delayed or extended into the future.*
- *An aspect of the upright meaning of the card needs to be released so you can move forward.*
- *This is not about the upright meaning, place another card on reversed one and read it.*

PAGE

WANDS

Page of Wands

REPRESENTS

- a messenger bringing creative ideas
- a message that will affect your current enterprise

NUMBER ELEVEN

- The number eleven reduces to two. (1+1=2)
- Two represents some type of union or partnership with another person, a spiritual entity, or two parts of you.
- Associated with the balance of polarities such as yin/yang, male/female and public/separate.
- Two builds on the opportunity presented by one (*the ace*).
- Two can represent sensitivity to others sometimes to the point of considering their wellbeing over your own.
- Representative of immersing yourself into another person, an idea, or a project.
- Two is associated with choices and decisions.

ASTROLOGICALLY

- Ruled by the Moon, two (*the Page*) is associated with relationships, cooperation, emotions and feelings.
- Two corresponds to FIXED SIGNS Taurus, Leo, Scorpio and Aquarius. Resistant to change these people are faithful and persevering seeing projects through to the end. They attempt to adapt the environment to themselves and above all they want to maintain things.
- Wands are represented by FIRE SIGNS, Aries, Leo and Sagittarius. Born leaders they display vital energy, action, and creative talent.
- Fire signs MASCULINE ENERGY primarily motivated by external concerns is outward looking, action-oriented and protective. Seeking to dominate the outside world, it can be hard, firm, logical, strong, rational, rough and loud.

SYMBOLISM INCLUDES

- **Orange and yellow clothing** - symbolizes enthusiasm, optimism and warmth.
- **Ouroborus designs on clothing** - an ancient symbol of a serpent or a salamander biting its tail and in so doing creating a circle which symbolizes the never ending perpetual motion of the universe. The ancients thought the salamander, the elemental spirit of the suit of Wands, survived fire by quenching it with its frigid body. As one of the alchemical symbols for primal material, its purpose was to help the substance under transformation give up its secret fire. The salamander symbolizes optimism and creative vision and its earth energy represents high potential for manifestation. Symbolizing the Page's dedication to higher service and self development the ouroborus links the royalty of the Wand suit with the Magician, who also wears the ouroborus on his belt. Because the Page is young, the ouroborus does not quite connect with its tail.
- **Page's hat** – hats symbolize thinking and this one implies a certain carefree jovialness, associated to youthfulness.
- **Page's stance** – implies he is still a youth and as yet does not have a lot of responsibilities.
- **Pyramids in the background** - symbolize new territories or ideas to investigate, indicates a place of inspiration, and suggests the presence of hidden or unexplored emotions.
- **Desert** – with the pyramids in the background this is Egypt so depicts a pathway of ancient, hidden knowledge or ideas to be learned.

UPRIGHT MEANING
PAGES BRING MESSAGES

- After laying out the entire spread, lay the first extra card that was selected on the Page, this clarifies the message.

PAGES AS A SITUATION

- Your intuition is at work, new ideas are emerging that will lead to creative activity.
- An idea representing potential or possibilities is gestating within you but it needs time to become grounded.

- A business or family matter requiring moral support may occur and help will be provided from a sensitive young friend or relative.
- The spirit of excitement and adventure surrounds you. Feel free to express your individuality and power with light-hearted abandonment.

PAGE AS A PERSONALITY

- Represents a lovely, inquisitive child or youth with a lively nature who is easy to manage. Possibly your own child, a relative, or a child that will be impacting your life.
- A young person who is faithful, loyal and a friend.
- May personify you implying you have an immature manner of looking at your experiences.

REVERSED MEANING

- The message you are waiting for is delayed and or does not come at all.
- *The meaning of the card is delayed or extended into the future.*
- *An aspect of the upright meaning of the card needs to be released so you can move forward.*
- *This is not about the upright meaning, place another card on reversed one and read it.*

KNIGHT

WANDS

Knight of Wands

REPRESENTS
- change
- possibility of a different job or relationship
- energy and action
- a possible journey

NUMBER TWELVE
- The number twelve reduces to three. (1+2=3)
- Cosmic energy is embedded in threes.
- Three, a mystic number, represents Spirit.
- Threes possess celestial power – the sun stands still for three days at the solstices before resuming its motion; threes encompass past, present and future; the moon looks full for three days and disappears as dark for three days. Threes make up the trinity of mind, body and spirit.
- Group activities, movement, action, growth and development are expressed by threes.
- Sometimes with threes expansion occurs too quickly causing you to spread yourself too thin or for your energies to scatter.
- Paying attention to what you are doing results in threes vibration being cheerful, optimistic and pleasant, representing a period of happiness and benefits.

ASTROLOGICALLY
- The Knight is represented by SAGITTARIUS, ruled by JUPITER and characterizes the Revolutionary.
- Jupiter symbolizes expansion, optimism, foresight and fortune. It rules good luck and good cheer, health, wealth, happiness, success and joy. The symbol of opportunity Jupiter is associated with gambling and games of chance. Jupiter rules acting, publishing, philosophy, religion, sports and travel.

- Three corresponds to MUTABLE SIGNS Gemini, Virgo, Sagittarius and Pisces. Seeing both sides of a situation they adjust their attitudes and adapt to almost any circumstances. Versatility allows mutable sign people to accept change and thereby end what was.
- Wands are represented by FIRE SIGNS, Aries, Leo and Sagittarius. Born leaders they display vital energy, action, and creative talent.
- Fire signs MASCULINE ENERGY primarily motivated by external concerns is outward looking, action-oriented and protective. Seeking to dominate the outside world, it can be hard, firm, logical, strong, rational, rough and loud.

SYMBOLISM INCLUDES

- **Dressed in armour** – symbolizes the possession of necessary traits and tools to get the job done.
- **Yellow clothing** - yellow denotes enthusiasm and optimism.
- **Ouroborus designs on clothing** - an ancient symbol of a serpent or a salamander biting its tail and in so doing creating a circle which symbolizes the never ending perpetual motion of the universe. The ancients thought the salamander, the elemental spirit of the suit of Wands, survived fire by quenching it with its frigid body. As one of the alchemical symbols for primal material, its purpose was to help the substance under transformation give up its secret fire. The salamander symbolizes optimism and creative vision and its earth energy represents high potential for manifestation. Symbolizing the Knight's dedication to higher service and self development the ouroborus links the royalty of the Wand suit with the Magician, who also wears the ouroborus on his belt.
- **Red plumes on helmet and armour's sleeves** – red symbolizes passion, this Knight indicates a fiery energy and desire for action.
- **Horse's stance** - represents action, the horses haunches are gathered up and he is rearing back. Animals always represent instincts which signify making decisions from "a gut feeling."
- **Body Language** – appears confident, ready to do his duty, an air of cockiness to him; he emits a feeling of recklessness.

- **Pyramids in the background** - symbolize new territories or ideas to investigate, indicates a place of inspiration, and suggests the presence of hidden or unexplored emotions.
- **Desert** – with the pyramids in the background this is Egypt so depicts a pathway of ancient, hidden knowledge or ideas to be learned.

UPRIGHT MEANING
KNIGHTS MEAN CHANGE IS COMING

- Usually this indicates a long-term condition of life that is about to become better, worse or end.
- Plans and intrigues are occurring in the background of which you may or may not be aware, and in which you are about to become involved with whether you want to or not.
- The horse's stance indicates the timing of the change, this horse is rearing and ready to go so it means the change is coming soon.

KNIGHT AS A SITUATION

- May represent a journey or change of residence.
- Could represent spontaneous changes and impulsive behaviour resulting in a tendency not to think too long if at all before making a response.
- Your intuition and instincts about your surroundings are magnified at this time.
- You may be asked to give up something that matters to you.
- Someone may perform an unselfish act on your behalf.

KNIGHT AS A PERSONALITY

- Represents a trustworthy, unselfish and faithful young person who will give up something for you.
- Represents an honest, intelligent young person who is friendly towards you. Perhaps a brother, a friend, or a lover.
- Someone whose advice you can trust and whose help you can take if you are in need.
- May personify you.

REVERSED MEANING

- The Knight has fallen off his horse, whatever change was coming has been delayed.
- *The meaning of the card is delayed or extended into the future.*
- *An aspect of the upright meaning of the card needs to be released so you can move forward.*
- *This is not about the upright meaning, place another card on reversed one and read it.*

QUEEN

WANDS

Queen of Wands

REPRESENTS
- endurance and maintenance
- generosity and strength
- an honourable, intelligent, friendly woman
- receiving valuable assistance

NUMBER THIRTEEN
- The number thirteen reduces to four. (1+3 = 4)
- Four is the number associated to "matter."
- Four is a time to build a foundation that will support your ideas and projects.
- Hard work and self discipline are required with fours.
- A stabilizing time for creating structures and order.
- Representing manifestation of your ideas, fours represent prosperity, peace, happiness, abundance and even triumph.
- Sometimes fours represent a stage in personal development when a stalemate has been reached, a period that often seems necessary for unacknowledged emotions or dilemmas to come into consciousness so we can experience them and get on with growth or healing.

ASTROLOGICALLY
- The Queen of Wands is represented by ARIES, ruled by MARS and characterizes the Seer.
- The exemplar of all the traditional aspects that we esteem in the male Mars is related to sexual prowess, courage, energy, action, protectiveness, valour and being an able provider.
- Four corresponds to CARDINAL SIGNS which are about new beginnings, enterprise and getting things started. Aries for spring, Cancer for summer, Libra for autumn, and Capricorn for winter.

- Wands are represented by FIRE SIGNS, Aries, Leo and Sagittarius. Born leaders they display vital energy, action, and creative talent.

- Fire signs MASCULINE ENERGY primarily motivated by external concerns is outward looking, action-oriented and protective. Seeking to dominate the outside world, it can be hard, firm, logical, strong, rational, rough and loud.

SYMBOLISM INCLUDES

- **Yellow clothing** - denotes enthusiasm, optimism, creativity and joy.

- **Purple coloured robe** – symbolizes royalty and indicates that the person wields the type of authority that brings them respect from others.

- **Fox clasp on her robe** - symbolizes feminine energy, as well as the fox's attributes of cleverness, observational skills, cunning, intelligence and persistence. Animals always represent instincts which signify making decisions from "a gut feeling."

- **Crown is topped with green sprigs** - indicates earth energy, manifestation is very possible.

- **Spirals on crown** - symbolize life energy, renewal and movement toward the centre.

- **Cat** – because they see in the dark they are symbolic of a "seer," a knower of mysteries. Being black this cat is associated with the darker shadow side of the feminine and it represents the Queen's intuitive skills.

- **Holding a sunflower** - indicates truthfulness. Sunflowers are connected to the energy of the (*Sun*) Sol the great feminine sun goddess. Avebury, England was one of the places where this sun goddess was worshipped.

- **Throne is in the desert** – this desert is Egypt so denotes a place of inspiration and a pathway to ancient, hidden knowledge or ideas to be learned.

- **Throne is on a grey slab** - symbolizes wisdom.

- **Red lions on the throne** - symbolize alchemy (*alchemy is the process of becoming personally enlightened or spiritually awakened*).

- **Lions' heads as part of the throne** - symbolizes majesty, strength, courage, justice and military might; these lions related to the Great Mother symbolize protection, fertility, care and vigilance.

- **Body language** - the Queen appears calm, caring, relaxed, gentle and serious. She seems to be a deep thinker.
- **Pyramids** - symbolize the highest point of or connection with spiritual attainment. Denoting a pathway of ancient, hidden knowledge or ideas to be learned they call attention to our desire for spiritual aspirations and represent the introduction to an esoteric system of learning. These pyramids are in the distance and denote wisdom has been internalized.

UPRIGHT MEANING
QUEEN AS A SITUATION

- This is a good time to make your move in an important endeavour, especially one involving business or finance.
- Your ideas have a high likelihood of coming to fruition at this time.
- Your current environment supports inspiration and advancement.
- You may find your intuition and instincts are more prevalent right now.

QUEEN AS A PERSONALITY

- A woman who is entering or affecting your life at this moment with the qualities of the Queen of Wands. She could be a parent, boss, relative, counsellor or a confidant.
- A career minded, headstrong woman who knows what she wants and she wants it now.
- An honourable, friendly and intelligent woman who is comfortable with her position in life.
- Displaying a love of luxury while demonstrating she is economical and serious this woman knows how to manage money to the advantage of herself or her family.
- A woman who is sympathetic towards you and is willing to help with either money or advice.
- Accomplishing things in her own right this educated woman did not just inherit things from her family or husband.

- A lover of life this woman displays self-confidence, self-determination and a willingness to become more mature. Working easily with inner visions or fantasies she demonstrates the potential for deep spirituality.
- May personify you.

REVERSED MEANING
- You will not receive any advice or assistance from influential people however if you work hard your personal efforts will not be blocked.
- *The meaning of the card is delayed or extended into the future.*
- *An aspect of the upright meaning of the card needs to be released so you can move forward.*
- *This is not about the upright meaning, place another card on reversed one and read it.*

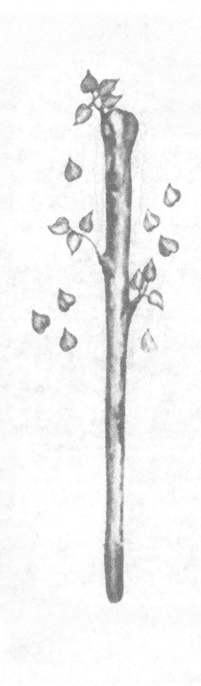

KING

WANDS

King of Wands

REPRESENTS
- a charismatic leader
- a time to take action in business matters
- a creative and inspiring time

NUMBER FOURTEEN
- The number fourteen reduces to five. (1+4=5)
- Fives always represent some type of difficulty, tension or crisis.
- Challenges often result in a winner or loser with fives.
- Fives suggest a sense of being on a roller coaster ride or being caught up in a whirlwind.
- Fluctuation, unrest and sometimes clashes create a sense of instability and can cause stress.
- Impulsive and impatient behaviours occur but resourcefulness and curiosity are also present.
- Fives indicate we have the quality of mind, but lack the maturity and knowledge to transform old ways into new patterns of being.
- We may be forced to make a choice in order to end the anxiety that is associated with fives.

ASTROLOGICALLY
- The King of Wands is represented by LEO, ruled by the SUN and characterizes the Seeker.
- Symbolizing strength, vigour, generosity and the ability to function as a mature individual the Sun represents a creative force facilitating the complete potential of every human being.
- Five corresponds to FIXED SIGNS Taurus, Leo, Scorpio and Aquarius. Resistant to change these people are faithful and persevering seeing projects through to the end. They attempt

to adapt the environment to themselves and above all they want to maintain things.

- Wands are represented by FIRE SIGNS Aries, Leo and Sagittarius. Born leaders they display vital energy, action, and creative talent.
- Fire signs MASCULINE ENERGY primarily motivated by external concerns is outward looking, action-oriented and protective. Seeking to dominate the outside world, it can be hard, firm, logical, strong, rational, rough and loud.

SYMBOLISM INCLUDES

- **Crown** - represents authority, the right to this authority, and the awareness and acceptance of others that the person wearing the crown is entitled to this authority.
- **Dressed in orange** – represents warmth, energy, activity, drive and confidence.
- **Green on clothing** – represent earth energies implying manifestation of ideas and projects.
- **Salamander on clothing** – symbolize earth energy implying manifestation of ideas and projects.
- **Salamander near his feet** - the ancients thought the salamander, the elemental spirit of the suit of wands, survived fire by quenching it with its frigid body. As one of the alchemical symbols for the primal material, its purpose was to help the substance under transformation give up its secret fire. Like the salamander on his clothing this denotes earth energy.
- **Ouroborus designs on clothing and throne** - an ancient symbol of a serpent or a salamander biting its tail and in so doing creating a circle which symbolizes the never ending perpetual motion of the universe. The salamander symbolizes optimism and creative vision and its earth energy represents high potential for manifestation. Symbolizing the King's dedication to higher service and self development the ouroborus links the royalty of the Wand suit with the Magician, who also wears the ouroborus on his belt.
- **Moon looking amulet around King's neck with asymmetrical pieces on the chain** - the moon a feminine sign represents inner looking, secrets, intuition, and emotions. The asymmetrical pieces symbolize the unexpected.

- **Lions on his throne** - lions symbolize majesty, strength, courage, justice and military might; these lions signify the King possesses the necessary ability to provide protection.

- **Throne is yellow** - represents intellect, positive mental activity and awareness, willpower, intention, outer self-expression, change and radiant energy; yellow can be seen as protection for its wearer (*stems from yellow insects that sting thus making others avoid it*).

- **Throne is on a slab of grey coloured stone** - the colour grey signifies wisdom, the stone permanence and stability.

- **King's head is facing the left side of the card** – the left signifies the unconscious and the need to delve into it. This symbolizes the King is intuitive.

- **Body Language** – he appears contemplative.

UPRIGHT MEANING
KING AS A SITUATION

- There is a high likelihood of your ideas or projects coming to fruition at this time.

- You may find your intuitiveness is enhanced.

- The environment around you is motivating and supportive of your endeavours.

- Surrounded by advantages and fairness this is a favourable time for you.

KING AS A PERSONALITY

- A man who is entering or affecting your life at this moment with the qualities of the King of Wands. He could be a parent, boss, relative, counsellor or a confidant.

- Someone with authority such as an ambitious businessman, a politician, a boss figure.

- An intuitive, optimistic man who demonstrates creative vision.

- A man who possesses the necessary abilities and resources to be supportive of your ideas.

- A man of status and wealth who excels in the areas of business and finance.

- A strong willed and self disciplined man.

- Usually a man of humble origin who has succeeded by using his own intelligence and determination.
- Likely someone you admire for both his position and his accomplishments.
- His word is good and his advice can be trusted.
- If you are male this may represent a rival, but a generous and honest one.
- If you are female, this man is either a relative or close family friend, but always a good advisor.
- May personify you.

REVERSED MEANING

- You will not receive any help from wealthy or influential people however your own hard work and personal efforts will not be blocked.
- *The meaning of the card is delayed or extended into the future.*
- *An aspect of the upright meaning of the card needs to be released so you can move forward.*
- *This is not about the upright meaning, place another card on reversed one and read it.*

The Suit of
Cups

26. THE SUIT OF CUPS

- Cups represent the power of love and faith.
- Focused on emotions, relationships and matters of the heart this suit is about good fortune, love, relationships and family.
- Cups, a water sign, are represented by Cancer, Scorpio and Pisces. Waters energy is receptive, inner-directed, reflective, connected with the emotions, creative, and intuitive.
- The feminine energy of water is inward looking, internally driven, intuitive, sensitive, and emotional while seeking to create co-existence and consensus it is introspective and nurturing.
- In medieval times the cups suit represented the clergy, mainly the local priests, who did what they could to alleviate the hardships and suffering of the peasant class.
- In a reading cups indicate there are individuals, groups or forces who will work in your favour for no other reason than they care about you.
- Cups are often seen as the second suit of the Minor Arcana. As the emotional stage they bridge the gap between ideas and action.

REVERSED CARDS

Sometimes cards are upside down when they are chosen. Readers have preferences as to interpreting the meanings of cards in this position. I have listed some reversed meanings and also provided some other options. It is up to you as a reader to determine which meaning fits best. Some readers simply turn the cards right side up and do not deal with reversed meanings. It is a good idea to choose a standard method to follow and deviate only when circumstances in the reading seem to dictate a need to do so.

ACE

CUPS

ACE OF CUPS

REPRESENTS
- opportunities come out of the blue

NUMBER ONE
- One's energy is individual, solitary and self-contained.
- Representing the beginning of form number one relates to the active principle of creation.
- One represents the mystic centre core of mysterious, inscrutable, symbolic, secretive and hidden knowing.
- One represents self-development, creativity, action, progress, a new chance, and rebirth.

ASTROLOGICALLY
- The Ace of Cups is the root of the powers of water.
- The Ace (1) ruled by the Sun is very egocentric quite often representing a person who is somewhat of a loner.
- One corresponds to CARDINAL SIGNS which are about new beginnings, enterprise and getting things started. Aries for spring, Cancer for summer, Libra for autumn, and Capricorn for winter.
- Cups are represented by the element of water a feminine energy. Intuitive and attuned to subtle vibrations WATER SIGN people are quick to sum up others, often at a first meeting. Emotional and sensitive they are a capable of great compassion.
- Inward looking, internally driven and intuitive FEMININE ENERGY is sensitive and emotional, while seeking to create co-existence and consensus it is introspective and nurturing.

SYMBOLISM INCLUDES
- **Hand holding an elaborate golden cup** - sometimes considered the Holy Grail this symbolizes possibilities of connecting to a source greater than oneself.

- **Halo around the hand** - denotes energy coming from Spirit.
- **Water pouring out of the cup** - represents the never ending supply of energy coming from the universe.
- **A dove** - symbolizes peace, reconciliation, promise and is highly associated to spirituality.
- **Round disc with a cross on it** - a symbol for "terra" meaning earth and with the dove holding it this symbol means peace on earth.
- **The letter W on the golden cup** - a symbol for the Mother Goddess, or Earth Mother.
- **Yods** – droplets representing divine grace and healing. Translated yod means "open hand," and represents the new possibility of divine energy or intelligence coming through us and manifesting in our ideas, thoughts and actions.
- **Water** – denotes feminine energy, intuitiveness and hidden knowledge.
- **Green lily pads floating on water** - earth energy denoting the high likelihood of manifestation of your plans or ideas. The lilies symbolize the mystic path or way.
- **Green coloured mountain in the background** - mountains represent stability and a connection to spirituality, this mountain being green contains earth energy so manifestation especially associated to spirituality is highly probable.

UPRIGHT MEANING
- A gift from the universe.
- About new beginnings.
- It is the starting point of a whole new cycle.
- You have the choice to initiate something and the time is right for this.
- It may mean a new job, promotion, or acceptance into a school or program.
- It could mean artistic endeavours such as writing, painting, pottery, etc.
- It could mean starting your own business.

REVERSED MEANING

- Think "thumbs down" on a particular project suggesting the need to start over, rethink, or regroup.
- *The meaning of the card is delayed or extended into the future.*
- *An aspect of the upright meaning of the card needs to be released so you can move forward.*
- *This is not about the upright meaning, place another card on reversed one and read it.*

TWO

CUPS

Two of Cups

REPRESENTS
* bonding
* relationships
* making connection
* acknowledging attractions
* friendship and unions based in harmony

NUMBER TWO
* Some type of union or partnership with another person, a spiritual entity, or two parts of you.
* Associated with the balance of polarities such as yin/yang, male/female and public/separate.
* Two builds on the opportunity presented by one (*the ace*).
* Two can represent sensitivity to others sometimes to the point of considering their wellbeing over your own.
* Representative of immersing yourself into another person, an idea, or a project.
* Two is associated with choices and decisions.

ASTROLOGICALLY
* Ruled by the Moon, two is associated with relationships, cooperation, emotions and feelings.
* Two corresponds to FIXED SIGNS Taurus, Leo, Scorpio and Aquarius. Resistant to change these people are faithful and persevering seeing projects through to the end. They attempt to adapt the environment to themselves and above all they want to maintain things.
* Cups are represented by the element of water a feminine energy. Intuitive and attuned to subtle vibrations WATER SIGN people are quick to sum up others, often at a first meeting. Emotional and sensitive they are a capable of great compassion.

- Inward looking, internally driven and intuitive FEMININE ENERGY is sensitive and emotional, while seeking to create co-existence and consensus it is introspective and nurturing.

SYMBOLISM INCLUDES

- **Man and woman exchanging vows** – symbolizing marriage, it represents the forming of a sacred union based on a relationship in which the sum is greater than its individual parts.
- **Green laurel wreath on woman's head** - the wreath itself symbolises current or past accomplishments and being green affords it earth energy and therefore manifestation.
- **Red beaded band on man's head** - red signifies passion, the band being on his head signifies passionate thoughts.
- **Head gear** - together the woman's and man's head gear symbolize the wholeness that comes from the alchemical marriage. Alchemical referring to the ability to transform one element into a higher element and or some aspect of life into a greater aspect of life.
- **Chalices** - in alchemy a vessel symbolizes the power to bring about transformation.
- **Winged lion** – an alchemical symbol representing the transmutation of the lower self to a higher realm. Representing both the process and the result the winged lion symbolizes one's relationship with oneself whether that comes through individual work or is influenced through a relationship with another person.
- **Caduceus** - the two interlacing serpents which represent the balancing of opposing forces.
- **Spiral formed by the caduceus** – symbolizing life energy and renewal spirals convey the motion created through the experiences that are forever occurring in our lives.
- **Green grass and hills** – represent earth energy, new beginnings and the manifestation of ideas.
- **House in the distance** – symbolizes stability and resources.
- **Blue sky** – signifies that things look positive.

UPRIGHT MEANING

- This card is about transformation, becoming more than you have been either through a more enlightened relationship with yourself or with others.
- It could indicate that a commitment has been made in a relationship.
- It can indicate a favourable offer has been made to you.
- Can indicate it's time to look for connections in your life – now is not the time to stay apart.
- Can indicate that two heads are better than one.

REVERSED MEANING

- A breakdown in a relationship.
- Delays in a relationship.
- Some reason why the relationship needs to be kept secret.
- *The meaning of the card is delayed or extended into the future.*
- *An aspect of the upright meaning of the card needs to be released so you can move forward.*
- *This is not about the upright meaning, place another card on reversed one and read it.*

THREE

CUPS

Three of Cups

REPRESENTS
- valuing community
- celebrations
- group activity
- caring and sharing
- success in business or relationships

NUMBER THREE
- Cosmic energy is embedded in threes.
- Three, a mystic number, represents Spirit.
- Threes possess celestial power – the sun stands still for three days at the solstices before resuming its motion; threes encompass past, present and future; the moon looks full for three days and disappears as dark for three days. Threes make up the trinity of mind, body and spirit.
- Group activities, movement, action, growth and development are expressed by threes.
- Sometimes with threes expansion occurs too quickly causing you to spread yourself too thin or for your energies to scatter.
- If you pay attention to what you are doing threes vibration is cheerful, optimistic and pleasant, representing a period of happiness and benefits.

ASTROLOGICALLY
- JUPITER, considered a major benefit, rules three.
- With Jupiter's influence over the number three money often comes and goes easily.
- Three corresponds to MUTABLE SIGNS Gemini, Virgo, Sagittarius and Pisces. Seeing both sides of a situation they adjust their attitudes and adapt to almost any circumstances. Versatility allows mutable sign people to accept change and thereby end what was.

- Cups are represented by the element of water a feminine energy. Intuitive and attuned to subtle vibrations WATER SIGN people are quick to sum up others, often at a first meeting. Emotional and sensitive they are a capable of great compassion.
- Inward looking, internally driven and intuitive FEMININE ENERGY is sensitive and emotional, while seeking to create co-existence and consensus it is introspective and nurturing.

SYMBOLISM INCLUDES

- **Women dancing** – denotes a celebration, a joyous time.
- **Orange clothing** – orange symbolizes warmth, energy, and optimism.
- **Yellow clothing** – yellow symbolizes enthusiasm, creativity and intuitiveness.
- **White clothing** - white symbolizes purity.
- **Fruits and vegetables** – symbolize bountifulness, earth energy with the high likelihood for manifestation of ideas and projects.

UPRIGHT MEANING:

- About good news and can mean success, perfection, plenty, merriment, happiness, fulfillment and victory.
- It can mean the achievement of great things.
- If you have begun a new endeavour or recent relationship then things are off to a good start.
- Could represent a celebration possibly a graduation, an engagement, a wedding or even an office party.
- Could indicate it is time to examine the groups in your life – possibly you need to reach out to them and spend more time with friends.
- Can mean expansion in a relationship, possibly a child is conceived.
- Could indicate a time for rituals.
- A reminder to enjoy the moment.
- Could be about a time of emotional healing.
- Could be about the happy conclusion to some phase or stage of life.

REVERSED MEANING

- Possible back biting or issues arising within the family group.
- *The meaning of the card is delayed or extended into the future.*
- *An aspect of the upright meaning of the card needs to be released so you can move forward.*
- *This is not about the upright meaning, place another card on reversed one and read it.*

FOUR

CUPS

Four of Cups

REPRESENTS

- contemplation
- lost opportunity
- your negative outlook is keeping you from attaining what you need or could hope for
- self absorption and discontent

NUMBER FOUR

- Four is the number associated to "matter."
- Four is a time to build a foundation that will support your ideas and projects.
- Hard work and self discipline are required with fours.
- A stabilizing time for creating structures and order.
- Representing manifestation of your ideas, fours represent prosperity, peace, happiness, abundance and even triumph.
- Sometimes fours represent a stage in personal development when a stalemate has been reached, a period that often seems necessary for unacknowledged emotions or dilemmas to come into consciousness so we can experience them and get on with growth or healing.

ASTROLOGICALLY

- Four is ruled by URANUS the eccentric and unusual natured planet.
- Where the number four is prominent invention and ingenuity are very important elements to any given situation.
- Four corresponds to CARDINAL SIGNS which are associated with new beginnings, enterprise and getting things started. Aries for spring, Cancer for summer, Libra for autumn and Capricorn for winter.
- Cups are represented by the element of water a feminine energy. Intuitive and attuned to subtle vibrations WATER SIGN people

are quick to sum up others, often at a first meeting. Emotional and sensitive they are a capable of great compassion.

- Inward looking, internally driven and intuitive FEMININE ENERGY is sensitive and emotional, while seeking to create co-existence and consensus it is introspective and nurturing.

SYMBOLISM INCLUDES

- **Hand offering a chalice** – this is somewhat like the Ace, the universe is offering a gift.
- **Beige tunic over red clothing** - the red indicates passion but this passion has been covered over with a beige coloured tunic so no longer is prevalent in the person's feelings.
- **Person staring at three chalices** - this fellow is so focused on the three chalices that he fails to see the opportunity being presented to him by the universe.
- **Green grass, tree, green leaves** – denotes earth energy is present here indicating a great deal of potential for manifestation of ideas or projects.
- **Mountain in the background** - symbolizes spirituality and stability.

UPRIGHT MEANING

- About how your negative outlook is keeping you from recognizing available opportunities.
- About feelings you have regarding situations or certain relationships that have left you feeling lethargic and apathetic. The focus on these feelings is keeping you from noticing all the positive things going on around you.
- Perhaps boredom or becoming so wrapped up in your own issues has resulted in feelings of despondency and an overall withdrawal for you from life in general. Help is available if you want it.
- About help from an unseen source.
- About spending so much time in deep contemplation and inaction that opportunities are passing by you.

REVERSED MEANING

- An unforeseen event.

- *The meaning of the card is delayed or extended into the future.*
- *An aspect of the upright meaning of the card needs to be released so you can move forward.*
- *This is not about the upright meaning, place another card on reversed one and read it.*

FIVE

CUPS

Five of Cups

REPRESENTS
- loss of something that cannot be recovered
- deep sorrow
- despair
- regret
- bereavement

NUMBER FIVE
- Fives always represent some type of difficulty, tension or crisis.
- Challenges often result in a winner or loser with fives.
- Fives suggest a sense of being on a roller coaster ride or being caught up in a whirlwind.
- Fluctuation, unrest and sometimes clashes create a sense of instability and can cause stress.
- Impulsive and impatient behaviours occur but resourcefulness and curiosity are also present.
- Fives indicate we have the quality of mind but lack the maturity and knowledge to transform old ways into new patterns of being.
- We may be forced to make a choice in order to end the anxiety that is associated with fives.

ASTROLOGICALLY
- MERCURY, the planet associated with communication, rules five.
- If five is significant in a reading it may mean this individual needs to make adjustments in order to fit in.
- Five corresponds to FIXED SIGN Taurus, Leo, Scorpio and Aquarius. Resistant to change these people are faithful and persevering seeing projects through to the end. They attempt

to adapt the environment to themselves and above all they want to maintain things.

- Cups are represented by the element of water a feminine energy. Intuitive and attuned to subtle vibrations WATER SIGN people are quick to sum up others, often at a first meeting. Emotional and sensitive they are a capable of great compassion.

- Inward looking, internally driven and intuitive FEMININE ENERGY is sensitive and emotional, while seeking to create co-existence and consensus it is introspective and nurturing.

SYMBOLISM INCLUDES

- **Cloak** - symbolizes being cut off from the world, they are shrouds to keep things out.
- **Deep blue colour** – this is indigo and represents wisdom.
- **Three cups are over turned** – these symbolize that much of what was is no longer viable.
- **Wine is spilled on the ground** - wine and blood are intermingled in symbolism, so something has occurred that has "cost blood," even if symbolically, sorrow and sadness are present here and possibly regret.
- **Two cups are standing behind the person** - these cups are upright, they are in the past, but represent he has not lost everything and therefore he has something to work with.
- **Flowing water** – symbolic of purification and healing properties.
- **Person facing left side of card** – represents reflective, inward looking thoughts.
- **Bridge** - symbolizes communication.
- **Large house in background** – signifies there are abundant resources and security, or it could symbolize a healing temple, somewhere to rest and get better.
- **Green in the foreground and trees in the distance** – represents earth energy which indicates the possibility for the materialization or realized outcome of an idea or project.

UPRIGHT MEANING

- About disappointment.

- About something that has been lost, perhaps a relationship may have taken a down turn, or ended altogether.
- This card speaks to deep sorrow or despair about the loss of something that cannot be recovered. But it also indicates that focusing on what is gone is interfering with the ability to appreciate what is still there.
- About taking time to grieve as out of what seems hurtful may arise something special and valued if you identify and acknowledge it.
- About a time when the feeling of loss is most acute.
- This card is telling you that the more you struggle to keep what is gone, the more you suffer.
- About cherished hopes that have slipped away.
- It may indicate that success has not come as planned or at too great an expense if at all.

REVERSED MEANING:
- Something from the past is revisiting you and brings sorrow.
- *The meaning of the card is delayed or extended into the future.*
- *An aspect of the upright meaning of the card needs to be released so you can move forward.*
- *This is not about the upright meaning, place another card on reversed one and read it.*

Six of Cups

REPRESENTS

- nostalgic sentiments
- valuing past memories
- future dreams
- childhood
- good will
- innocence
- understanding that happiness can be relearned

NUMBER SIX

- Sixes are always favourable.
- Sixes vibration is cooperative.
- Six represents the ability to transcend difficulties and a sense of peace and quiet after the storm.
- Following the conflicts experienced with fives, sixes demonstrate the integration of newly acquired skills. Improved coping mechanisms and overcoming challenges has resulted in stability.
- Six is a time of balance and respite that creates a base and a pivot for new experiences.
- Six, an important ceremonial number, refers to Spirit's connection to life in all directions (*north, south, east and west, above and below*).
- Because three (3) is a cosmic number its attributes are amplified by six (6).

ASTROLOGICALLY

- Ruled by the planet VENUS, six is a pleasant harmonious number that governs the arts and music. Relationships are of paramount importance with tact and diplomacy figuring prominently.

- When number six is significant money plays an important role.
- Six enables a free flow of energy, which allows many opportunities for success.
- Six corresponds to MUTABLE SIGNS Gemini, Virgo, Sagittarius and Pisces. Seeing both sides of a situation they adjust their attitudes and adapt to almost any circumstances. Versatility allows mutable sign people to accept change and thereby end what was.
- Cups are represented by the element of water a feminine energy. Emotional and sensitive WATER SIGN people are capable of great compassion. Intuitive and attuned to subtle vibrations they are quick to sum up others, often at a first meeting.
- Inward looking, internally driven and intuitive FEMININE ENERGY is sensitive and emotional, while seeking to create co-existence and consensus it is introspective and nurturing.

SYMBOLISM INCLUDES
- **Children in the foreground** – symbolizes innocence and the presence of loving actions.
- **Cups full of flowers** – represent pleasantness and peacefulness.
- **Cross of St. Andrew** - this cross acts as an amulet against danger, a weapon against monsters, even the Devil. It is the union between male and female, earth and sky and signifies integration and manifestation.
- **Large castle type home** - symbolizes wealth, resources and stability.
- **Man walking toward house** – represents the "father," which symbolizes the protector and provider.
- **Green grass, green on the flower's leaves** – represents earth energy, manifestation, moving ahead with a plan that has great potential for its final realization.

UPRIGHT MEANING
- A time to attend to everyday needs as any previous misunderstandings or upheavals can now be harmoniously resolved.

- About someone or some event forcing you to recognize the good in your life.
- About nostalgia and sentimental values.
- About simple goodness, being kind, generous and forgiving.
- About the carefree, playful and secure feelings of being loved associated to childhood and youth.
- Can indicate a time to focus on a sibling.
- This card could indicate a rekindling of an old love affair or a friendship from the past.

REVERSED MEANING
- An important event is coming soon.
- *The meaning of the card is delayed or extended into the future.*
- *An aspect of the upright meaning of the card needs to be released so you can move forward.*
- *This is not about the upright meaning, place another card on reversed one and read it.*

CUPS

Seven of Cups

REPRESENTS
- dreaming
- wishful thinking
- imagination
- visions
- moving into disorganization
- possibly entering into addictive patterns
- facing an array of options

NUMBER SEVEN
- Sevens are sacred numbers made up of three, the number of Spirit and cosmic energy and four, the number of matter, that which is necessary for the manifestation of ideas or projects.
- Relating to the development of the soul, sevens deal with wisdom, completeness and perfection.
- Indicating a need to deal with your inner life, seven is a time of introspection and soul searching that will require solitude.
- A reflective time, seven indicates a period when you will find it necessary to seriously consider how and why specific events occur.
- Sevens represent a turning point as they begin a new cycle of threes. One, two and three the first cycle was followed by four, five and six, and now we have seven, eight and nine.
- Sevens bring about a new restlessness possibly indicating a breakthrough in awareness which causes us to re-evaluate and willingly try new things, which may result in a changed understanding or perspective.

ASTROLOGICALLY
- Ruled by the planet NEPTUNE, seven a spiritual number with surreal qualities, is connected to mystics, visionaries and seers. Associated with idealism the number seven can represent

depression when our expectations of others and our personal goals are not met.

- Seven corresponds to CARDINAL SIGNS which are about new beginnings, enterprise and getting things started. Aries for spring, Cancer for summer, Libra for autumn, and Capricorn for winter.

- Cups are represented by the element of water a feminine energy. Emotional and sensitive WATER SIGN people are capable of great compassion. Intuitive and attuned to subtle vibrations they are quick to sum up others, often at a first meeting.

- Inward looking, internally driven and intuitive FEMININE ENERGY is sensitive and emotional, while seeking to create co-existence and consensus it is introspective and nurturing.

SYMBOLISM INCLUDES

- **Man in the foreground** – represents someone having a vision or imagining things.
- **Cups in the air** - symbolizes the imagination or a fantasy.
- **Each cup holding a different symbol** - represents countless hopes, desires and wishes.
- **Jewels in the cup** - represent wealth.
- **Laurel wreath in cup** – symbolizes success and victory.
- **Dragon in cup** – symbolizes fear or adventure.
- **Blue castle in cup** – symbolizes wealth and power.
- **Snake in cup** – symbolizes knowledge and wisdom.
- **Baccus "the god of wine" in cup** - Baccus was the promoter of civilization, so this is about relationships and friends.
- **Radiant ghostly figure in cup** - symbolizes the connection to the spirit world.

UPRIGHT MEANING

- About self indulgences and excesses.
- About the presence of personal fantasies and desires.
- About being connected with Spirit, you should write down your dreams and interpret them as this is a good time to connect with your soul guides.
- Can indicate experiencing heightened intuitiveness and even some psychic visions.

- About daydreaming, imagination and visions, either fantastic or reflective.
- Could be a warning about "pie in the sky thoughts," that indulging in endless daydreams will get you nowhere. You need to decide what is practical, what has possibilities, and what constitutes a waste of time.

REVERSED MEANING

- *The meaning of the card is delayed or extended into the future.*
- *An aspect of the upright meaning of the card needs to be released so you can move forward.*
- *This is not about the upright meaning, place another card on reversed one and read it.*

EIGHT

CUPS

Eight of Cups

REPRESENTS
* retiring
* retreating
* regeneration
* seeking deeper meaning
* realizing the current cycle is over

NUMBER EIGHT
* Eight, the sign of infinity represents death and regeneration.
* The number of cosmic balance, eight's beneficial qualities are rarely diluted, they represent two times greater the benefits of four, the number of manifestation.
* Placed on its side eight becomes the lemniscate, the symbol of infinity representing the eternal spiralling movement of the heavens.
* The hour glass shape of eight symbolizes the passage of time and cycles by representing the four seasons the two solstices and two equinoxes.
* Eights vibration is linked with abundance, material prosperity, worldly power, influence, leadership, authority, possibility, options and potential.

ASTROLOGICALLY
* Ruled by the planet SATURN, the hard task master, eight is a solid and very stable number.
* When eight is prominent in an individual's life they often are presented with many harsh lessons and must learn by experience.
* Eight corresponds to FIXED SIGN Taurus, Leo, Scorpio and Aquarius. Resistant to change these people are faithful and persevering seeing projects through to the end. They attempt

to adapt the environment to themselves and above all they want to maintain things.

- Cups are represented by the element of water a feminine energy. Emotional and sensitive WATER SIGN people are capable of great compassion. Intuitive and attuned to subtle vibrations they are quick to sum up others, often at a first meeting.
- Inward looking, internally driven and intuitive FEMININE ENERGY is sensitive and emotional, while seeking to create co-existence and consensus it is introspective and nurturing.

SYMBOLISM INCLUDES

- **Eight cups neatly stacked up** - this represents orderliness, care and attention.
- **Man with walking stick** – symbolizes a journey ahead.
- **Orange coloured clothing** – symbolizes warmth, determination and willingness for action.
- **Cups are behind the man** – symbolizes leaving something behind.
- **Night time** – symbolizes things are not as they appear and the presence of hidden meanings.
- **Full moon with crescent moon in it** – represents a time of mystery, not all the answers are available.
- **Water** – symbolizes feminine energy, intuitiveness, hidden knowledge, caring, and is all about emotions.
- **Large mountains** – represents connection to higher thoughts and spirituality.
- **Green** - the mountains and ground are green, representing earth energy, manifestation and potential for success.

UPRIGHT MEANING

- About moving on and taking a new direction. Nothing in life is permanent.
- The situation or issue you are currently focused on does not hold the importance you have currently assigned it, by taking action this will be revealed to you allowing you to move on.
- About moving away from old beliefs or possibly rejecting the value of material objects for the spiritual search or quest.

- Can indicate there comes a time when something has run its course it's time to move on.
- Can mean leaving something behind that you spent a great deal of time and effort on but that no longer holds its relevance for you.
- Can mean a physical change such as leaving a job, location, or relationship.
- Can be a warning that a failure to act now could lead to stagnation.

REVERSED MEANING

- *The meaning of the card is delayed or extended into the future.*
- *An aspect of the upright meaning of the card needs to be released so you can move forward.*
- *This is not about the upright meaning, place another card on reversed one and read it.*

CUPS

Nine of Cups

REPRESENTS
- sensual satisfaction
- everything you hoped for will soon come to be
- indulging in a bit of smugness
- satisfaction and contentment

NUMBER NINE
- Nine's vibrations let you see beyond the physical into the limitlessness of the universe.
- Nine is the number of fulfillment, it triples the effect of three the number of cosmic power.
- Representing the end of a cycle nine indicates it is time to tie up loose ends.
- Generally nine depicts completion, wholeness and the sense of satisfaction that comes from reaching a hard worked for goal.
- Sometimes nine can demonstrate regrets as it's the end of a cycle and things may not have gone well, when this is the case you may experience anxiety about not knowing what to expect next.

ASTROLOGICALLY
- The planet MARS which is related to sexual prowess, courage, energy, action, protectiveness, valour and being an able provider rules nine. Forceful and dominating nine creates stability and is a good number when attempting to build foundations.
- When nine is prominent, quite often people will need to overcome obstacles before they will be able to reach their highest potential.
- Nine corresponds to MUTABLE SIGNS Gemini, Virgo, Sagittarius and Pisces. Seeing both sides of a situation they adjust their attitudes and adapt to almost any circumstances. Versatility

allows mutable sign people to accept change and thereby end what was.

- Cups are represented by the element of water a feminine energy. Emotional and sensitive WATER SIGN people are capable of great compassion. Intuitive and attuned to subtle vibrations they are quick to sum up others, often at a first meeting.
- Inward looking, internally driven and intuitive FEMININE ENERGY is sensitive and emotional, while seeking to create co-existence and consensus it is introspective and nurturing.

SYMBOLISM INCLUDES

- **Person's crossed arms** - symbolizes the "ego" or personal satisfaction rather than true inner self satisfaction.
- **Flamboyant red hat** - hats represent authority and power, red indicates passionate energy.
- **Person's clothing** – looking like a genie he is symbolic of someone who can grant a wish.
- **Cups are above and behind the person** – represents things are in place and ready for business.
- **Blue table cloth** - blue symbolizes spirit and intellect, loyalty, insight, inspiration and independence.
- **Yellow foreground and background** – represents immense enthusiasm and energy.

UPRIGHT MEANING

- Everything you hoped for will soon come to be, expect triumph and complete success.
- Expect fulfillment, harmony and success with the projects or situations described by other cards in the reading.
- About feeling satisfied with the abundance present in your life.
- There is a belief which has been influenced by the Romany gypsies that this card can grant desires. So rub the man's belly and make a silent wish.

REVERSED MEANING

- Possibly some people taking advantage of your hospitality.
- *The meaning of the card is delayed or extended into the future.*

- *An aspect of the upright meaning of the card needs to be released so you can move forward.*
- *This is not about the upright meaning, place another card on reversed one and read it.*

TEN

CUPS

Ten of Cups

REPRESENTS

- happy endings
- this is as good as it gets
- joy, peace, and family
- real love
- domestic bliss
- satisfaction in your accomplishments

NUMBER TEN

- The number ten reduces to one. (1 + 0 = 1)
- One's energy is individual, solitary and self-contained.
- Represents the beginning of form; the active principle of creation.
- Represents the mystic centre.
- Represents self-development, creativity, action, progress, a new chance, and rebirth.

ASTROLOGICALLY

- Ruled by the SUN, ten reduced to one is egocentric often representing a person who is somewhat of a loner.
- One corresponds to CARDINAL SIGNS which are about new beginnings, enterprise, and getting things started. Aries for spring, Cancer for summer, Libra for autumn, and Capricorn for winter.
- Cups are represented by the element of water a feminine energy. Emotional and sensitive WATER SIGN people are capable of great compassion. Intuitive and attuned to subtle vibrations they are quick to sum up others, often at a first meeting.
- Inward looking, internally driven and intuitive FEMININE ENERGY is sensitive and emotional, while seeking to create co-existence and consensus it is introspective and nurturing.

SYMBOLISM INCLUDES

- **Man, woman and children** - represents joy, happiness, satisfaction, a sense of accomplishment and completeness.
- **Cups up in the air surrounded by a rainbow** - rainbows signify renewal, hope, happiness and they are an act of divine benevolence. Cups up in the air represent a connection with Spirit.
- **Blue sky** – signifies that things look positive.
- **Water** - symbolizes feminine energy, relationships, emotions, hidden meanings and intuitiveness.
- **Green grass and trees** - symbolize earth energy and the high likelihood of manifestation of ideas or projects.
- **House in the distance** - symbolizes security and resources.

UPRIGHT MEANING

- About permanent relationships and a happy home life that has been well tended to.
- Can mean feeling comfortable with whom you are.
- About experiencing happiness and a sense of wholeness.
- About caring for the people in your life and the peace and harmony they create for you.
- If this reading is about work this card implies work can wait, family comes first.
- This card strengthens positive cards in a reading and helps to negate negative cards.

REVERSED MEANING

- Family relationships are troubled.
- *The meaning of the card is delayed or extended into the future.*
- *An aspect of the upright meaning of the card needs to be released so you can move forward.*
- *This is not about the upright meaning, place another card on reversed one and read it.*

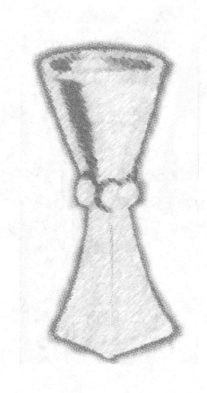

PAGE

CUPS

Page of Cups

REPRESENTS
* messages arriving
* new beginning on a feeling level
* intuitiveness is increased

NUMBER ELEVEN
* The number eleven reduces to two. (1+1 = 2)
* Some type of union or partnership with another person, a spiritual entity, or two parts of you.
* The balance of polarities such as yin/yang, male/female and public/separate.
* Builds on the opportunity presented by one (*the ace*).
* Sensitivity to others sometimes to the point you consider their wellbeing over your own.
* Becoming immersed in another person an idea or a project.
* Choices and decisions.

ASTROLOGICALLY
* Ruled by the MOON, two (*the Page*) is associated with relationships, cooperation, emotions and feelings.
* Two corresponds to FIXED SIGNS Taurus, Leo, Scorpio and Aquarius. Resistant to change these people are faithful and persevering seeing projects through to the end. They attempt to adapt the environment to themselves and above all they want to maintain things.
* Cups are represented by the element of water a feminine energy. Emotional and sensitive WATER SIGN people are capable of great compassion. Intuitive and attuned to subtle vibrations they are quick to sum up others, often at a first meeting.
* Inward looking, internally driven and intuitive FEMININE ENERGY is sensitive and emotional, while seeking to create co-existence and consensus it is introspective and nurturing.

SYMBOLISM INCLUDES

- **Blue coloured tunic** - symbolizes purity, serenity, mental clarity and compassion.
- **Lilies on his tunic** – symbolize purity.
- **Carefree blue hat** - hats denote authority and thinking. The blue hat indicates he has mental clarity and his thoughts are pure, serene and compassionate. The hat's design represents a sense of light-heartedness, relaxation and cheerfulness.
- **Orange clothing** - orange symbolizes warmth, enthusiasm and optimism.
- **Fish coming out of cup** – fish symbolize spirituality.
- **Waves in the background** – symbolize emotions are running high, feminine energy, intuitiveness, caring, and sensitivity.

UPRIGHT MEANING
PAGES BRING MESSAGES

- After laying out the entire spread, lay the first extra card that was selected on the Page, this clarifies the message.

PAGES AS A SITUATION

- Your intuition is at work, new ideas are emerging that will lead to creative activity.
- An idea representing potential or possibilities is gestating within you but it needs time to become grounded.
- Possibly the birth of a child.

PAGE AS A PERSONALITY

- Represents a sweet natured child who likely enjoys his (*her*) home life and will not be the cause of problems. This child may not be particularly academic and may struggle somewhat in school but later in life he or she will get by and go on to hold responsible employment.
- Possibly your child, a relative, or a child that will be impacting your life.
- An endearing child that any family would be proud to have as part of it.
- May personify you implying you have an immature manner of looking at your experiences.

REVERSED MEANING

- *The meaning of the card is delayed or extended into the future.*
- *An aspect of the upright meaning of the card needs to be released so you can move forward.*
- *This is not about the upright meaning, place another card on reversed one and read it.*

KNIGHT

CUPS

Knight of Cups

REPRESENTS

- methodical change
- the romantic knight in shining armour
- a messenger of true love

NUMBER TWELVE

- The number twelve reduces to three. (1+2=3)
- Cosmic energy is embedded in threes.
- Three, a mystic number, represents Spirit.
- Threes possess celestial power; the sun stands still for three days at the solstices; threes encompass past, present and future; the moon looks full for three days and disappears as dark for three days. Threes make up the trinity of mind, body and spirit.
- Group activities, movement, action, growth and development are expressed by threes.
- Sometimes with threes expansion occurs quickly causing you to spread yourself too thin or for your energies to scatter.
- Paying attention to what you are doing results in threes vibration being cheerful, optimistic and pleasant, representing a period of happiness and benefits.

ASTROLOGICALLY

- The Knight of Cups is represented by CANCER, ruled by the MOON, and characterizes the High Flyer.
- Governing emotions and intuition the Moon is a metaphor for all that is instinctive. Cyclical and constantly changing the Moon is called the soul of life, mediator between the planes of the spiritual (*Sun*) and the material (*Earth*).
- Three corresponds to MUTABLE SIGNS Gemini, Virgo, Sagittarius and Pisces. Seeing both sides of a situation they adjust their attitudes and adapt to almost any circumstances.

Versatility allows mutable sign people to accept change and thereby end what was.

- Cups are represented by the element of water a feminine energy. Emotional and sensitive WATER SIGN people are capable of great compassion. Intuitive and attuned to subtle vibrations they are quick to sum up others, often at a first meeting.
- Inward looking, internally driven and intuitive FEMININE ENERGY is sensitive and emotional, while seeking to create co-existence and consensus it is introspective and nurturing.

SYMBOLISM INCLUDES

- **Dressed in armour** –symbolizes a readiness to fight or defend as well as possessing the necessary skills, tools, and traits to succeed.
- **Wings on his helmet and at his ankles** – wings symbolize movement and action as well as denoting an improvement for the subject wearing them.
- **Fish and waves on the clothing** – symbolize feminine energy, intuitiveness, emotions, caring and a connection to spirituality.
- **White horse** – the horse denotes animal instincts (*connection to the unconscious and making gut decisions*) and the colour white signifies innocence, divinity, and victory.
- **Sitting on a horse** - a rider on a horse can symbolize the workings of conscious (*rider*) and unconscious (*instincts of horse*) mind.
- **Stream of water** – symbolizes feminine energy, intuitiveness, emotions and caring.
- **Green on trees and hills** – indicates earth energy and the possibility of manifestation.
- **Hills** - symbolize ancient wisdom; they depict mountains that have worn down with age.
- **Mountains in the background** – symbolize stability and connection to spirituality.

UPRIGHT MEANING
KNIGHTS MEAN CHANGE IS COMING

- Usually indicating a long-term condition of life that is about to become better, worse or end.

- Plans and intrigues are occurring in the background of which you may or may not be aware and in which you are about to become involved with whether you want to or not.
- The horse's stance indicates the speed of that process and this horse is walking so you should have time to prepare for the change.

KNIGHT AS A SITUATION

- Your intuition and instincts about your surroundings are magnified at this time.
- You may receive an invitation concerning a positive event.
- You may receive good sound advice from someone you can trust.
- You have shown great dedication to a project, have taken risks and are now focusing your energies toward accomplishing a goal.
- In modern times this main mean you will be getting a new car (*horses are equated to cars*).
- You may be asked to give up something that matters to you.
- Someone may perform an unselfish act on your behalf.

KNIGHT AS A PERSONALITY

- Represents an honest intelligent young person who is friendly towards you. Perhaps a brother, a friend, or a lover.
- A trustworthy and unselfish person.
- If this person is your lover they will share true reciprocated love with you.
- May personify you.

REVERSED MEANING

- The Knight has fallen off his horse, whatever change was coming has been delayed.
- *The meaning of the card is delayed or extended into the future.*
- *An aspect of the upright meaning of the card needs to be released so you can move forward.*
- *This is not about the upright meaning, place another card on reversed one and read it.*

QUEEN

CUPS

Queen of Cups

REPRESENTS
- the beloved and tender-hearted
- a secure environment
- someone who is intelligent cultured and intuitive
- someone who has a well developed sixth sense
- anticipation and foresight

NUMBER THIRTEEN
- The number thirteen reduces to four. (1+3 = 4)
- Four is the number associated to "matter."
- Four is a time to build a foundation that will support your ideas and projects.
- Hard work and self discipline are required with fours.
- A stabilizing time for creating structures and order.
- Representing manifestation of your ideas, fours represent prosperity, peace, happiness, abundance and even triumph.
- Sometimes fours represent a stage in personal development when a stalemate has been reached, a period that often seems necessary for unacknowledged emotions or dilemmas to come into consciousness so we can experience them and get on with growth or healing.

ASTROLOGICALLY
- The Queen of Cups is represented by PISCES, ruled by NEPTUNE and characterizes the Feeler.
- Neptune represents dreams, imagination, inspiration, spirituality and deception. It is related to all that is unreal, ethereal, mystical, otherworldly, invisible, imaginative and creative. As the planet of emotional genius, Neptune has dominance over many of the arts and inspirational thought. Neptune rules theatre, sensationalism, poetry, music, and transcendent modes of creativity.

- Four corresponds to CARDINAL SIGNS which are about new beginnings, enterprise and getting things started. Aries for spring, Cancer for summer, Libra for autumn, and Capricorn for winter.
- Cups are represented by the element of water a feminine energy. Emotional and sensitive WATER SIGN people are capable of great compassion. Intuitive and attuned to subtle vibrations they are quick to sum up others, often at a first meeting.
- Inward looking, internally driven and intuitive FEMININE ENERGY is sensitive and emotional, while seeking to create co-existence and consensus it is introspective and nurturing.

SYMBOLISM INCLUDES
- **White gown** – the colour white symbolizes purity.
- **Wearing a golden crown** – crowns symbolize authority and power. The colour gold is associated with the Sun and thus the highest stage of spiritual development. Gold is also found at the heart of the earth and symbolizes superiority, wealth, abundance, immortality and incorruptibility.
- **Grey throne** – the colour grey symbolizes wisdom.
- **Undines (cherub looking mermaids on top of and carved into throne)** - the lower half of their body is a fish and the upper part is a human making them water nymphs or mermaids, they represent the perilous nature of water (*the unconscious*). They symbolize attempts to reconcile our unconscious thoughts (*untamed part of our nature*) with our conscious thoughts (*tamed or humanized part of us*).
- **Ornate container with victory wreathes and a cross on top** – signifies the Queen values her possessions which includes her sense of spirituality. The victory wreath indicates that the Queen personally earned or won many of her possessions, they were not all presents.
- **Winged figures on the ornate container** – signifies that the contents of the container are linked with Spirit.
- **Ornate container is closed** - symbolizes that what it contains is not to be seen by all.
- **Colourful rocks at Queen's feet** - rocks denote stability and safety. Possibly the rocks colour indicates the Queen's ability to see auras.

- **Water** – symbolizes feminine energy which is receptive, intuitive, inward looking, internally driven, sensitive and emotional.
- **Yellow** - yellow symbolizes optimism, enthusiasm and positive energy.
- **Green** – an earth energy which symbolizes the likelihood of manifestation of ideas or projects.
- **The Queen is facing left** - signifies the unconscious and the need or desire to delve into it.

UPRIGHT MEANING
QUEEN AS A SITUATION
- About feeling emotionally secure and making wise choices especially in personal relationships.
- This is a time of success, happiness and pleasure.
- If you are planning an important endeavour, especially one that involves relationships this is a good time to do it.
- About being posed for success as a result of your dedication and well developed skills.
- Your understanding of universal truths is enhanced at this time.
- This is a time to draw upon your emotional integrity and authenticity.
- Self nurturance and forgiveness plays a bigger role in your life right now.
- Could indicate that your intuitions are heightened at this time and that you may even have some psychic experiences.

QUEEN AS A PERSONALITY
- Evoking feelings of affection and love this woman is an honest and devoted female friend or relative who will perform a service for you.
- Motherly, intuitive and in-touch with her own and other's feelings this woman represents a great parent and excellent spouse.
- Using authenticity, forgiveness and full emotional understanding this woman models emotional integrity. Her

inner world is highly developed and she is a master at healthy self nurturance.

- This woman could be entering or affecting your life at the moment. She could be a parent, boss, relative, counsellor or confident.
- May personify you.

REVERSED MEANING

- You may be playing with dangerous psychic matters you do not understand.
- *The meaning of the card is delayed or extended into the future.*
- *An aspect of the upright meaning of the card needs to be released so you can move forward.*
- *This is not about the upright meaning, place another card on reversed one and read it.*

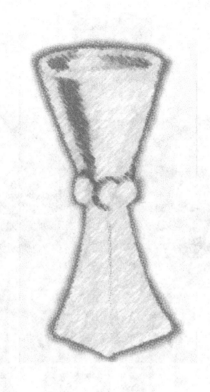

KING

CUPS

King of Cups

REPRESENTS
- a just and good man
- a situation involving justice, intelligence or honour
- diplomacy
- wisdom
- calmness
- ability to manage well while surrounded with turmoil and emotions

NUMBER FOURTEEN
- The number fourteen reduces to five. (1+4=5)
- Fives always represent some type of difficulty, tension or crisis.
- Challenges often result in a winner or loser with fives.
- Fives suggest a sense of being on a roller coaster ride or being caught up in a whirlwind.
- Fluctuation, unrest and sometimes clashes create a sense of instability and can cause stress.
- Impulsive and impatient behaviours occur but resourcefulness and curiosity are also present.
- Fives indicate we have the quality of mind, but lack the maturity and knowledge to transform old ways into new patterns of being.
- We may be forced to make a choice in order to end the anxiety that is associated with fives.

ASTROLOGICALLY
- The King of Cups is represented by SCORPIO, ruled by PLUTO and characterizes Rebirth.
- Ruling the forces of creation and destruction Pluto symbolizes the capacity to change totally and forever one's lifestyle, thought and behaviour. As the planet of beginnings and endings, Pluto

can effect total transformation. Pluto can also bring a lust for power with strong obsessions.

- Five corresponds to FIXED SIGNS Taurus, Leo, Scorpio and Aquarius. Resistant to change these people are faithful and persevering seeing projects through to the end. They attempt to adapt the environment to themselves and above all they want to maintain things.

- Cups are represented by the element of water a feminine energy. Emotional and sensitive WATER SIGN people are capable of great compassion. Intuitive and attuned to subtle vibrations they are quick to sum up others, often at a first meeting.

- Inward looking, internally driven and intuitive FEMININE ENERGY is sensitive and emotional while seeking to create co-existence and consensus it is introspective and nurturing.

SYMBOLISM INCLUDES

- **King dressed in blue gown** – symbolizes purity of spirit.

- **King's robe is yellow with orange trim** – represents vitality, energy, optimism and enthusiasm.

- **Magnificent crown** – represents royalty, power, authority, he deserves his place in life, he has earned it and those around him recognize it.

- **Green shoes, some green in the water** – signifies earth energy thus manifestation is possible.

- **One foot close to the water** - water is a feminine energy which means intuition and caring, this King can be very emotional and caring if he needs to be.

- **Golden fish necklace** – covering his heart chakra it suggests the orderly recognition of feelings and a feminine instinct which has yet to be fully incorporated. The colour gold is associated with the sun and thus the highest stage of spiritual development. Gold is also found at the heart of the earth and symbolizes superiority, wealth, abundance, immortality and incorruptibility.

- **Body language** - this King appears focused and absorbed but approachable.

- **Throne is grey stone** - stone symbolizes stability and the colour grey signifies wisdom.

- **Waves surrounding throne** - symbolizes turmoil and emotional problems to deal with as well as representing the King's mastery of his emotions. This can be a reminder of how easily we can be overcome by our emotions.
- **Ship with red sails** – signifies resources, the presence of commerce, the introduction of cultural information as well as material gain - "your ship is coming in." Red represents passion.

UPRIGHT MEANING
KING AS A SITUATION

- The situation you may find yourself in involves justice, honour, learning and understanding, intelligence and intelligent action.
- If you are involved with any authority figures your issues will be dealt with fairly.
- About a favourable time for you especially for any artistic pursuits.
- Through your dedication your work skills have become highly developed.
- Even if surrounded with issues and emotional turmoil you will stay afloat.
- You need to use diplomacy, tolerance and patience when approaching a situation.

KING AS A PERSONALITY

- This man is a motivator and innovator.
- A just and honest man who is kindly disposed toward you.
- Represents a responsible, mature, intelligent, well educated man that possess the skills and connections which you may require at this time.
- This is a man willing to help you in some way however you may need to ask him.
- Compassionate and in touch with his feelings this is a fatherly man or a husband.

REVERSED MEANING

- Someone is trying to dump you and the romance is over.

- *The meaning of the card is delayed or extended into the future.*
- *An aspect of the upright meaning of the card needs to be released so you can move forward.*
- *This is not about the upright meaning, place another card on reversed one and read it.*

The Suit of
Swords

27. THE SUIT OF SWORDS

- The suit of swords represents events, conditions, situations or attitudes that may be difficult or challenging. When swords appear in a reading you may be experiencing stress or problems but these make you think.
- Swords, an air sign, are represented by Gemini, Libra and Aquarius. Intellectual and good at conceptualizing air signs are great communicators constantly coming up with new ideas
- Representing masculine energy air signs are outward looking, primarily motivated by external concerns, action-oriented and protective. Seeking to dominate the outside world air sign people can be hard, firm, logical, strong, rational, rough and loud.
- Swords represent the medieval nobility, the most influential class, who held absolute power with the ability, resources and tendency to wage war and fickly control the lives and deaths of all other classes.
- Swords can represent anyone or anything wishing to harm or control you for their own ends.
- Demonstrating ill fortune and strife swords sometime represent your ability to harm others.
- In a reading this suit is sometimes associated to health issues.
- Swords are associated with spades in playing cards.
- Swords are often seen as the third suit of the Major Arcana. They are the stage of action, movement, struggle and effort.

REVERSED CARDS

Sometimes cards are upside down when they are chosen. Readers have preferences when interpreting the meanings of cards in this position. I have listed some reversed meanings and also provided some other options. It is up to you as a reader to determine which meaning best fits. Some readers simply turn the cards right side up and do not deal with reversed meanings. It is a good idea to choose a standard method to follow and deviate only when circumstances in the reading seem to dictate a need to do so.

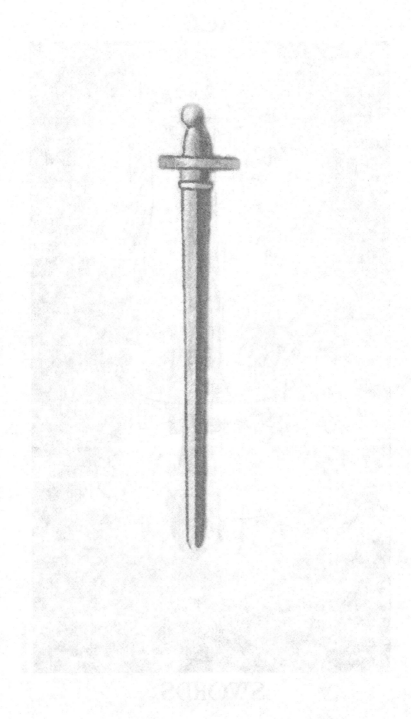

ACE

SWORDS

Ace of Swords

REPRESENTS
- success and victory, following strife, which seemingly comes from nowhere

NUMBER ONE
- One's energy is individual, solitary and self-contained.
- Representing the beginning of form number one relates to the active principle of creation.
- One represents mystery, secret information, hidden knowledge, and the mystic centre.
- One is about self-development, creativity, action, progress, a new chance, and rebirth.

ASTROLOGICALLY
- The Ace of Swords is the root of the powers of air.
- Ruled by the Sun one's egocentrism often represents people who are somewhat loners.
- One corresponds to CARDINAL SIGNS which are about new beginnings, enterprise and getting things started. Aries for spring, Cancer for summer, Libra for autumn, and Capricorn for winter.
- The suit of swords represented by AIR SIGNS are intellectuals and good at conceptualizing. All about thinking they are great communicators constantly coming up with new ideas.
- Representing MASCULINE ENERGY air signs are outward looking, primarily motivated by external concerns, action-oriented and protective. Seeking to dominate the outside world air sign people can be hard, firm, logical, strong, rational, rough and loud.

SYMBOLISM INCLUDES
- **Hand surrounded by clouds with a halo emanating from it** - symbolizes the hand of Spirit.

- **Right hand** – represents the honourable, good, truthful and trustworthy side and symbolizes assertive, active masculine energy.
- **Golden crown** – a crown signifies authority and power. Gold's association with the Sun represents the highest stage of spiritual development. Gold as a metal symbolizes superiority, wealth, abundance, immortality and incorruptibility.
- **Olive branch suspended from the crown** – a symbolic metaphor for spiritual light it symbolizes peace, fruitfulness, mercy and purification.
- **Palm branch suspended from the crown** – represents triumphal victory.
- **Six yellow yods** – yods are shaped like dew drops and represent the primary Hebrew letter as all other Hebrew letters are a variation of it. Associated with the astrological sign Virgo yods symbolize creative seeds representing divine grace and healing. Translated yod means "open hand" and signifies new possibility of divine energy or intelligence coming through us and manifesting in our thoughts and deeds. Six a cosmically powerful number enhances the yod's symbolization of the potency of activity, power and direction. Their yellow color denotes enthusiasm, opportunity and energy.
- **Purple mountains** - symbolizes stability, wisdom and authority.

UPRIGHT MEANING
- A gift from the universe.
- About new beginnings and starting a whole new cycle.
- Higher guidance is inherent in this card.
- Something has begun even if you are not aware of it.
- If you initiate something now the circumstances are favourable for you to succeed.
- About being surrounded with opportunity.
- May be about a new job, promotion or acceptance into a school or program.
- May be about engaging in artistic endeavours such as writing, painting, pottery, etc.
- This could mean starting your own business.

REVERSED MEANING

- Think "thumbs down" on a particular project, you need to start over, rethink, or regroup.
- *The meaning of the card is delayed or extended into the future.*
- *An aspect of the upright meaning of the card needs to be released so you can move forward.*
- *This is not about the upright meaning, place another card on reversed one and read it.*

TWO

SWORDS

Two of Swords

REPRESENTS
* blocked emotions
* avoidance
* a stalemate
* tension
* anxiety

NUMBER TWO
* Some type of union or partnership with another person, a spiritual entity, or two parts of you.
* Associated with the balance of polarities such as yin/yang, male/female and public/separate.
* Two builds on the opportunity presented by one (*the ace*).
* Two can represent sensitivity to others sometimes to the point of considering their wellbeing over your own.
* Representative of immersing yourself into another person, an idea, or a project.
* Two is associated with choices and decisions.

ASTROLOGICALLY
* Ruled by the MOON, two is associated with relationships, cooperation, emotions and feelings.
* Two corresponds to FIXED SIGNS Taurus, Leo, Scorpio and Aquarius. Resistant to change these people are faithful and persevering seeing projects through to the end. They attempt to adapt the environment to themselves and above all they want to maintain things.
* The suit of swords represented by AIR SIGNS are intellectuals and good at conceptualizing. All about thinking they are great communicators constantly coming up with new ideas.
* Representing MASCULINE ENERGY air signs are outward looking, primarily motivated by external concerns, action-

oriented and protective. Seeking to dominate the outside world air sign people can be hard, firm, logical, strong, rational, rough and loud.

SYMBOLISM INCLUDES

- **Blindfold** - symbolizes the inability to see or find one's way.
- **White dress** – white symbolizes purity.
- **Arms are crossed with a sword in each hand** – represents a sense of being closed down, holding things close to the heart.
- **Sitting on a grey bench with a grey foreground** - denotes wisdom (*she is sitting on information she does not realize – she is wiser than she thinks*).
- **Crescent moon** - the moon symbolizes mysteriousness, the unknown, and being crescent shaped it denotes a warning about not revealing too much information as the psyche may not be able to handle it. It may also indicate emotional factors and unconscious habit patterns that need to be changed.
- **Green grass behind her** – denotes earth energy, manifestation, creating and seeing things through to fruition is possible.
- **Water** - a large body of water, a great deal of feminine energy is present, feelings, emotion, intuition and hidden information.
- **Rocks** - these rocks rise out of the water near the shoreline so represent a need to be careful of hazards.
- **Mountains in the background** – represent stability, constancy, warmth and a connection to spirituality.

UPRIGHT MEANING

- About feeling like you are between a rock and a hard place, all options seem poor.
- About situations when feeling you do not have all the answers, but not sure if you want to go looking for the answers, you try and maintain your current balance between all the opposing forces believing enduring the present is better than acting blindly.
- If the situation can be opened up and the fear honestly faced, something can be done to resolve the issue. What is unacknowledged cannot be changed.

- About determining whether to move into action and be assertive versus in-action and passivity.
- About situations in which you feel intellectually immobilized.

REVERSED MEANING

- Don't be pushed into making decisions, now is not the time.
- *The meaning of the card is delayed or extended into the future.*
- *An aspect of the upright meaning of the card needs to be released so you can move forward.*
- *This is not about the upright meaning, place another card on reversed one and read it.*

THREE

SWORDS

Three of Swords

REPRESENTS
- deep hurt
- releasing of tension
- heartbreak
- loneliness
- betrayal
- the disintegration of alliances

NUMBER THREE
- Cosmic energy is embedded in threes.
- Three, a mystic number, represents Spirit.
- Threes possess celestial power – the sun stands still for three days at the solstices before resuming its motion; threes encompass past, present and future; the moon looks full for three days and disappears as dark for three days. Threes make up the trinity of mind, body and spirit.
- Group activities, movement, action, growth and development are expressed by threes.
- Sometimes with threes expansion occurs too quickly causing you to spread yourself too thin or for your energies to scatter.
- If you pay attention to what you are doing threes vibration is cheerful, optimistic and pleasant, representing a period of happiness and benefits.

ASTROLOGICALLY
- JUPITER, considered a major benefit, rules three.
- With Jupiter's influence over the number three money often comes and goes easily.
- Three corresponds to MUTABLE SIGNS Gemini, Virgo, Sagittarius and Pisces. Seeing both sides of a situation they adjust their attitudes and adapt to almost any circumstances.

Versatility allows mutable sign people to accept change and thereby end what was.

- The suit of swords represented by AIR SIGNS are intellectuals and good at conceptualizing. All about thinking they are great communicators constantly coming up with new ideas.

- Representing MASCULINE ENERGY air signs are outward looking, primarily motivated by external concerns, action-oriented and protective. Seeking to dominate the outside world air sign people can be hard, firm, logical, strong, rational, rough and loud.

SYMBOLISM INCLUDES

- **Heart pierced with swords** - represents being emotionally hurt and feeling devastated.
- **Rain clouds** – symbolize tears and sadness.
- **Rain** – according to intensity it can be life giving or life destroying. Depicting revitalization, fertilization and connection to the heavens it often marks acts of purification. This rain appears to be more of a light shower symbolizing healing, renewing and perhaps a time of releasing tension.
- **Lots of grey** - denotes wisdom, something will be learned by all the hurt that is occurring.

UPRIGHT MEANING

- About an acute sense of sorrow.
- About heart ache, strife, disappointment, sadness, also an underlying sense that this is inevitable, perhaps even necessary.
- Sadness which we must endure for new understanding, insight or wisdom.
- Feelings associated with discovering a painful truth and finding your trust was misplaced.
- Can be about feelings associated with having let someone else down.
- Can be a flash of insight, it hurts and is painful, but it provides new perspective for a sorrow or loss you are experiencing.
- Can mean it is time to release some aspect of the painful past.

- Can be about a relationship or alliance that is disintegrating and ending. There are quarrels, opposing interests and conflicts between the parties. This was not a stable alliance to begin with as it was based on selfish interests for at least one if not both parties involved. Ensure you protect your interests in this breakup as this is what your former partner will definitely be doing. Stay on top of things, this will be a confusing and upsetting time, but things can go very wrong as a result of this breakup if you don't keep your wits about you.
- About separation, severance, removal, divorce, ruptures in personal or business relationships. Dispersion of property and power. This involves quarrels, infidelity and sorrow.
- A possible "love triangle" some other party or some other event or interests entering into the picture may be the reason for the breakup. The breakup will not be amicable; expect quarrels, anger, even hatred.
- If you are not sure what this card is referring to during the reading take it as a warning, examine your situation carefully, talk to people in your life, and don't take anything for granted. Listen to your inner voice; it will help you locate the problem.

REVERSED MEANING
- Don't get bogged down with what might have been.
- *The meaning of the card is delayed or extended into the future.*
- *An aspect of the upright meaning of the card needs to be released so you can move forward.*
- *This is not about the upright meaning, place another card on reversed one and read it.*

FOUR

SWORDS

Four of Swords

REPRESENTS
* a time for quiet preparation and contemplation
* recuperation
* convalescence
* rest

NUMBER FOUR
* Four is the number associated to "matter."
* Four is a time to build a foundation that will support your ideas and projects.
* Hard work and self discipline are required with fours.
* A stabilizing time for creating structures and order.
* Representing manifestation of your ideas, fours represent prosperity, peace, happiness, abundance and even triumph.
* Sometimes fours represent a stage in personal development when a stalemate has been reached, a period that often seems necessary for unacknowledged emotions or dilemmas to come into consciousness so we can experience them and get on with growth or healing.

ASTROLOGICALLY
* Four is ruled by URANUS the eccentric and unusual natured planet.
* Where the number four is prominent invention and ingenuity are very important elements to any given situation.
* Four corresponds to CARDINAL SIGNS which are associated with new beginnings, enterprise and getting things started. Aries for spring, Cancer for summer, Libra for autumn and Capricorn for winter.
* The suit of swords represented by AIR SIGNS are intellectuals and good at conceptualizing. All about thinking they are great communicators constantly coming up with new ideas.

- Representing MASCULINE ENERGY air signs are outward looking, primarily motivated by external concerns, action-oriented and protective. Seeking to dominate the outside world air sign people can be hard, firm, logical, strong, rational, rough and loud.

SYMBOLISM INCLUDES

- **Person lying down** - symbolizes a time of introspection either through quiet prayer or meditation – represents our need to go within for spiritual teaching and regeneration.
- **Dressed in armour** – denotes that protection is in place for this person.
- **Position of person's hands** – represents prayer and meditation.
- **Coffin or sarcophagus** - suggests that change needs to come about during a respite.
- **Stained glass window** – symbolizes a place of spirituality and calmness.
- **Three swords hanging above person and one below** - the number four has been separated into three and one (3 + 1). Three is embedded with cosmic energy and represents Spirit while one denotes the individual.
- **Gold colour** – gold is associated with the Sun and symbolizes the highest stage of spiritual development, it also represents an amulet (*talisman*) for wounded people.
- **Purple** - symbolizes authority and grants permission for the action of resting.

UPRIGHT MEANING

- This card indicates you need to rest. Almost a hermit's retreat.
- It also indicates a necessary period of recuperation from the situation you just passed through. Take this time to work things out on your own and plan more wisely.
- You have been through a crisis – take time alone to think, plan, and revaluate what you had been doing before the crisis. It's time to get your inner house in order.

- This is also considered a health card; it is not indicative of a serious problem, probably a minor virus and you may need to take a sick day or some time off from work.
- Can mean you should "sleep on your problem."

REVERSED MEANING

- By refusing to heed the advice in the upright meaning this will only worsen the situation.
- *The meaning of the card is delayed or extended into the future.*
- *An aspect of the upright meaning of the card needs to be released so you can move forward.*
- *This is not about the upright meaning, place another card on reversed one and read it.*

FIVE

SWORDS

Five of Swords

REPRESENTS

- self defence
- accepting the limits of both victory and defeat
- being in a hostile environment
- allowing ends to justify the means

NUMBER FIVE

- Fives always represent some type of difficulty, tension or crisis.
- Challenges often result in a winner or loser with fives.
- Fives suggest a sense of being on a roller coaster ride or being caught up in a whirlwind.
- Fluctuation, unrest and sometimes clashes create a sense of instability and can cause stress.
- Impulsive and impatient behaviours occur but resourcefulness and curiosity are also present.
- Fives indicate we have the quality of mind, but lack the maturity and knowledge to transform old ways into new patterns of being.
- We may be forced to make a choice in order to end the anxiety that is associated with fives.

ASTROLOGICALLY

- Mercury the planet associated with communication rules five.
- If five is significant in a reading it may mean this individual needs to make adjustments in order to fit in.
- Five corresponds to FIXED SIGN Taurus, Leo, Scorpio and Aquarius. Resistant to change these people are faithful and persevering seeing projects through to the end. They attempt to adapt the environment to themselves and above all they want to maintain things.

- The suit of swords represented by AIR SIGNS are intellectuals and good at conceptualizing. All about thinking they are great communicators constantly coming up with new ideas.

- Representing MASCULINE ENERGY air signs are outward looking, primarily motivated by external concerns, action-oriented and protective. Seeking to dominate the outside world air sign people can be hard, firm, logical, strong, rational, rough and loud.

SYMBOLISM INCLUDES

- **Man holding three swords** - he has taken something from the others against their will or desire.

- **Two swords lie on the ground** – this man has not only taken things away he has made sure the others have nothing.

- **Man with swords appears to be smirking** - this was a ruthless act, like a bully.

- **Man with swords wearing green** – green an earth energy means likelihood of fruition of your ideas and deeds, this man seems to have achieved his goal.

- **Man in middle has a cloak over his shoulder, his back to us** - cloaks symbolize being cut off from the world; they are shrouds to keep out things. This might be symbolizing an attempt for the man to cover up his feelings. As well his back is turned to us meaning he is not interested in communicating right now.

- **Most distance man's back is to us and he appears defeated** – he appears upset, perhaps he is crying and he looks to be feeling a lot of emotion.

- **Middle and distance men are facing the water** – water symbolize feminine energy – turning inward, relying on intuition, gaining insight (*the unconscious*).

- **Jagged clouds in the sky** – symbolizes tension is present.

- **Water** - feminine energy, inward thinking, hidden information and intuitiveness.

- **Purple mountains in the distance** - stability, connection to spirituality, could mean life continues regardless of circumstances facing people.

UPRIGHT MEANING

- Can be about the fear of defeat.
- About someone losing out, either you are the victor or the defeated.
- This card warns that if you try to get ahead at the expense of others your actions will come back to haunt you one way or another.
- Can be a warning against treachery, deceit and arrogance regarding victory, yours or others.
- Could indicate being bullied at work, or being physically or mentally abused in your relationship.
- Can be about learning to accept boundaries we all must face and live with.
- Could be about adjusting to some kind of change brought on by distress or loss, though uncomfortable it is necessary.
- This card can indicate defeat of your plans, possible monetary loss and mental anxiety.

REVERSED MEANING

- *The meaning of the card is delayed or extended into the future.*
- *An aspect of the upright meaning of the card needs to be released so you can move forward.*
- *This is not about the upright meaning, place another card on reversed one and read it.*

SIX

SWORDS

Six of Swords

REPRESENTS
* a flight to safety, either away from or towards something
* picking up the pieces after a tough time
* a possible journey

NUMBER SIX
* Sixes are always favourable.
* Sixes vibration is cooperative.
* Six represents the ability to transcend difficulties and a sense of peace and quiet after the storm.
* Following the conflicts experienced with fives, sixes demonstrate the integration of newly acquired skills. Improved coping mechanisms and overcoming challenges has resulted in stability.
* Six is a time of balance and respite that creates a base and a pivot for new experiences.
* Six, an important ceremonial number, refers to Spirit's connection to life in all directions (*north, south, east and west, above and below*).
* Because three (3) is a cosmic number its attributes are amplified by six (6).

ASTROLOGICALLY
* Ruled by the planet VENUS, six is a pleasant, harmonious number that governs the arts and music. Relationships are of paramount importance with tact and diplomacy figuring prominently.
* When number six is significant money plays an important role.
* Enabling a free flow of energy six allows many opportunities for success.

- Six corresponds to MUTABLE SIGNS Gemini, Virgo, Sagittarius and Pisces. Seeing both sides of a situation they adjust their attitudes and adapt to almost any circumstances. Versatility allows mutable sign people to accept change and thereby end what was.
- The suit of swords represented by AIR SIGNS are intellectuals and good at conceptualizing. All about thinking they are great communicators constantly coming up with new ideas.
- Representing MASCULINE ENERGY air signs are outward looking, primarily motivated by external concerns, action-oriented and protective. Seeking to dominate the outside world air sign people can be hard, firm, logical, strong, rational, rough and loud.

SYMBOLISM INCLUDES
- **Six swords standing upright** – represents orderliness and the presence of planning.
- **Man poling with two passengers** – denotes moving forward, the man poling the boat seems to be expectant of something new, the other two seem huddled and a bit despondent, possibly in the recovery stage after a crisis.
- **Calm water in front of boat with waves behind the boat** – represents that the troubled times are behind you, calmness and better times are coming.
- **Water all around** – feminine energy, the significant amount of water represents a large degree of feminine energy is present, as are emotions, intuitiveness, and hidden knowledge.
- **Land on the horizon** – represents moving towards something new.
- **Green clothing a few trees in the distance** – represents earth energy, possibility for manifestation and the concrete realization of our ideas and projects.

UPRIGHT MEANING
- About slowly moving out of a bad situation in which you recently found yourself.
- About having plans in place and moving towards an improved situation.

- About a time when harmony and ease prevails. New people you can trust come into your life.
- About feeling optimistic and balanced following a trying time you have come through.
- About moving onto better things, luck is on your side, things are getting better.
- Can represent physical moves as well as mental movement.
- This card is considered a TRAVEL CARD so it may indicate a journey, often over water, a visitor may be coming or a message is on its way.

REVERSED MEANING

- Six is always positive so this just means a delay of the above.
- *The meaning of the card is delayed or extended into the future.*
- *An aspect of the upright meaning of the card needs to be released so you can move forward.*
- *This is not about the upright meaning, place another card on reversed one and read it.*

© 2003 USGAMES

Seven of Swords

REPRESENTS

- escaping undetected
- covering your tracks
- a time for using tact and not aggression
- keeping something to yourself

NUMBER SEVEN

- Sevens are sacred numbers made up of three, the number of Spirit and cosmic energy and four, the number of matter, that which is necessary for the manifestation of ideas or projects.
- Relating to the development of the soul, sevens deal with wisdom, completeness and perfection.
- Indicating a need to deal with your inner life, seven is a time of introspection and soul searching that will require solitude.
- A reflective time, seven indicates a period when you will find it necessary to seriously consider how and why specific events occur.
- Sevens represent a turning point as they begin a new cycle of threes. One, two and three the first cycle was followed by four, five and six, and now we have seven, eight and nine.
- Sevens bring about a new restlessness possibly indicating a breakthrough in awareness. Through re-evaluating and willingly trying new things we sometimes experience a change in understanding or perspective.

ASTROLOGICALLY

- Ruled by the planet NEPTUNE, seven a spiritual number with surreal qualities, is connected to mystics, visionaries and seers. Associated with idealism the number seven can represent depression when our expectations of others and our personal goals are not met.
- Seven corresponds to CARDINAL SIGNS which are about new beginnings, enterprise and getting things started. Aries for

spring, Cancer for summer, Libra for autumn, and Capricorn for winter.

- The suit of swords represented by AIR SIGNS are intellectuals and good at conceptualizing. All about thinking they are great communicators constantly coming up with new ideas.

- Representing MASCULINE ENERGY air signs are outward looking, primarily motivated by external concerns, action-oriented and protective. Seeking to dominate the outside world air sign people can be hard, firm, logical, strong, rational, rough and loud.

SYMBOLISM INCLUDES

- **Man is carrying off five swords** - looks like he is escaping quietly, trying not to be detected.

- **Two swords left standing** - he never took all the swords so he is not a thief, possibly taking back what is his.

- **Man's apparel looks like circus clothing** - he either works for the carnival or is dressed in camouflage to fit into the surroundings.

- **Carnival tents** – represent a temporary situation; also carnivals symbolize actors and can represent illusions and sometimes deceit.

- **Group of people in the far background** - they appear to be working on weapons, the main character is trying to get away without alerting the people in the background.

- **Cloud on the horizon** - harbinger of possible sad or difficult times ahead.

- **Smoke rising in the background** – symbolizes secret or coded messages that are being sent.

- **A great deal of orange and yellow colouring in the card** – these colours symbolize energy, optimism, warmth and enthusiasm.

UPRIGHT MEANING

- About exercising caution as underhanded, sneaky actions or indirect communications may be occurring.

- About having the upper hand in a tricky situation but nothing is quite what it seems so discretion and diplomacy and evasive tactics will be required.

- Can indicate a sense of futility believing despite your actions you cannot alter the situation.
- About looking behind the scenes as there is more going on here than meets the eye.
- In terms of work it can mean secrets are being leaked, or someone is not telling you everything.
- Could indicate a possible con job is occurring.
- If this card is next to a Page it may mean a child is stealing from you.
- Could also indicate a hidden dishonour, a choice you have made and are ashamed of.
- This may indicate either you or someone you know will experience a burglary or theft.

REVERSED MEANING

- Something that is lost may turn up.
- *The meaning of the card is delayed or extended into the future.*
- *An aspect of the upright meaning of the card needs to be released so you can move forward.*
- *This is not about the upright meaning, place another card on reversed one and read it.*

EIGHT

SWORDS

Eight of Swords

REPRESENTS
- feeling trapped physically or mentally
- restriction
- confusion
- a sense of powerlessness

NUMBER EIGHT
- Eight, the sign of infinity represents death and regeneration.
- The number of cosmic balance, eight's beneficial qualities are rarely diluted, they represent two times greater the benefits of four, the number of manifestation.
- Placed on its side eight becomes the lemniscate, the symbol of infinity representing the eternal spiralling movement of the heavens.
- The hour glass shape of eight symbolizes the passage of time and cycles by representing the four seasons the two solstices and two equinoxes.
- Eights vibration is linked with abundance, material prosperity, worldly power, influence, leadership, authority, possibility, options and potential.

ASTROLOGICALLY
- Ruled by the planet SATURN, a hard task master, eight is a solid and very stable number.
- When eight is prominent in an individual's life they often are presented with many harsh lessons and must learn by experience.
- Eight corresponds to FIXED SIGNS Taurus, Leo, Scorpio and Aquarius. Resistant to change these people are faithful and persevering seeing projects through to the end. They attempt to adapt the environment to themselves and above all they want to maintain things.

- The suit of swords represented by AIR SIGNS are intellectuals and good at conceptualizing. All about thinking they are great communicators constantly coming up with new ideas.

- Representing MASCULINE ENERGY air signs are outward looking, primarily motivated by external concerns, action-oriented and protective. Seeking to dominate the outside world air sign people can be hard, firm, logical, strong, rational, rough and loud.

SYMBOLISM INCLUDES

- **Woman is blindfolded** - blindfolds symbolize not being able to see and that things are hidden from us.

- **Arms are tied** - represents an inability to act. (*Interestingly one of the initiations in freemasonry involves blindfolding and tying up the acolyte with ropes followed by providing them with new truths and information - Arthur Waite may have used this imagery for this card*).

- **Orange clothing** – symbolizes warmth, enthusiasm, and energy.

- **Swords are partially around her** – represent prison bars (*she feels trapped*).

- **Swords are pushed into sand** – sand symbolizes a situation that is temporary in nature.

- **One foot in water, one on land** – represents being pulled between feelings (*water energies*) and actions (*earth energies*).

- **Water** - feminine energy, relates to emotions, feelings, intuition and hidden knowledge.

- **Castle on top of rock cliffs** – castles represent resources, wealth and stability.

- **Green hills in the distance, some green in foreground** – earth energy which indicates that the manifestation of ideas or projects is possible.

UPRIGHT MEANING:

- About feelings of interference, doubt and confusion in your environment.

- About feeling you are not in control of your life, a sense of being trapped in a situation that you can't see a way out of.

The important message here is you have resources and you are less trapped than you think.

- About situations in which you feel victimized and powerless however this card indicates you do have the personal skills and abilities to change this.
- Can indicate that a female around you is trying to exact revenge or hurt you in some way.
- About a situation causing you great unhappiness but you have the resources to change matters.
- About feelings associated with avoiding responsibility, feeling victimized and accepting inaction.
- About feeling distanced from the soul of self, you have the inner resources to change this.
- The situation you find yourself in is temporary in nature and it will soon pass.
- If this card falls in a "future" position, the problem or situation can even be avoided.

REVERSED MEANING

- *The meaning of the card is delayed or extended into the future.*
- *An aspect of the upright meaning of the card needs to be released so you can move forward.*
- *This is not about the upright meaning, place another card on reversed one and read it.*

NINE

SWORDS

Nine of Swords

REPRESENTS

- the pain of mental anguish
- worry
- guilt
- unfounded fears
- nightmares

NUMBER NINE

- Nine's vibrations let you see beyond the physical into the limitlessness of the universe.
- Nine is the number of fulfillment, it triples the effect of three the number of cosmic power.
- Representing the end of a cycle nine indicates it is time to tie up loose ends.
- Generally nine depicts completion, wholeness and the sense of satisfaction that comes from reaching a hard worked for goal.
- Sometimes nine can demonstrate regrets as it's the end of a cycle and things may not have gone well, when this is the case you may experience anxiety about not knowing what to expect next.

ASTROLOGICALLY

- The planet MARS which is related to sexual prowess, courage, energy, action, protectiveness, valour and being an able provider rules nine. Forceful and dominating nine creates stability and is a good number when attempting to build foundations.
- When nine is prominent, quite often people will need to overcome obstacles before they will be able to reach their highest potential.
- Nine corresponds to MUTABLE SIGNS Gemini, Virgo, Sagittarius and Pisces. Seeing both sides of a situation they adjust their

attitudes and adapt to almost any circumstances. Versatility allows mutable sign people to accept change and thereby end what was.

- The suit of swords represented by AIR SIGNS are intellectuals and good at conceptualizing. All about thinking they are great communicators constantly coming up with new ideas.

- Representing MASCULINE ENERGY air signs are outward looking, primarily motivated by external concerns, action-oriented and protective. Seeking to dominate the outside world air sign people can be hard, firm, logical, strong, rational, rough and loud.

SYMBOLISM INCLUDES

- **Woman sitting up in bed** - she looks very upset; she is holding her head and possibly crying.
- **White gown** – white symbolizes purity.
- **Swords are hanging on the wall above woman's head** - whatever she thinks is going to happen has not yet happened – these swords are placed very orderly so this woman practices structure in her life.
- **Black background** - black symbolizes mourning, loss and despair; it is a symbol of the unknown and the workings of the unconscious. The scene in this card appears very bleak, foreboding, and depressing.
- **Orange bed** - orange denotes warmth, optimism, energy, and enthusiasm – the orange is below her so this signifies that she has experienced these and they are still there to draw upon.
- **Action figures carved into bed frame** - symbolizes the enthusiasm and the opportunity of the colour orange.
- **Yellow pillow** – yellow symbolizes enthusiasm, so her pillow is symbolic of demonstrating that she is supported by enthusiasm, energy and potential even if she does not feel it right now.
- **Quilt with red roses** – represent sorrow and may have to do with the loss of love.
- **Zodiac signs on the quilt** - the zodiac symbolizes cycles, the passage of time, a map of consciousness, or the combination of personality traits in general.

UPRIGHT MEANING

- This card can represent self-cruelty due to your own hurtful thinking about yourself.

- About the pain of mental anguish, misery, desolation, or receiving bad news. It can be anguish over another's cruelty, dishonesty or even slander.

- About being extremely upset over a situation that hasn't happened and may not even happen. The fear associated to these thoughts may we worse than whatever it is you are afraid of.

- Can be about nightmares, but nightmares aren't real.

- Can be about worries regarding your children or other loved ones, this type of fear leaves you feeling impotent because there is nothing you can do for someone else while you can always find something to do for yourself if you want to.

- If this pain and anguish is about changes you are making in your attitudes and beliefs you can be assured that you will experience a better future.

- Can indicate you are repeating the same problem, choice or situation over and over (*ties it to the zodiacal signs on the quilt*) and are unhappy with the results.

- Whatever the issue, it is not long standing and will soon pass.

- This card can foretell death if the tower is beside it or crosses it.

REVERSED MEANING

- *The meaning of the card is delayed or extended into the future.*
- *An aspect of the upright meaning of the card needs to be released so you can move forward.*
- *This is not about the upright meaning, place another card on reversed one and read it.*

331

TEN

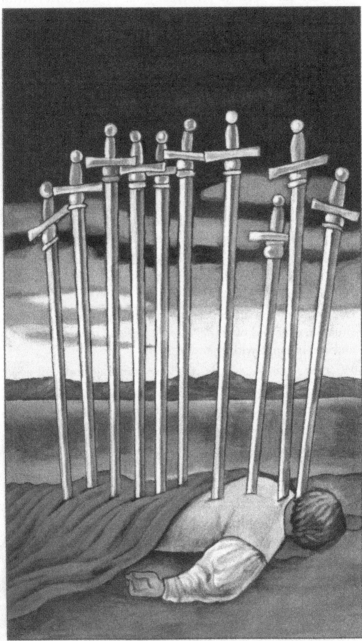

SWORDS

Ten of Swords

REPRESENTS
- betrayal
- defeat but NOT DEATH
- at your lowest point with nowhere to go but up
- martyrdom
- self-deprecation
- the end of a situation or phase

NUMBER TEN
- Ten reduces to one. (1 + 0 = 1)
- One's energy is individual, solitary and self-contained.
- Representing the beginning of form number one relates to the active principle of creation.
- One represents the mystic centre core of mysterious, inscrutable, symbolic, secretive and hidden knowing.

ASTROLOGICALLY
- Ruled by the SUN, ten which reduces to one is egocentric often representing a person who is somewhat of a loner.
- One corresponds to CARDINAL SIGNS which are about new beginnings, enterprise and getting things started. Aries for spring, Cancer for summer, Libra for autumn, and Capricorn for winter.
- The suit of swords represented by AIR SIGNS are intellectuals and good at conceptualizing. All about thinking they are great communicators constantly coming up with new ideas.
- Representing MASCULINE ENERGY air signs are outward looking, primarily motivated by external concerns, action-oriented and protective. Seeking to dominate the outside world air sign people can be hard, firm, logical, strong, rational, rough and loud.

SYMBOLISM INCLUDES

- **Man lying face down with ten swords in his back** – denotes he has been "stabbed in the back," and betrayed.
- **Swords are not aligned** – being out of alignment could represent the death of a variety of old ideas.
- **Swords piercing the body** - these swords could represent "acupuncture," a healing process. These swords would be providing a generous jolt of endorphins that would cause old memories stored in the spinal cord to be sent up to the brain where they can be consciously recognized, expressed and integrated.
- **Covered with an orange blanket and wearing a yellow shirt** - there is no blood spilled, his head is lying on part of the blanket. He was covered before being stabbed. This is a symbolic death not a real one – the colours orange and yellow denote enthusiasm, energy, and optimism so he has resources to start over.
- **Position of the fingers on the man's right hand** - in some cultures (*Japanese for one*) the positioning of his fingers symbolizes good fortune or joy. The fingers represent chakras. The ring finger (*denotes the second chakra – one of decision*) touches the thumb (*the fifth chakra – one of communication*) of the right hand, signalling a conscious decision to evolve toward emotional integration, integrity and harmony.
- **Large body of water** – denotes feminine energy, intuitiveness, inward thinking and hidden knowledge.
- **Black sky** – represents sorrow and depressing feelings.
- **Yellow sunrise** - promises of new beginnings, things are now going to improve.
- **Purple mountains** – stability and an enduring connection to spirituality.

UPRIGHT MEANING

- Can be about your fear of ruin.
- About betrayal and defeat but not about death. It indicates tears, pain and sorrow will need to be experienced before the situation in question is over.
- Can be about the end of something very significant to you, but it is not a physical death. Possibly the end of relationship or a

job. Indicated here is that change occurs because whatever has been operating is no longer valid.

- Can be about experiencing a whole new outlook on things following a mental anguish.
- About the need to make a clean break with your past and its attendant pain and suffering. Whether this means a divorce, moving across the country, changing careers or changing a traditional belief system the break needs to be complete, it is time to move on.
- About the ending of something that didn't turn out well for you. Your thoughts and behaviours contributed to the situation but it is time to end this. You will feel sad emotions but will also experience a cathartic release that takes your life in a new direction. Things will be better.
- IF THE TEN OF SWORDS AND THE DEATH CARD appear anywhere in the same spread, then the death of someone or something is highly probable.
- This card can also imply ill health, a need for a stay in the hospital, and possibly a sickness.

REVERSED MEANING
- Steady improvement in health, any losses are now in the past. New horizons and positive cycles can begin.
- *The meaning of the card is delayed or extended into the future.*
- *An aspect of the upright meaning of the card needs to be released so you can move forward.*
- *This is not about the upright meaning, place another card on reversed one and read it.*

PAGE

SWORDS

Page of Swords

REPRESENTS
- a message
- heeding early warning signals
- new beginnings associated with mental activity
- facing problems squarely

NUMBER ELEVEN
- Number eleven reduces to two. (1+1=2)
- Two represents some type of union or partnership with another person, a spiritual entity, or two parts of you.
- Associated with the balance of polarities such as yin/yang, male/female and public/separate.
- Two builds on the opportunity presented by one (*the ace*).
- Two can represent sensitivity to others sometimes to the point of considering their wellbeing over your own.
- Representative of immersing yourself into another person, an idea, or a project.
- Two is associated with choices and decisions.

ASTROLOGICALLY
- Ruled by the MOON, two (*the Page*) is associated with relationships, cooperation, emotions and feelings.
- Two corresponds to FIXED SIGNS Taurus, Leo, Scorpio and Aquarius. Resistant to change these people are faithful and persevering seeing projects through to the end. They attempt to adapt the environment to themselves and above all they want to maintain things.
- The suit of swords represented by AIR SIGNS are intellectuals and good at conceptualizing. All about thinking they are great communicators constantly coming up with new ideas.
- Representing MASCULINE ENERGY air signs are outward looking, primarily motivated by external concerns, action-

oriented and protective. Seeking to dominate the outside world air sign people can be hard, firm, logical, strong, rational, rough and loud.

SYMBOLISM INCLUDES

- **Page's casual stance** – represents immaturity and a lack of confidence.
- **Orange and yellow clothing** - denotes energy, enthusiasm and opportunity.
- **Standing on a green hill** – signifies earth energy, denoting the likelihood of manifestation.
- **Water in the background** – symbolizes feminine energy, emotions, intuition and hidden knowledge.
- **Clouds** – symbolize the air sign but have a variety of meanings. They can obscure our vision and thereby dim our optimism, they are a symbol of change, constantly coming and going so represent transitory and short lived circumstances, their colour and form usually dictate their meaning. These clouds are cumulus and the wind is blowing, they represent intellect and draw our minds upward into higher thinking.
- **Windy** - wind symbolizes a creative force is at work, so could suggest that new thinking and conceptualizing is occurring.
- **Birds in the sky** - symbolize the element of air, as well as representing the drive toward developing a thoughtful sense of ethics.
- **Purple mountains in the background** – symbolize stability and a link to spirituality.

UPRIGHT MEANING
PAGES BRING MESSAGES

- After laying out the entire spread, lay the first extra card that was selected on the Page, this clarifies the message.

PAGES AS A SITUATION

- Your intuition is at work, new ideas are emerging that will lead to creative activity.
- An idea representing potential or possibilities is gestating within you but it needs time to become grounded.

- As this is the swords suit it could mean tension is surrounding you.
- Possibly there are malicious rumours or someone is spying on you or your work.
- Feelings of being at cross purposes.

PAGE AS A PERSONALITY

- Represents a difficult, wilful child whose parents constantly battle to gain control of.
- May be a youth in trouble with the law.
- A youth who can be malicious, cunning and capable of hurting you.
- A youth who is capable of making you an enemy even if you are not aware of it.

REVERSED MEANING

- The message you are waiting for is delayed and or does not come at all.
- *The meaning of the card is delayed or extended into the future.*
- *An aspect of the upright meaning of the card needs to be released so you can move forward.*
- *This is not about the upright meaning, place another card on reversed one and read it.*

KNIGHT

© 2003 USGAMES

SWORDS

Knight of Swords

REPRESENTS
- change is coming fast
- the presence of aggressive and assertive behaviours
- a warning about opposition
- possible disruptions

NUMBER TWELVE
- The number twelve reduces to three. (1+2=3)
- Cosmic energy is embedded in threes.
- Three, a mystic number, represents Spirit.
- Threes possess celestial power; the sun stands still for three days at the solstices; threes encompass past, present and future; the moon looks full for three days and disappears as dark for three days. Threes make up the trinity of mind, body and spirit.
- Group activities, movement, action, growth and development are expressed by threes.
- Sometimes with threes expansion occurs too quickly causing you to spread yourself too thin or for your energies to scatter.
- Paying attention to what you are doing results in threes vibration being cheerful, optimistic and pleasant, representing a period of happiness and benefits.

ASTROLOGICALLY
- The Knight of Swords is represented by GEMINI, ruled by MERCURY and characterizes the Decider.
- Mercury, the planet that carries the awareness or level of communication from one person to another represents communication, intellect, reasoning power and discernment. Mercury rules speaking, language, mathematics, logic, drafting and design.

- Three corresponds to MUTABLE SIGNS Gemini, Virgo, Sagittarius and Pisces. Seeing both sides of a situation they adjust their attitudes and adapt to almost any circumstances. Versatility allows mutable sign people to accept change and thereby end what was.
- The suit of swords represented by AIR SIGNS are intellectuals and good at conceptualizing. All about thinking they are great communicators constantly coming up with new ideas.
- Representing MASCULINE ENERGY air signs are outward looking, primarily motivated by external concerns, action-oriented and protective. Seeking to dominate the outside world air sign people can be hard, firm, logical, strong, rational, rough and loud.

SYMBOLISM INCLUDES

- **Dressed in armour** – represents being ready for action, this knight possesses the necessary tools and traits to get the job done.
- **Orange coloured clothing** - symbolizes energy, action, enthusiasm, optimism and opportunity.
- **White horse** - white signifies innocence, divinity, and victory. The horse signifies animal instincts which symbolically denote the unconscious.
- **Knight on the horse** - a rider on a horse can symbolize the workings of conscious (*rider*) and unconscious (*instincts of horse*) mind. This horse provides the vehicle for the knight to do his work – thus in modern readings this is associated with cars.
- **Jagged clouds in the sky** – represent tension, someone's feelings are hurt.
- **Trees bent over by the wind** – wind symbolizes a creative force at work, this suggests that new thinking and conceptualizing is occurring.
- **Birds in the sky** – symbolize higher consciousness and Spirit itself. Birds also are closely tied to air and thus the associations connected to this element.

UPRIGHT MEANING
KNIGHTS MEAN CHANGE IS COMING

- Usually this indicates a long-term condition of life that is about to become better, worse or end.
- Plans and intrigues are occurring in the background of which you may or may not be aware, and in which you are about to become involved with whether you want to or not.
- The horse's stance indicates the speed of that process; this charging horse means change is coming soon.

KNIGHT AS A SITUATION

- Someone is about to rush headlong into your life, or a change will happen so quickly you may not have time to prepare for it.
- Your intuition and instincts about your surroundings are magnified at this time.
- A caution about the tendency of over using mannerisms which are blunt and too self-assured.
- A dose of clear sightedness is required.
- You may be asked to give up something that matters to you.
- Someone may perform an unselfish act on your behalf.

KNIGHT AS A PERSONALITY

- Represents someone who has the capacity to undermine and hurt you.
- A person who will stop at nothing to achieve their goals not caring whose toes they tread on along the way.
- Someone who is rather full of themselves.

REVERSED MEANING

- The Knight has fallen off his horse, whatever change was coming has been delayed.
- *The meaning of the card is delayed or extended into the future.*
- *An aspect of the upright meaning of the card needs to be released so you can move forward.*
- *This is not about the upright meaning, place another card on reversed one and read it.*

QUEEN

SWORDS

Queen of Swords

REPRESENTS
- dominance
- dignity
- an astute, honest, forthright, witty, and experienced woman

NUMBER THIRTEEN
- The number thirteen reduces to four. (1+3=4)
- Four is the number associated to "matter."
- Four is a time to build a foundation that will support your ideas and projects.
- Hard work and self discipline are required with fours.
- A stabilizing time for creating structures and order.
- Representing manifestation of your ideas, fours represent prosperity, peace, happiness, abundance and even triumph.
- Sometimes fours represent a stage in personal development when a stalemate has been reached, a period that often seems necessary for unacknowledged emotions or dilemmas to come into consciousness so we can experience them and get on with growth or healing.

ASTROLOGICALLY
- The Queen of Swords is represented by LIBRA, ruled by VENUS and characterizes the Crystallizer.
- Venus symbolizes attraction, unity, balance, valuation and assets. Ruling the love of nature and pleasure, luck and wealth it represents that rare and elusive harmony and radiance that is true beauty.
- Four corresponds to CARDINAL SIGNS which are about new beginnings, enterprise and getting things started. Aries for spring, Cancer for summer, Libra for autumn, and Capricorn for winter.

- The suit of swords represented by AIR SIGNS are intellectuals and good at conceptualizing. All about thinking they are great communicators constantly coming up with new ideas.
- Representing MASCULINE ENERGY air signs are outward looking, primarily motivated by external concerns, action-oriented and protective. Seeking to dominate the outside world air sign people can be hard, firm, logical, strong, rational, rough and loud.

SYMBOLISM INCLUDES
- **Wearing a white gown** – white symbolizes purity.
- **Butterflies on crown and imbedded into throne** – butterflies symbolize transformation.
- **Cloak has clouds on it** - symbolizes thought.
- **The Queen is facing right** - represents conscious awareness of facing the future.
- **Throne is grey** - symbolizes wisdom.
- **Cupid inlaid on the throne** - depicts the soul's search for love and the many choices or problems it can encounter.
- **Water in the background** – symbolizes feminine energy, intuition, emotions and hidden knowledge.
- **Green trees in the background** – denotes the presence of earth energy the manifestation of ideas or projects into concrete realities.

UPRIGHT MEANING
QUEEN AS A SITUATION
- You need to utilize your problem solving, observational and communication skills to end the bogged down feeling you have been experiencing.
- By using logic and courage you can redirect the fear and emotional distress currently surrounding you into focused energy.
- Use your keen observations of people to assist you in your problem solving.

QUEEN AS A PERSONALITY

- The quintessential problem solver this organized woman has highly developed leadership skills.
- A woman who is able to contain her emotions when dealing with difficulties.
- Agile minded and good with words this woman can be sharp tongued.
- This woman admires honesty and she lives by her commitment to being truthful.
- A skilful communicator, forthright and direct with candid observations she however is never hurtful.
- This woman could be entering or affecting your life soon, she could be a parent, boss, relative, counsellor or a confidant.
- She is a very good teacher, directing and guiding, carefully observing her students' progress.

REVERSED MEANING

- Someone around you may be intolerant, interfering, and oblivious to other's opinions.
- *The meaning of the card is delayed or extended into the future.*
- *An aspect of the upright meaning of the card needs to be released so you can move forward.*
- *This is not about the upright meaning, place another card on reversed one and read it.*

KING

SWORDS

King of Swords

REPRESENTS

* patience
* endurance
* a man with power and authority which he administers with firmness and fairness
* a potentially harmful situation

NUMBER FOURTEEN

* The number fourteen reduces to five. (1+4=5)
* Fives always represent some type of difficulty, tension or crisis.
* Challenges often result in a winner or loser with fives.
* Fives suggest a sense of being on a roller coaster ride or being caught up in a whirlwind.
* Fluctuation, unrest and sometimes clashes create a sense of instability and can cause stress.
* Impulsive and impatient behaviours occur but resourcefulness and curiosity are also present.
* Fives indicate we have the quality of mind, but lack the maturity and knowledge to transform old ways into new patterns of being.
* We may be forced to make a choice in order to end the anxiety that is associated with fives.

ASTROLOGICALLY

* The King of Swords is represented by AQUARIUS, ruled by URANUS and characterizes the Thinker.
* Uranus rules upheaval and revolution and signifies sudden drastic change for good or evil. Destroying old ideologies concepts and structures that have outlived their usefulness Uranus's role is to usher in a new order. Representing the advanced thinker, modern scientist and esoteric occultist, as

well as nonconformists such as the hippie, revolutionaries, anarchists, rebels and radical humanitarians Uranus influences humanity's great forward leaps.

- Five corresponds to FIXED SIGNS Taurus, Leo, Scorpio and Aquarius. Resistant to change these people are faithful and persevering seeing projects through to the end. Attempting to adapt the environment to themselves they above all want to maintain things.
- The suit of swords represented by AIR SIGNS are intellectuals and good at conceptualizing. All about thinking they are great communicators constantly coming up with new ideas.
- Representing MASCULINE ENERGY air signs are outward looking, primarily motivated by external concerns, action-oriented and protective. Seeking to dominate the outside world air sign people can be hard, firm, logical, strong, rational, rough and loud.

SYMBOLISM INCLUDES
- **Wearing a blue gown** - symbolizes purity of spirit, serenity, mental clarity and compassion.
- **Purple robe** - represents authority to make decisions.
- **Orange clothing** - denotes energy, action, optimism and opportunity.
- **Crown** - represents his authority, the right to this authority, and the awareness and acceptance of others that he is entitled to this authority.
- **Holding the sword in his right hand** – symbolizes masculine energy and conscious awareness.
- **Throne is grey** – grey symbolizes wisdom.
- **Throne has butterflies** – butterflies symbolize transformation.
- **Crescent moons on the throne** – this symbolizes a warning that too much information is not good for the psyche.
- **Green hill, green trees in the background** - green represents earth energy and the high likelihood of manifestation of ideas or projects.
- **Mountain** – symbolize stability and a connection to spirituality.

UPRIGHT MEANING
KING AS A SITUATION

- You could experience a potentially harmful situation involving worry, grief, chagrin and possibly even physical danger. Clear thinking and clear expression is required, do not use haste and seriously consider consulting an expert.
- You may need to consult a professional such as a lawyer, doctor or someone who possesses special knowledge.

KING AS A PERSONALITY

- Representing a motivator and innovator this man comes up with great new ideas that others will develop and put into practice.
- Representing power, authority and intelligence this man is in a position to issue and carry out judgements; perhaps he is someone with legal authority or political connections.
- Could represent someone currently in your life.
- A person of great emotional reserve this man is the strong and silent type and has no time for emotions or psychic insights into problem solving.
- Using his great analytical skills he cuts through chaos and confusion working out solutions quickly while lucidly explaining the way forward to others.
- Demonstrating high ethical standards this eloquent speaking man is often sought out by others to present their cases as they know his truthfulness can be relied on.
- Could personify you.

REVERSED MEANING

- This card can represent a bully who misuses his power, a stern husband or father, or disloyal and secretive man.
- *The meaning of the card is delayed or extended into the future.*
- *An aspect of the upright meaning of the card needs to be released so you can move forward.*
- *This is not about the upright meaning, place another card on reversed one and read it.*

The Suit of Pentacles

28. The Suit of Pentacles

- The pentacles suit focuses on finances, family, home, and health. All about financial, physical and material success this suit corresponds to your physical or material status.
- Pentacles, an earth sign, are represented by Taurus, Virgo and Capricorn. Grounded and oriented towards what is real earth signs are here to bring form to ideas. Practical, solid, dependable, productive, reasonable and persistent earth signs don't rush into things.
- The feminine energy of earth is receptive, intuitive, internally driven, and sensitive striving to create co-existence and consensus it is introspective and nurturing.
- In medieval times pentacles represented the merchant class. Buying, selling and opening trade routes merchants provided financing for many ventures. Controlling the power of money they were prosperous and often became rich.
- In a reading pentacles represent the influences for good or bad of material wealth in your life.
- Pentacles are associated with diamonds in playing cards.
- Often seen as the fourth suit in the Minor Arcana pentacles focus on results, fruition, realization and prosperity.

Reversed Cards

Sometimes cards are upside down when they are chosen. Readers have preferences as to interpreting the meanings of cards in this position. I have listed some reversed meanings and also provided some other options. It is up to you as a reader to determine which meaning best fits. Some readers simply turn the cards right side up and do not deal with reversed meanings. It is good practice to choose a standard method of reading reversed cards and deviate only when circumstances in the reading make it sensible to do so.

ACE

PENTACLES

Ace of Pentacles

REPRESENTS
* receiving money from unexpected sources

NUMBER ONE
* One's energy is individual, solitary and self-contained.
* Representing the beginning of form number one relates to the active principle of creation.
* One represents the mystic centre core of mysterious, inscrutable, symbolic, secretive and hidden knowing.
* One represents self-development, creativity, action, progress, a new chance, and rebirth.

ASTROLOGICALLY
* The Ace of Pentacles represents the root of the powers of the earth.
* Ruled by the Sun, one is egocentric often representing a person who is somewhat of a loner.
* One corresponds to CARDINAL SIGNS which are about new beginnings, enterprise and getting things started. Aries for spring, Cancer for summer, Libra for autumn, and Capricorn for winter.
* Pentacles, an EARTH SIGN, are represented by Taurus, Virgo and Capricorn. Grounded and oriented towards what is real earth signs are here to bring form to ideas. Practical, solid, dependable, productive, reasonable and persistent earth signs don't rush into things.
* The intuitive, internally driven and sensitive FEMININE ENERGY of earth signs is introspective and nurturing while it strives to create co-existence and consensus.

SYMBOLISM INCLUDES
* **Hand holding a pentacle** - gift from the universe; the gift is a pentacle so it is related to money, material possessions, physical or material status.

- **Halo around the hand** - blessings of the universe, a gift from Spirit.
- **Red rose bushes** - symbolize the occult path (*relating to or dealing with supernatural influences, agencies or phenomena; secret information available only to the initiate; hidden from view; concealed*). The colour red symbolizes passion.
- **Lilies** - symbolize the mystical path (*finding a direct connection to God through experience*).
- **Mountains** – represent spirituality, divine inspiration and achievement.
- **Path** - most commonly symbolizes life, this path is smooth so is about an easier time right now, it leads to the mountains which symbolizes this path will lead to achievement.

UPRIGHT MEANING

- A gift from the Universe.
- Whatever you are thinking about is possible especially things to do with money or acquiring material possessions.
- This card is about new beginnings, so it may indicate a new job starting, a promotion, or acceptance into a program or school.
- It could mean success with artistic endeavours such as writing, painting, pottery etc.
- This can mean a starting point of a whole new cycle.
- It may mean starting your own business.
- The time is right for you to initiate something and there is a high likelihood of success.
- Obstacles have been removed and your plans should proceed smoothly.

REVERSED MEANING

- *The meaning of the card is delayed or extended into the future.*
- *An aspect of the upright meaning of the card needs to be released so you can move forward.*
- *This is not about the upright meaning, place another card on reversed one and read it.*

TWO

PENTACLES

Two of Pentacles

REPRESENTS
* balancing assets and liabilities
* flexibility
* versatility
* doing something you enjoy

NUMBER TWO
* Some type of union or partnership with another person, a spiritual entity, or two parts of you.
* Associated with the balance of polarities such as yin/yang, male/female and public/separate.
* Two builds on the opportunity presented by one (*the ace*).
* Two can represent sensitivity to others sometimes to the point of considering their wellbeing over your own.
* Representative of immersing yourself into another person, an idea, or a project.
* Two is associated with choices and decisions.

ASTROLOGICALLY
* Ruled by the Moon, two is associated with relationships, cooperation, emotions and feelings.
* Two corresponds to FIXED SIGNS Taurus, Leo, Scorpio and Aquarius. Resistant to change these people are faithful and persevering seeing projects through to the end. They attempt to adapt the environment to themselves and above all they want to maintain things.
* Pentacles, an EARTH SIGN, are represented by Taurus, Virgo and Capricorn. Grounded and oriented towards what is real earth signs are here to bring form to ideas. Practical, solid, dependable, productive, reasonable and persistent earth signs don't rush into things.

- The intuitive, internally driven and sensitive FEMININE ENERGY of earth signs is introspective and nurturing while it strives to create co-existence and consensus.

SYMBOLISM INCLUDES

- **Two pentacles held in a material shaped like a leminscate** - lemniscates symbolize infinity – the eternal spiralling movement of the heavens – they represent the ongoing problems associated to establishing and maintaining balance and harmony.
- **Green coloured lemniscate and shoes** - green is an earth energy colour, it represents growth and the potential for manifestation of our ideas or projects.
- **Clothing, orange and yellow colours** - the man is dressed as a performer, he displays a certain amount of playfulness which is required to adapt to the ups and downs that we face in life while trying to establish equilibrium. The orange colors symbolize warmth and good will. The yellow color symbolizes enthusiasm, optimism and energy.
- **Red belt** - symbolizes his instinctual vitality which creates a temporary separation from other issues so he can pursue chosen interests. Red symbolizes passion.
- **Juggling** - symbolizes indecisiveness; this person appears to be trying to keep his options open as he attempts to establish and keep an equilibrium.
- **Rolling seas** – symbolize the fluctuations of emotional life.
- **Wavy water** – symbolizes feminine energy, feelings, emotions, hidden information and some sense of disturbance in the immediate emotional environment.
- **Ships on the ocean** - symbolize action, and commerce.

UPRIGHT MEANING

- The opportunity presented by the ace has been initiated.
- About possessing the necessary mental and physical energy to juggle all the demands currently being presented to you.
- About dealing with some fluctuation and change.
- You may be presented with several proposals and you possess the necessary focus to decide which one to go with.

- About your ability to maintain your balance at this time.
- About utilizing some playfulness while dealing with life's emotional ups and downs.

REVERSED MEANING
- *The meaning of the card is delayed or extended into the future.*
- *An aspect of the upright meaning of the card needs to be released so you can move forward.*
- *This is not about the upright meaning, place another card on reversed one and read it.*

THREE

PENTACLES

Three of Pentacles

REPRESENTS
* achieving prosperity
* the initial completion of work
* competence
* planning
* teamwork
* proficiency that could prove profitable

NUMBER THREE
* Cosmic energy is embedded in threes.
* Three, a mystic number, represents Spirit.
* Threes possess celestial power – the sun stands still for three days at the solstices before resuming its motion; threes encompass past, present and future; the moon looks full for three days and disappears as dark for three days. Threes make up the trinity of mind, body and spirit.
* Group activities, movement, action, growth and development are expressed by threes.
* Sometimes with threes expansion occurs quickly causing you to spread yourself too thin or for your energies to scatter.
* If you pay attention to what you are doing threes vibration is cheerful, optimistic and pleasant, representing a period of happiness and benefits.

ASTROLOGICALLY
* Considered a major benefit, JUPITER rules three.
* With Jupiter's influence over the number three money often comes and goes easily.
* Three corresponds to MUTABLE SIGNS Gemini, Virgo, Sagittarius and Pisces. Seeing both sides of a situation they adjust their attitudes and adapt to almost any circumstances.

Versatility allows mutable sign people to accept change and thereby end what was.

• Pentacles, an EARTH SIGN, are represented by Taurus, Virgo and Capricorn. Grounded and oriented towards what is real earth signs are here to bring form to ideas. Practical, solid, dependable, productive, reasonable and persistent earth signs don't rush into things.

• The intuitive, internally driven and sensitive FEMININE ENERGY of earth signs is introspective and nurturing while it strives to create co-existence and consensus.

SYMBOLISM INCLUDES

• **Three pentacles in the archway** - symbolizes the cosmic power of three, this power is amplified here as the three pentacles are built into an archway in a church.

• **Arches** - symbolic of the act of rebirth, of leaving the old behind and entering the new. This often marks an access into holy places. An open arch signifies the freedom to move on.

• **Church** - symbolizes spirituality.

• **Rose in the downward pointing triangle** - roses symbolize esoteric knowledge (*information only available to initiates and scholars*) and the downward pointing triangle symbolizes the divine feminine which includes all the attributes of feminine energy.

• **Craftsman standing on a bench** – standing higher in an elevated position over the two people speaking to him, signifies the craftsman in a senior position; he is a master in his trade.

• **Craftsman dressed in purple** - purple is the colour of kings and thus signifies authority; this further symbolizes the senior position of this craftsman.

• **Monk looking up to the craftsman** - signifies again the senior position of the craftsman.

• **Yellow and red in person's clothing** - yellow and red are enthusiastic colors, lots of positive energy occurring here.

UPRIGHT MEANING

• About being proficient in a craft, profession or trade and the profitability from this.

- About gaining proficiency in a saleable skill which will result in ultimate success.
- About possessing the necessary abilities to learn a skill.
- About self-employment, look at the cards surrounding this one to determine if the venture will be successful.
- About growing or sharpening up your professional skills and abilities.

REVERSED MEANING

- *The meaning of the card is delayed or extended into the future.*
- *An aspect of the upright meaning of the card needs to be released so you can move forward.*
- *This is not about the upright meaning, place another card on reversed one and read it.*

FOUR

PENTACLES

Four of Pentacles

REPRESENTS

- possessions
- ownership
- holding on too tightly
- possessiveness
- obstructing new developments
- feeling a need to protect possessions

NUMBER FOUR

- Four is the number associated to "matter."
- Four is a time to build a foundation that will support your ideas and projects.
- Hard work and self discipline are required with fours.
- A stabilizing time for creating structures and order.
- Representing manifestation of your ideas, fours represent prosperity, peace, happiness, abundance and even triumph.
- Sometimes fours represent a stage in personal development when a stalemate has been reached, a period that often seems necessary for unacknowledged emotions or dilemmas to come into consciousness so we can experience them and get on with growth or healing.

ASTROLOGICALLY

- Four is ruled by URANUS which is very eccentric and unusual in nature.
- Where number four is prominent invention and ingenuity are very important elements to any given situation.
- Four corresponds to CARDINAL SIGNS which are associated with new beginnings, enterprise and getting things started. Aries for spring, Cancer for summer, Libra for autumn and Capricorn for winter.

- Pentacles, an EARTH SIGN, are represented by Taurus, Virgo and Capricorn. Grounded and oriented towards what is real earth signs are here to bring form to ideas. Practical, solid, dependable, productive, reasonable and persistent earth signs don't rush into things.
- The intuitive, internally driven and sensitive FEMININE ENERGY of earth signs is introspective and nurturing while it strives to create co-existence and consensus.

SYMBOLISM INCLUDES

- **Wearing a crown and purple robe** - symbolizes he has authority to make decisions; he is in charge of his actions.
- **Pentacle on top of his crown** - he thinks a lot about money.
- **Pentacle clasped in his arms** - he is focused on holding onto his money.
- **Pentacles under his feet** - he is focused on keeping the money.
- **Body language** - he appears almost miserly in his clutching of his money.
- **Castle and buildings in the background** – symbolize resources and wealth, this man has access to these.
- **Seated on a grey slab** - symbolizes a strong foundation embedded with wisdom.
- **Green trees and grass** – denotes earth energy the manifestation of one's ideas or projects is possible.

UPRIGHT MEANING

- About holding on too tightly.
- About possessions and feeling there is a need to guard or protect them. Other cards in the reading will indicate whether or not that feeling is justified.
- Could be a caution that while resting on your laurels may be comfortable, it is not a way to go forward or prepare for your future.
- Could be about being exposed to a stingy or miserly person.
- Could indicate you are being stingy or miserly whether monetarily or in your interactions with others.

- Could be about experiencing problems with possessiveness or jealousy.

REVERSED MEANING

- You are spending too much money.
- *The meaning of the card is delayed or extended into the future.*
- *An aspect of the upright meaning of the card needs to be released so you can move forward.*
- *This is not about the upright meaning, place another card on reversed one and read it.*

FIVE

PENTACLES

Five of Pentacles

REPRESENTS
- a lack of support
- the effects of poor choices
- the breakdown of a belief system
- hard times
- ill health
- rejection

NUMBER FIVE
- Fives always represent some type of difficulty, tension or crisis.
- Challenges often result in a winner or loser with fives.
- Fives suggest a sense of being on a roller coaster ride or being caught up in a whirlwind.
- Fluctuation, unrest and sometimes clashes create a sense of instability and can cause stress.
- Impulsive and impatient behaviours occur but resourcefulness and curiosity are also present.
- Fives indicate we have the quality of mind, but lack the maturity and knowledge to transform old ways into new patterns of being.
- We may be forced to make a choice in order to end the anxiety that is associated with fives.

ASTROLOGICALLY
- Five is ruled by the planet Mercury which deals with communication.
- If five is significant in a reading it may mean this individual needs to make adjustments in order to fit in.
- Five corresponds to FIXED SIGNS Taurus, Leo, Scorpio and Aquarius. Resistant to change these people are faithful and persevering seeing projects through to the end. They attempt

to adapt the environment to themselves and above all they want to maintain things.

- Pentacles, an EARTH SIGN, are represented by Taurus, Virgo and Capricorn. Grounded and oriented towards what is real earth signs are here to bring form to ideas. Practical, solid, dependable, productive, reasonable and persistent earth signs don't rush into things.
- The intuitive, internally driven and sensitive FEMININE ENERGY of earth signs is introspective and nurturing while it strives to create co-existence and consensus.

SYMBOLISM INCLUDES

- **Church window** – symbolizing spirituality they denote that help is nearby and welcoming they say come in out of the cold.
- **Anchors between the pentacles in the window** – symbolize safety and security.
- **Snowing, wind blowing and snow on the ground** - represents harsh, cold and uncomfortable conditions.
- **Man on crutches without any gloves** - it appears this man has sustained some type of injury; he is not strong at this time and has few reserves or resources to call upon.
- **Barefoot woman** – represents someone without resources, she appears so focused on her misery she does not realize she walked past a church where she could have had sanctuary from the cold; perhaps she has lost her sense of spiritual connection.

UPRIGHT MEANING

- About worry.
- About feeling emotionally and perhaps physically destitute.
- About feeling lonely and abandoned.
- About feeling a loss of love, separation and heartache.
- About a breakdown in a belief system that has yet to be replaced with something else.
- About being in danger of losing a sense or belief in the goodness or meaning of life.

- Could be about material losses, you may soon be in a financially tight situation or one in which expected material gains have fallen through.
- About the wisdom of paying attention to both the financial and spiritual areas of your life.
- Could mean that even if you lack material possessions you can become warm and enlightened within.

REVERSED MEANING

- Do not take any financial risks at this time.
- *The meaning of the card is delayed or extended into the future.*
- *An aspect of the upright meaning of the card needs to be released so you can move forward.*
- *This is not about the upright meaning, place another card on reversed one and read it.*

SIX

PENTACLES

Six of Pentacles

REPRESENTS
* generosity
* giving financially
* giving spiritually
* offering charity
* receiving charity

NUMBER SIX
* Sixes are always favourable.
* Sixes vibration is cooperative.
* Six represents the ability to transcend difficulties and a sense of peace and quiet after the storm.
* Following the conflicts experienced with fives, sixes demonstrate the integration of new skills learned. Improved coping mechanisms and overcoming challenges has resulted in stability.
* Six is a time of balance and respite that creates a base and a pivot for new experiences.
* Six, an important ceremonial number, refers to Spirit's connection to life in all directions (*north, south, east and west, above and below*).
* Because three (3) is a cosmic number its attributes are amplified by six (6).

ASTROLOGICALLY
* Ruled by the planet VENUS, six is a pleasant, harmonious number that governs the arts and music. Relationships are of paramount importance with tact and diplomacy figuring prominently.
* When number six is significant money plays an important role.

- Enabling a free flow of energy six allows many opportunities for success.
- Six corresponds to MUTABLE SIGNS Gemini, Virgo, Sagittarius and Pisces. Seeing both sides of a situation they adjust their attitudes and adapt to almost any circumstances. Versatility allows mutable sign people to accept change and thereby end what was.
- Pentacles, an EARTH SIGN, are represented by Taurus, Virgo and Capricorn. Grounded and oriented towards what is real earth signs are here to bring form to ideas. Practical, solid, dependable, productive, reasonable and persistent earth signs don't rush into things.
- The intuitive, internally driven and sensitive FEMININE ENERGY of earth signs is introspective and nurturing while it strives to create co-existence and consensus.

SYMBOLISM INCLUDES
- **Man wearing a red robe** – red symbolizes passion.
- **Holding scales** - symbolizes fairness and justice.
- **Purple scarf on his head** – his thoughts are on spiritual matters and he possesses authority.
- **Red belt** - symbolizes instinctual vitality that creates a temporary separation from day to day chores so other interests may be pursued. Red symbolizes passion.
- **Green shoes and trees in background** - green symbolizes earth energy which denotes manifestation of ideas and projects are highly likely.
- **Handing out money** - denotes generosity, this man is doing what he believes is right.
- **Man in blue cloak with a hole in his garment** - blue symbolizes spirit and intellect; this person is poor but spiritual in nature.
- **Castle in the background** – symbolizes wealth and access to resources.

UPRIGHT MEANING
- About generosity and giving either financially or spiritually to others.
- Could mean a raise or bonuses being handed out work.

- About previous problems being solved.
- About the high likelihood of prosperity.
- About either you or someone you know using their prosperity to help others.
- About the need to give and take.
- Depending upon the reading, if the cards around this card are unfavourable it may be warning you not to loan money as it may be a long time being repaid if at all.

REVERSED MEANING

- Investments have lost their value.
- Do not throw good money after bad.
- *The meaning of the card is delayed or extended into the future.*
- *An aspect of the upright meaning of the card needs to be released so you can move forward.*
- *This is not about the upright meaning, place another card on reversed one and read it.*

SEVEN

PENTACLES

Seven of Pentacles

REPRESENTS

* profit on an investment
* reaping the rewards of your labours
* considering a different approach
* a need to make some decisions

NUMBER SEVEN

* Sevens are sacred numbers made up of three, the number of Spirit and cosmic energy and four, the number of matter, that which is necessary for the manifestation of ideas or projects.
* Relating to the development of the soul, sevens deal with wisdom, completeness and perfection.
* Indicating a need to deal with your inner life, seven is a time of introspection and soul searching that will require solitude.
* A reflective time, seven indicates a period when you will find it necessary to seriously consider how and why specific events occur.
* Sevens represent a turning point as they begin a new cycle of threes. One, two and three the first cycle was followed by four, five and six, and now we have seven, eight and nine.
* Sevens bring about a new restlessness possibly indicating a breakthrough in awareness which causes us to re-evaluate and willingly try new things. Sometimes this results in a changed understanding or perspective.

ASTROLOGICALLY

* Ruled by the planet NEPTUNE, seven a spiritual number with surreal qualities is connected to mystics, visionaries and seers.
* Associated with idealism the number seven can represent depression when our expectations of others and our personal goals are not met.

- Seven corresponds to CARDINAL SIGNS which are about new beginnings, enterprise and getting things started. Aries for spring, Cancer for summer, Libra for autumn, and Capricorn for winter.
- Pentacles, an EARTH SIGN, are represented by Taurus, Virgo and Capricorn. Grounded and oriented towards what is real earth signs are here to bring form to ideas. Practical, solid, dependable, productive, reasonable and persistent earth signs don't rush into things.
- The intuitive, internally driven and sensitive FEMININE ENERGY of earth signs is introspective and nurturing while it strives to create co-existence and consensus.

SYMBOLISM INCLUDES

- **Farmer leaning on his hoe** – linked with cycles and nature farmers represent "keepers of tradition" and exhibit the value of common sense. Alchemy is often called "celestial agriculture."
- **Orange tunic and shoes** - symbol of fertility, warmth, energy, action, drive and confidence.
- **Green vines with six pentacles attached** – denotes earth energy, manifestation, the pentacles and lushness of the vines symbolize success. Six is associated with allowing energy to flow and successfulness.
- **One pentacle at farmer's feet** - the farmer is thinking about "what if," with the one pentacle, and how this may generate other possibilities.
- **Farmer's body language** - he looks day dreamy, deep in thought.
- **Purple mountains** – symbolize loftiness, stability, connection and spirituality.

UPRIGHT MEANING

- Can be about a fear of failure.
- About making choices, staying with the tried and true that has been successful or going in another direction and attempting something new. You have proven you possess the necessary skills and abilities to succeed.

- About profits and more specifically about reaping the rewards of your labours.
- Usually the profit is financial but it may be in any area where you have laboured and done well.
- About taking a pause to appreciate, assess or plan, a time of preparation.
- About following natural cycles.

REVERSED MEANING

- Possibly investments have proven unprofitable or there has been little gain after much work.
- *The meaning of the card is delayed or extended into the future.*
- *An aspect of the upright meaning of the card needs to be released so you can move forward.*
- *This is not about the upright meaning, place another card on reversed one and read it.*

EIGHT

PENTACLES

Eight of Pentacles

REPRESENTS
- learning
- skill development
- working for wages
- diligence
- knowledge
- paying attention to detail
- goal you are working towards

NUMBER EIGHT
- Eight, the sign of infinity represents death and regeneration.
- The number of cosmic balance, eight's beneficial qualities are rarely diluted, they represent two times greater the benefits of four, the number of manifestation.
- Placed on its side eight becomes the lemniscate, the symbol of infinity representing the eternally spiralling movement of the heavens.
- The hour glass shape of eight symbolizes the passage of time and cycles by representing the four seasons the two solstices and two equinoxes.
- Eights vibration is linked with abundance, material prosperity, worldly power, influence, leadership, authority, possibility, options and potential.

ASTROLOGICALLY
- Ruled by the planet SATURN, the hard task master, eight is a solid and very stable number.
- When eight is prominent in an individual's life they often are presented with many harsh lessons and must learn by experience.
- Eight corresponds to FIXED SIGNS Taurus, Leo, Scorpio and Aquarius. Resistant to change these people are faithful and

persevering seeing projects through to the end. They attempt to adapt the environment to themselves and above all they want to maintain things.

- Pentacles, an EARTH SIGN, are represented by Taurus, Virgo and Capricorn. Grounded and oriented towards what is real earth signs are here to bring form to ideas. Practical, solid, dependable, productive, reasonable and persistent earth signs don't rush into things.

- The intuitive, internally driven and sensitive FEMININE ENERGY of earth signs is introspective and nurturing while it strives to create co-existence and consensus.

SYMBOLISM INCLUDES

- **Brown leather apron over clothing** – represents apprentice clothing, so is indicative of learning a new trade, this person is not yet a craftsman.

- **Body language** - he appears focused and to be concentrating on his task, he appears to be engaged in repetitive motions to learn his trade.

- **Village in the background with a road leading to it** – with no castles in the background existing wealth is not suggested, rather learning a trade and working towards a goal is being indicated.

- **Green grass in village** - symbolizes earth energy so manifestation is possible; the patch of grass is small so it will take a great deal of work to realize the goal.

UPRIGHT MEANING

- About the opportunity of following a direction which really inspires you, even it means undertaking a course of training or study to get there.

- About a chance to learn something you are really interested in as opposed to school children who have mandated study courses.

- Careful attention to detail is required, being painstakingly careful and precise.

- About approaching a task methodically.

- This could mean it is time for you to change directions and learn a new task.

REVERSED MEANING

- The apprentice would not be on the bench (*upside down card means he fell off the bench*) so possibly a work slowdown or strike.
- Someone is not putting in the necessary effort on a task so may fail an exam.
- Someone does not like the work they are engaged in.
- *The meaning of the card is delayed or extended into the future.*
- *An aspect of the upright meaning of the card needs to be released so you can move forward.*
- *This is not about the upright meaning, place another card on reversed one and read it.*

NINE

PENTACLES

Nine of Pentacles

REPRESENTS
- self reliance
- success
- enjoyment
- understanding the value of money
- security in possessions and relationships
- the wisdom and experience to handle problems

NUMBER NINE
- Nine's vibrations let you see beyond the physical into the limitlessness of the universe.
- Nine is the number of fulfillment, it triples the effect of three the number of cosmic power.
- Representing the end of a cycle nine indicates it is time to tie up loose ends.
- Generally nine depicts completion, wholeness and the sense of satisfaction that comes from reaching a hard worked for goal.
- Sometimes nine can demonstrate regrets as it's the end of a cycle and things may not have gone well, when this is the case you may experience anxiety about not knowing what to expect next.

ASTROLOGICALLY
- The planet MARS which is related to sexual prowess, courage, energy, action, protectiveness, valour and being an able provider rules nine. Forceful and dominating nine creates stability and is a good number when attempting to build foundations.
- When nine is prominent in a reading it can mean people will need to overcome obstacles before they will be able to reach their highest potential.

- Nine corresponds to MUTABLE SIGNS Gemini, Virgo, Sagittarius and Pisces. Seeing both sides of a situation they adjust their attitudes and adapt to almost any circumstances. Versatility allows mutable sign people to accept change and thereby end what was.
- Pentacles, an EARTH SIGN, are represented by Taurus, Virgo and Capricorn. Grounded and oriented towards what is real earth signs are here to bring form to ideas. Practical, solid, dependable, productive, reasonable and persistent earth signs don't rush into things.
- The intuitive, internally driven and sensitive FEMININE ENERGY of earth signs is introspective and nurturing while it strives to create co-existence and consensus.

SYMBOLISM INCLUDES

- **Red hat, red trim and red flowers on her robe** - hats represent authority and power and the covered head denotes nobility. Red is a color of passionate energy, it can also mean love and health.
- **Yellow robe** - yellow represents creativity, optimism and enthusiasm; in the Tarot it usually represents positive mental activity and awareness.
- **Holding a hooded falcon in her hand** - reflects the discipline required to create a good life; falcons also symbolize all that is dark and unruly in human nature (*she has mastered the falcon thus she has controlled her baser instincts*).
- **Body language** - her facial expression is calm; her stance is serene and contented.
- **Grape vines** - represent abundance, fruitfulness and the achievement that occurs when you have successfully attended to your work.
- **Grape vines wrapped around a fence** - the lushness here was created through effort and this symbolizes rewards for hard work.
- **Green grass, green trees, green vines** - green is an earth energy which means bountifulness and the high likelihood of the manifestation of our ideas or projects.
- **Orange hills in the background** - orange signifies warmth and energy.

- **Castle in the background** - symbolizes wealth and resources.

- **Snail in the foreground** – a lunar symbol it represents feminine energy and the cycle of death and rebirth, ending and beginning, continuity and fertility. Because the snail is in its shell it is linked to the symbolism of the spiral and to self sufficiency.

UPRIGHT MEANING

- About order, self-discipline, planning and the ability to see things through to the end.
- About material well being, accomplishment and wisdom.
- About enjoying the fruits of your labours through spending money on yourself earned from your past successes.
- Could be about a special occasion where you will need to be well dressed.
- About the completion of a successful financial project or a creative cycle.
- If the Ace of Pentacles crosses this card it could mean great wealth to come.

REVERSED MEANING

- Could indicate a fear of loss, usually material things you have worked to acquire.
- *The meaning of the card is delayed or extended into the future.*
- *An aspect of the upright meaning of the card needs to be released so you can move forward.*
- *This is not about the upright meaning, place another card on reversed one and read it.*

TEN

PENTACLES

Ten of Pentacles

REPRESENTS
* material wealth
* resources
* affluence
* permanence
* passing on positive traditions
* a possible inheritance

NUMBER TEN
* Ten reduces to one. (1 + 0 = 1)
* One's energy is individual, solitary and self-contained.
* Represents the beginning of form; the active principle of creation.
* Represents the mystic centre.
* Represents self-development, creativity, action, progress, a new chance, and rebirth.

ASTROLOGICALLY
* Ruled by the SUN, ten which reduces to one is egocentric often representing a person who is somewhat of a loner.
* One corresponds to CARDINAL SIGNS which are about new beginnings, enterprise and getting things started. Aries for spring, Cancer for summer, Libra for autumn, and Capricorn for winter.
* Pentacles, an EARTH SIGN, are represented by Taurus, Virgo and Capricorn. Grounded and oriented towards what is real earth signs are here to bring form to ideas. Practical, solid, dependable, productive, reasonable and persistent earth signs don't rush into things.
* The intuitive, internally driven and sensitive FEMININE ENERGY of earth signs is introspective and nurturing while it strives to create co-existence and consensus.

SYMBOLISM INCLUDES

- **Family, grandfather, parents and child** – symbolizes continuity, passing down information, well being and an overall sense of happiness and contentment.

- **Grapes on grandfather's decorative robe** - represent abundance, fruitfulness and the achievement that occurs when one has successfully attended to one's work.

- **Egyptian symbols on grandfather's robe** – indicates this man possesses esoteric (*obscure and mysterious*) knowledge; he is wise.

- **Purple on the man's robe** - purple is the colour of royalty and symbolizes authority and the ability to make decisions.

- **Orange colour of woman's robe** – symbolizes warmth, energy and comfort.

- **Wreath woven into woman's hair** - symbolizes that one's power or authority derives from natural awareness, from one's own connection to nature and one's own inner nature.

- **Castle symbol's on castle wall** - symbolize material wealth, resources and abundance.

- **Ship symbol's on castle wall** – ships symbolize commerce and the spread of cultural information.

- **Black and white checkerboard pattern on castle wall** – symbolizes duality, positive/negative, good/evil, spirit/ matter and all things that make up life cycles that lead to transformation.

- **Green on grandfather's robe and green trees in the distance** – represents earth energy which denotes the high likelihood of manifestation of our ideas or projects through to fruition.

- **Castle** - represents wealth and sufficient material resources to be comfortable.

- **Dogs** - symbolize loyalty, vigilance and companionship. Two dogs together also symbolize the importance of relationships. Animals always symbolize instincts at work.

UPRIGHT MEANING

- About the benefits of establishing a concrete foundation in order to create wealth and healthy relationships.

- Can indicate the time is right to purchase a home, start a family, or put something substantial in place for the future.
- About the importance of ensuring something lives on for the benefit of others after you are gone.
- About the importance of family traditions and passing down cultural nuances and information to upcoming generations.
- Can be about your need to concentrate on the long term and to work towards a lasting solution.
- It can mean inheritance, or the less tangible gifts of love and support offered by family.

REVERSED MEANING
- You may experience problems with a pension, a will, or perhaps have taxation difficulties.
- *The meaning of the card is delayed or extended into the future.*
- *An aspect of the upright meaning of the card needs to be released so you can move forward.*
- *This is not about the upright meaning, place another card on reversed one and read it.*

PAGE

PENTACLES

Page of Pentacles

REPRESENTS

- messages
- visions
- omens
- premonitions
- draw to you what you need
- seeking abundance

NUMBER ELEVEN

- The number eleven reduces to two. (1+1=2)
- Some type of union or partnership with another person, a spiritual entity, or two parts of you.
- The balance of polarities such as yin/yang, male/female and public/separate.
- Builds on the opportunity presented by one (*the ace*).
- Sensitivity to others sometimes to the point you consider their wellbeing over your own.
- Immersing yourself into another person, an idea, or a project.
- Choices and decisions.

ASTROLOGICALLY

- Ruled by the Moon, the Page (*two*) is associated with relationships, cooperation, emotions and feelings.
- Two corresponds to FIXED SIGNS Taurus, Leo, Scorpio and Aquarius. Resistant to change these people are faithful and persevering seeing projects through to the end. They attempt to adapt the environment to themselves and above all they want to maintain things.
- Pentacles, an EARTH SIGN, are represented by Taurus, Virgo and Capricorn. Grounded and oriented towards what is real earth signs are here to bring form to ideas. Practical, solid,

dependable, productive, reasonable and persistent earth signs don't rush into things.

- The intuitive, internally driven and sensitive FEMININE ENERGY of earth signs is introspective and nurturing while it strives to create co-existence and consensus.

SYMBOLISM INCLUDES

- **Flamboyant red hat** - hats represent authority and power, the covered head denotes nobility. Red indicative of passionate energy can also mean love and health.
- **Green tunic** – represents earth energy, denoting possibility for the manifestation of our ideas or projects.
- **Orange footwear** -symbolizes warmth, enthusiasm and energy.
- **Body language** - this Page appears focused and he is probably studious.
- **Green grass and trees** – the green shown here coupled with his tunic indicates the Page possesses great potential for success in his endeavours.
- **Ploughed field** – symbolize fertility, waiting for information and a keenness to learn; a ploughed field also implies labour and the work and commitment involved in making something come to fruition.
- **Mountain in the background** – symbolizes stability, positive influences and a connection to spirituality.

UPRIGHT MEANING
PAGES BRING MESSAGES

- After laying out the entire spread, lay the first extra card that was selected on the Page, this clarifies the message.

PAGES AS A SITUATION

- Your intuition is at work, new ideas are emerging that will lead to creative activity.
- An idea representing potential or possibilities is gestating within you but it needs time to become grounded.
- The environment surrounding you is very positive with a high potential of good things occurring for you.

PAGE AS A PERSONALITY

- Represents a child or youth who enjoys reading and learning, one who studies hard and is often considered the "teacher's pet."
- This child or youth can be counted upon to complete tasks they either initiate or are assigned.
- Could represent your child, a relative, or someone who will be impacting your life.
- May personify you as someone who demonstrates an immature manner of looking their experiences.

REVERSED MEANING

- The message you are waiting for is delayed and or does not come at all.
- *The meaning of the card is delayed or extended into the future.*
- *An aspect of the upright meaning of the card needs to be released so you can move forward.*
- *This is not about the upright meaning, place another card on reversed one and read it.*

KNIGHT

© 2003 USGAMES

PENTACLES

Knight of Pentacles

REPRESENTS

- responsible change
- defensive behaviours
- unwavering
- fixed on a chosen course
- realistic young man with great potential
- slow but steady progress

NUMBER TWELVE

- The number twelve reduces to three. (1+2=3)
- Cosmic energy is embedded in threes.
- Three, a mystic number, represents Spirit.
- Threes possess celestial power – the sun stands still for three days at the solstices before resuming its motion; threes encompass past, present and future; the moon looks full for three days and disappears as dark for three days. Threes make up the trinity of mind, body and spirit.
- Group activities, movement, action, growth and development are expressed by threes.
- Sometimes with threes expansion occurs quickly causing you to spread yourself too thin or for your energies to scatter.
- Paying attention to what you are doing results in threes vibration being cheerful, optimistic and pleasant, representing a period of happiness and benefits.

ASTROLOGICALLY

- The Knight of Pentacles is represented by VIRGO, ruled by MERCURY and characterizes the Healer.
- Mercury is the planet of intellect, cleverness, dexterity, quickness, and changeability. Associated with communication, intellect, reasoning power and discernment Mercury is the

planet of the mind and the power of communication. It rules speaking, language, mathematics, logic, drafting and design.

- Three corresponds to MUTABLE SIGNS Gemini, Virgo, Sagittarius and Pisces. Seeing both sides of a situation they adjust their attitudes and adapt to almost any circumstances. Versatility allows mutable sign people to accept change and thereby end what was.

- Pentacles, an EARTH SIGN, are represented by Taurus, Virgo and Capricorn. Grounded and oriented towards what is real earth signs are here to bring form to ideas. Practical, solid, dependable, productive, reasonable and persistent earth signs don't rush into things.

- The intuitive, internally driven and sensitive FEMININE ENERGY of earth signs is introspective and nurturing while it strives to create co-existence and consensus.

SYMBOLISM INCLUDES

- **Knight is dressed in armour** – symbolic of being ready for action if necessary and indicates that the wearer possesses the necessary skills and talents to succeed

- **Red tunic** - symbolizes passion, this could be about his work.

- **Green plume on his helmet** – represents earth energy, the opportunity to succeed and for the manifestation of one's ideas and projects.

- **Sitting on an orange blanket** - symbolizes warmth, enthusiasm and energy.

- **Large black horse with a grey mane** - the horse symbolizes animal instincts thus the workings of the unconscious mind. Black can symbolize the underworld, the night, and is a symbol of hidden knowledge and the workings of the unconscious. The horse's grey mane can indicate wisdom.

- **Knight sitting on a horse** - a rider on a horse can symbolize the workings of conscious (*rider*) and unconscious (*instincts of horse*) mind. This horse provides the vehicle for the knight to do his work. Animals symbolize instincts at work.

- **Horse and rider are facing right** – this symbolizes conscious thought.

- **Body language** – this knight appears confident, contemplative and ready to do his duty.
- **Yellow sky in the background** – symbolizes enthusiasm and optimism.
- **Standing on green grass** – green is earth energy and symbolizes opportunity for success.
- **Ploughed field** - symbolizes fertility, waiting for information, and a keenness to learn; also implies labour and the work and commitment involved in making something come to fruition.
- **Mountains in the background** – symbolize stability and a connection to spirituality.

UPRIGHT MEANING
KNIGHTS MEAN CHANGE IS COMING
- Usually this indicates a long-term condition of life that is about to become better, worse or end.
- Plans and intrigues are occurring in the background of which you may or may not be aware and in which you are about to become involved with whether you want to or not.
- The horse's stance indicates the speed of that process and this horse is standing very still so it means the change is in the future.

KNIGHT AS A SITUATION
- Expect a departure or an arrival.
- Intuitive thoughts are occurring and your ideas have a high potential of success.
- You may be asked to give up something that matters to you.
- Someone may perform an unselfish act on your behalf.
- You may begin secondary studies or start a new job; you possess the keenness and commitment to succeed.

KNIGHT AS A PERSONALITY
- A youth with an adventurous spirit who possesses great potential but has yet to fulfill this.
- Materially minded this youth likely does not look beyond the surface and may engage in gambling.

- Given a task to perform this youth demonstrates responsibility and follow through but is not yet able to set personal goals and follow them to fruition.

REVERSED MEANING

- The knight has fallen off his horse, whatever change was coming has been delayed.
- *The meaning of the card is delayed or extended into the future.*
- *An aspect of the upright meaning of the card needs to be released so you can move forward.*
- *This is not about the upright meaning, place another card on reversed one and read it.*

QUEEN

PENTACLES

Queen of Pentacles

REPRESENTS

- resourcefulness
- being down to earth
- a wise, understanding woman
- a love of luxury
- security
- prudence
- wealth

NUMBER THIRTEEN

- The number thirteen reduces to four. (1+3= 4)
- Four is the number associated to "matter."
- Four is a time to build a foundation that will support your ideas and projects.
- Hard work and self discipline are required with fours.
- A stabilizing time for creating structures and order.
- Representing manifestation of your ideas, fours represent prosperity, peace, happiness, abundance and even triumph.
- Sometimes fours represent a stage in personal development when a stalemate has been reached, a period that often seems necessary for unacknowledged emotions or dilemmas to come into consciousness so we can experience them and get on with growth or healing.

ASTROLOGICALLY

- The Queen of Pentacles is represented by CAPRICORN, ruled by SATURN and characterizes the Succeeder.
- Associated with restriction, obstacles and discipline Saturn creates limits and boundaries and shows the consequences of being human. Saturn rules time, old age and sobriety and symbolizes ambition, selfishness, depression, jealousy and greed. Sometimes a harsh task master Saturn's lessons

once learned lead to wisdom and understanding with lasting rewards often being granted after a long struggle.

- Four corresponds to CARDINAL SIGNS which are about new beginnings, enterprise and getting things started. Aries for spring, Cancer for summer, Libra for autumn, and Capricorn for winter.

- Pentacles, an EARTH SIGN, are represented by Taurus, Virgo and Capricorn. Grounded and oriented towards what is real earth signs are here to bring form to ideas. Practical, solid, dependable, productive, reasonable and persistent earth signs don't rush into things.

- The intuitive, internally driven and sensitive FEMININE ENERGY of earth signs is introspective and nurturing while it strives to create co-existence and consensus.

SYMBOLISM INCLUDES

- **Her gown is red** – symbolizes passion.
- **Her veil is green** – represents earth energy which means the manifestation of one's ideas or projects is highly likely.
- **Wearing a crown** – denotes nobility and indicates that the wearer possesses the necessary authority to accomplish what she sets out to.
- **Holding a pentacle** – this signifies that the Queen is good with money, knows its value, but does not worship it.
- **Body language** - this Queen appears calm, caring and somewhat reflective.
- **Her throne is grey** – symbolizes wisdom.
- **Cupids inlaid in the throne** - depict the soul's search for love and the many choices or problems it can encounter.
- **Fruit inlaid in throne** – symbolizes abundance and earth energy, which means that one's ideas or projects have a high likelihood of materializing into something concrete.
- **Goats head inlaid in throne** – likely associated to Capricorn, an earth sign, signifying the high likelihood of manifestation of one's ideas or projects.
- **Rabbit** – symbolizes guile, quick thinking, intuition, fertility and alertness. Also represents animal instincts (*making decisions from a gut feeling*).

- **Green grass, flowers and vines** - abundance of earth energy, great potential for manifestation.
- **Water in the background** – symbolizes feminine energy, intuitiveness and hidden knowledge.
- **Mountains in the background** – symbolizes spiritual influences and stability.
- **Yellow sky** – represents enthusiasm, optimism, creativity and joy.

UPRIGHT MEANING
QUEEN AS A SITUATION

- Security, wisdom, wealth and opulence are currently possible for you.
- Your ideas have a high likelihood of fruition at this time.
- You will get your way if you use your intuition and focus on pragmatic solutions.

QUEEN AS A PERSONALITY

- A kind, generous, excellent and careful manager this woman possesses both intelligence and intuitive knowledge.
- Diligent and practical this woman is concerned with health and nutritional issues.
- Enjoying abundance this woman gives great attention to her physical surroundings while willingly sharing and nurturing others.
- Persuasive and attractive this reliable and steadfast woman gets her way not through feminine wiles but through demonstrating the mastery of her highly developed skills.
- This woman is in harmony with nature.
- This woman may represent someone who is entering or affecting your life at this moment. She can be a parent, boss, relative, counsellor or a confidant.
- This woman may personify you.

REVERSED MEANING

- Be careful who you trust.
- *The meaning of the card is delayed or extended into the future.*
- *An aspect of the upright meaning of the card needs to be released so you can move forward.*
- *This is not about the upright meaning, place another card on reversed one and read it.*

KING

PENTACLES

King of Pentacles

REPRESENTS

- a man who has reached the top through hard work, intelligence and ethical behaviours
- adeptness
- reliability
- a sponsor of worthwhile projects
- financial security
- stability

NUMBER FOURTEEN

- The number fourteen reduces to five. (1+4=5)
- Fives always represent some type of difficulty, tension or crisis.
- Challenges often result in a winner or loser with fives.
- Fives suggest a sense of being on a roller coaster ride or being caught up in a whirlwind.
- Fluctuation, unrest and sometimes clashes create a sense of instability and can cause stress.
- Impulsive and impatient behaviours occur but resourcefulness and curiosity are also present.
- Fives indicate we have the quality of mind but lack the maturity and knowledge to transform old ways into new patterns of being.
- We may be forced to make a choice in order to end the anxiety that is associated with fives.

ASTROLOGICALLY

- The King of Pentacles is represented by TAURUS, ruled by VENUS and characterizes the Builder.
- Venus symbolizes attraction, unity, balance, valuation and assets. Ruling the love of nature and pleasure, luck and wealth it represents the harmony and radiance of true beauty.

411

- Five corresponds to FIXED SIGNS Taurus, Leo, Scorpio and Aquarius. Resistant to change these people are faithful and persevering seeing projects through to the end. They attempt to adapt the environment to themselves and above all they want to maintain things.
- Pentacles, an EARTH SIGN, are represented by Taurus, Virgo and Capricorn. Grounded and oriented towards what is real earth signs are here to bring form to ideas. Practical, solid, dependable, productive, reasonable and persistent earth signs don't rush into things.
- The intuitive, internally driven and sensitive FEMININE ENERGY of earth signs is introspective and nurturing while it strives to create co-existence and consensus.

SYMBOLISM INCLUDES

- **Grapevine pattern on his robe** - symbolizes a great deal of abundance and prosperity.
- **Ornate crown** - symbolizes his authority and his right to that authority, he has earned it.
- **Laurel wreath on his head** - symbolizes his victorious spirit.
- **Pentacle lightly kept in place with his left hand** - prosperity is such a part of him he is not overly conscious of it.
- **Wearing armour under his robe** - symbolizes hidden strength; this King will do battle if required and is always ready.
- **Body language** – this King appears serious, honest looking, and he exudes a sense of kindness.
- **Throne has rams** – these rams represent Aries, a fire sign, which symbolizes leadership qualities and an inclination and readiness for action.
- **Throne has a bull** – the bull represents Taurus, an earth sign, signifying a high likelihood for the manifestation of one's ideas or projects; Taurus also represents a love of material possessions.
- **Royal orb in king's right hand** - this is a round ball held by a royal figure, it is a feminine symbol of temporal power and sovereignty. Orbs represent not only human domination of the physical world, but also the soul of the world, which the king holds in his hand. As a circle it is a symbol of completeness and fertility and suggests that we create our own lives.

- **Wall between king and his castle** - depicts a separation between his wealth and himself, he is more than his wealth.
- **Vines on the walls and greenery around his throne** - prosperity brought about by successful efforts and labour.
- **Animal skull at his feet** - sovereignty over the animal world, he is close to nature.
- **Castle in the background** – symbolizes a great deal of material wealth and access to unlimited resources.
- **Yellow sky** - symbolizes enthusiasm, creativity and joy.

UPRIGHT MEANING
KING AS A SITUATION

- You may be involved with an enterprise where intelligence and business acumen will be present.
- You may be involved in something mathematical that results in success in the areas of finance.
- Cunning action will lead to tangible results and an increase in your social status.
- You may possibly realize an inheritance.

KING AS A PERSONALITY

- Wealthy, powerful and cultured this man can provide wise counsel, help and inspiration.
- Refined, knowledgeable about money and finance this man is a true patron of the arts and sciences.
- This man may or may not be well disposed towards you but the cards around him will reveal what you need to do to acquire his patronage of you require it.
- Practical minded this man gets things done rather than theorizing about them.
- This man has the ability to turn insights and ideas into material comfort.

REVERSED MEANING

- You may be exposed to a shady deal so ensure you read the small print.
- *The meaning of the card is delayed or extended into the future.*

- *An aspect of the upright meaning of the card needs to be released so you can move forward.*
- *This is not about the upright meaning, place another card on reversed one and read it.*

PART IV

SPREADS

29. How are spreads used?

A spread refers to the way in which the cards are laid down (*arranged*) prior to a reading. Tarot spreads create a format from which to read the cards. The meaning of the card is interpreted in connection to where it is placed within the overall spread. Choosing a spread format depends upon the type of information someone wants to gain from the Tarot.

The Tarot is often consulted to provide information regarding a particular question. When formulating questions it is best to use open ended queries as gaining information from yes and no questions is not suited to the Tarot. Some question examples are "what do I need to know so I can get this job?" - "what do I need to understand about my relationship with my boyfriend?" "what can I expect the next few months to look like?" Sometimes a Querent is unable to formulate a question so many readers will use the Celtic Cross spread (*an example of this is provided*) with the first card becoming the question seeking an answer.

Creating one's own spreads is highly recommended.

30. Spread examples

THREE CARD SPREAD

This spread can handle "when" (*time questions*), example is "when will my marriage get better?"

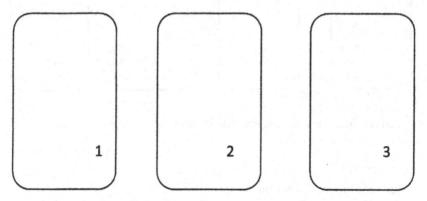

Draw three cards. Lay them side by side and interpret each card as an issue the Querent needs to resolve before the "when" question will occur.

THREE CARD SPREAD

This spread is appropriate for quick answers and insights into situations.

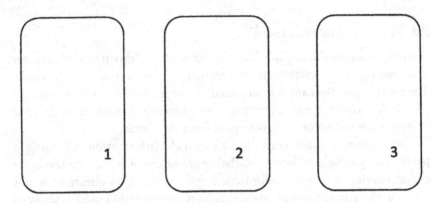

Draw three cards. Lay them side by side.
1. Nature of the present situation.
2. Querent's attitude towards what is happening.
3. Key elements to consider.

FOUR CARD SPREAD

This spread is appropriate for specific concerns.

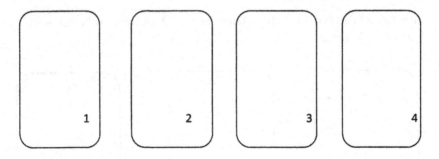

Draw four cards. Lay them side by side.
1. situation
2. obstacle
3. recommended action
4. expected outcome if the Querent does not change any thoughts or behaviours in connection to the situation

FIVE CARD SPREAD

This spread is appropriate for questions such as:

- will I get ......?
- what do I need to know so ...... will happen?
- is .... going to happen?

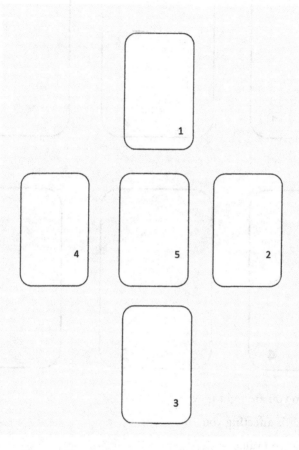

1. current situation

2. the waning influence

3. the hidden influence

4. the emerging influence

5. synthesis of previous 4 cards (*the expected outcome – should the Querent not change any beliefs or behaviours regarding the situation*)

Six Card Spread

This spread is appropriate for understanding personal issues.

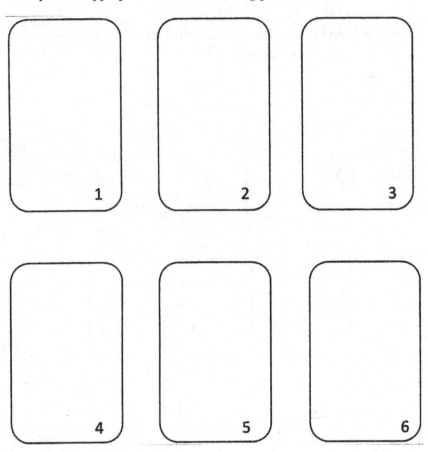

1. who you are right now
2. what is affecting you
3. what you value
4. what is bothering you
5. the short term
6. the long term

SIX CARD SPREAD

Appropriate for questions such as:

- what can I expect the next few months to look like?
- what can I expect the outcome of .... to look like?

1. the past
2. the recent past
3. the present
4. challenge you are facing
5. possible action
6. the result or outcome if you do not change any of your current beliefs or behaviours

SEVEN CARD SPREAD

Appropriate for quick answers.

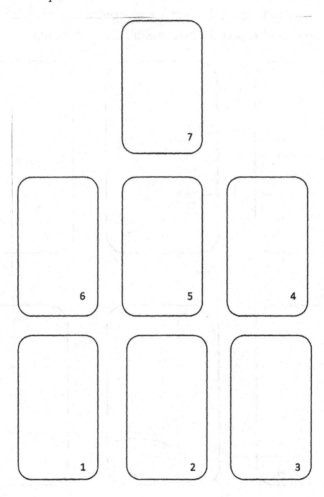

1. concern

2. immediate past

3. immediate future

4. Querent's state of mind

5. obstacle

6. help

7. outcome if Querent does not change beliefs or behaviours regarding the concern

THE HORSE SHOE SPREAD

Appropriate when more detailed information is being sought for a particular question.

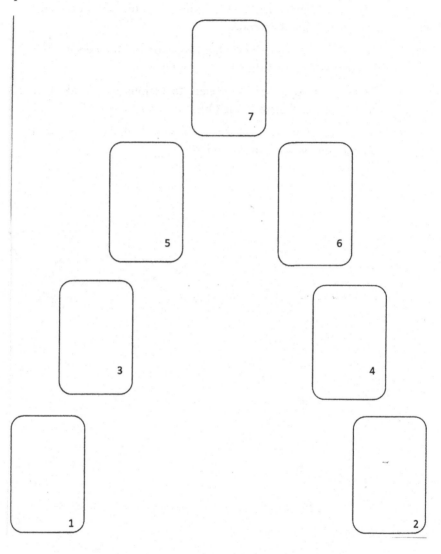

1. THE PAST. Describes what past events, emotions and actions pertain to the question being asked.

2. THE PRESENT. Refers to what is happening now or the Querent's current state of mind regarding what has occurred.

3. HIDDEN INFLUENCES. Unexpected occurrences or expectations about which the Querent is unaware.

4. OBSTACLES. Refers to what is standing in the Querent's way of attaining her goals. This may be external conditions or problems with the Querent's attitude.

5. ENVIRONMENT. Describes other people or another persona and their attitude toward the Querent and her issues.

6. WHAT SHOULD BE DONE. Refers to actions to be taken or recommends a change in the Querent's current attitude.

7. MOST LIKELY OUTCOME. Refers to what will likely occur if Querent follows the advice from #6.

THE CELTIC CROSS

This is one of the most popular spreads for reading the Tarot. This spread differs somewhat between readers. It is appropriate for almost any question. As well if the Querent does not have a question the card in the first position can be used as the question. I usually have the Querent draw 4 extra cards. These are used to clarify issues, an example is a Page, Pages always bring messages and the extra card will identify the message. Sometimes cards just don't seem to meld into the general message so extra cards can often assist with the overall meaning.

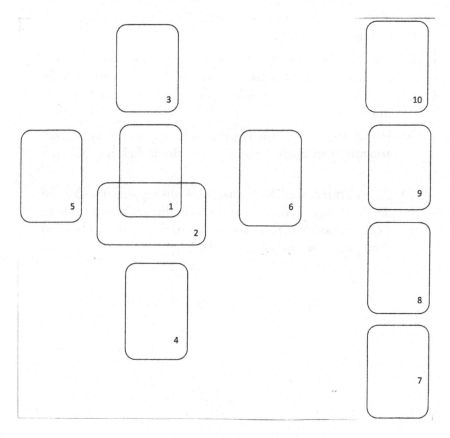

1. THE QUESTION. If the Querent doesn't have one start with saying this card deals with (*this becomes the question*).

2. WHAT CROSSES THE QUERENT. Describes obstacles the Querent currently faces.

3. WHAT IS ABOVE. Ideas currently in the air, these are the Querent's ideals and or what they want.

4. WHAT IS BENEATH. Immediate past circumstances in the Queren'ts life that are the direct cause of the situation under consideration. This may also indicate what is unknown.

5. WHAT IS BEHIND YOU. The environment the Querent was working in while the "question" or "situation" under consideration was occurring. This environment is now fading away.

6. WHAT IS BEFORE YOU. New circumstances coming into being, this is what will be happening around the Querent in the next while.

7. THIS IS THE QUERENT (INTERNAL). This describes the Querent's current state of mind.

8. THIS IS THE QUERENT (EXTERNAL). This describes the environment and circumstances surrounding the situation under consideration, it can include how others perceive the Querent's situation.

9. HOPES AND FEARS. The Querent is hoping for something but also fears what might be lost; this can also include the Querent's worries.

10. FUTURE OUTCOME. This is what likely will happen if the Querent doesn't change anything in the present. This outcome needs to be a culmination of the theme and pattern that has been identified throughout the reading.

31. A reading example

This is representative of readings I have done. Typically I receive an email requesting a reading from clients I have previously read for or from someone who has been referred by an existing client. Usually the Querent (*client I am reading for*) has a question but sometimes they don't. As the Querents live in different areas I focus my energies on them, shuffle the cards and generally use a Celtic Cross spread for the reading. Depending upon the Querent's question, in addition to the Celtic Cross, I will use various other spreads to ensure the information from the Tarot is more complete. I email the Querent the reading.

For this example while shuffling the cards my intuition suggested that the reading would be for a male. After laying out this particular Celtic Cross spread I read the cards with that in mind.

The cards were:

1. 7 of Cups — (*the question*)

2. 10 of Wands — (*obstacles the Querent currently faces*)

3. Queen of Cups — (*ideas currently in the air, the Querent's ideal, what s/he wants*)

4. Queen of Pentacles — (*immediate past circumstances, the direct cause of current situation*)

5. 8 of Swords — (*Querent's working environment when situation arose, now fading*)

6. Lovers Card — (*what lies ahead, new circumstances coming into being*)

7. Hanged Man — (*describes Querent's current internal state of mind*)

8. 4 of Swords — (*describes external circumstances currently surrounding situation*)

9. King of Wands — (*Querent's hopes, fears, desires and worries of what may be lost*)

10. Knight of Swords — (*outcome, what likely will happen if Querent does not change anything*)

To begin a reading I look at the cards as a whole. In this spread the element air was prominent indicating thinking and mental processing. The cardinal quality was prevalent indicating new beginnings and the fixed quality only came up twice showing this was not about keeping things the same. As well being mutable and adapting to the circumstances was not significant here. There was a greater tendency towards utilizing masculine energies than feminine energies. Two threes (*Hanged Man and Knight of Swords*) and a six (*Lovers*) indicated that movement and action were significant. Even more significant were the three fours (*Queen of Cups, Queen of Pentacles, Four of Swords*) and one eight (*Eight of Swords*). These indicated a significant possibility for the manifestation of the Querent's ideas or projects. The three sword cards indicated that the Querent would be facing some distress and hurdles. Swords also indicate a search for truth no matter what the consequences.

Major Arcana cards often represent themes striving to be realized. The Lovers card is about relationships and the Hanged Man is about sacrifice and looking at things differently.

The subject matter seemed to be overcoming current issues to realize something better. I based this on the first card which is about imagining things and the second card (*the obstacle*) was about burdens. Because pentacles only came up once I did not think this was associated with money. Money is usually tied to work so this did not seem to be an employment issue. Cups came up twice as did two Queens (*one was from the cups suit*) and the Lovers card so I sensed this had to do with relationship issues.

So with the theme being about relationships I began interpreting the cards with that in mind.

<u>Here is the reading I would have emailed the Querent.</u>
You have been spending a great deal of time thinking and pondering and trying to figure a way out of your present situation. Lots of "what if" scenarios have been going through your head. Idealistic thoughts of what should be and even bouts of despondency have been present. You have been feeling restless and there is a strong urge within you to start something new. You have reached a turning point.

It appears that the current relationship you are in is no longer bringing you a sense of joy. The sparkle and spontaneity that was once there seems to have vanished. I get the sense you are feeling pressured or that something is not sitting right with you and this is making you feel emotionally worn out. That you have made a commitment is evident but the focus and purpose of this commitment seems to have become lost.

You have been considering what it is you want in a relationship. You place a high value on honesty and affection as well as authenticity and you admire women who display emotional integrity. Recently you have spent a great deal of time thinking and mentally processing ideas and this action has not left a place for your feelings and intuitions in your decision making. The time is right to plan something but it needs to feel right now not just sound right.

Probably what you started you down this road of desiring a release from your current situation was observing someone you admire. This is likely a woman who is kind and generous and creates a warm environment for those close to her. She likely exudes a maturity and self reliance you find very attractive. It's not that you have a roving eye its more you have been observing characteristics you desire in others but that seem to be lacking in your current relationship. The time is right for you to gain what you desire but you need to use your intuition and to focus on practical solutions.

You are being presented with a harsh lesson to learn. Your intelligence will help but this time you need to feel your way through this and come out on the other side wiser. Currently you sense things occurring around you that are being hidden from you. Discomfort is putting it mildly. Feeling trapped you have moved into almost a victimized and powerless position. You have felt pulled between emotions and actions. What you clearly need to understand is that you possess the internal resources to rectify this situation. Take off the blinders you have been wearing and face the situation, it may be unpleasant but the relief you will experience will more than make up for the temporary discomfort involved.

The lesson being presented to you here is that in order to have a healthy and meaningful relationship with someone you also have to be in one with yourself. If being in union with a particular individual causes you to feel disjointed or ill at ease within yourself than this is not someone you want to merge your energies with. There needs to be mutual respect, shared values and some common goals for relationships to grow and thrive. This is definitely the time you need to make a wise decision about love. Something you need to know is once you have learned this lesson you can fully expect a happy outcome.

Currently you are willing to make some sacrifices as intuitively you are aware of better things to come as a result. It is time to break some old patterns of thinking and behaving and embrace new ways and perspectives. The way in which you have participated in relationships needs to change. Some of your rigidly held beliefs need to be released and old attachments to some ideas need to be let go. With all of your recent pondering and reflecting you have been working towards change even though you may not be consciously aware of it.

Take a bit a time to work things out in your mind. You need to get your inner life in order so that you can develop a plan to sort out the external aspects of your life. Once you feel connected again within yourself and with the universe and whatever higher spiritual presence you experience then you can begin to start something new.

Portraying yourself as someone who can be counted on and whose word is good is important to you. That is who you are so when you make a commitment you plan to keep it. You do not want others to lose any respect they have for you, nor do you want to lose self respect. Your intuitiveness is enhanced right now, use it and you will find that the environment around you supports your decisions.

If everything remains as it is right now then you can expect change coming for you and coming fast. It may even take you by surprise. Things have been occurring in the background and you can't stop them even if you wanted to. Someone or something is about to rush headlong into your life, this occurrence will be very decisive and things will be different as a result. This difference will very likely be an improvement for you.

Always remember that the cards prediction is based on everything remaining as it is. If you don't want the predicted outcome then you must alter something in the present. Nothing is written in stone. It is not the bad news but how you react or respond to the news that gives you control over your destiny.

The cards in this reading as a whole are very positive. There is an abundance of energy here urging you to move forward and start something new and a great deal of promise that things will turn out well for you.

PART V

Index

A

abyss 27
Ace of Cups 233
Ace of Pentacles 357, 391
Ace of Swords 297
Ace of Wands 169
Acolytes 59, 60, 326
Adonai 91
affirmations 1, 21, 22, 28, 34, 49, 54,
    62, 68, 75, 81, 87, 93, 99, 104, 110,
    117, 122, 129, 135, 141, 146, 152,
    158
alchemy 59, 91, 220, 238, 382
amulet 73, 174, 226, 254, 310
anchors 128, 174, 374
animal skull 413
ankh 52
arcane 9, 21, 39, 73
arched bridge 182
arches 182, 366
Archetype Chaos (*16 - The Tower*)
    125
Archetype Endurance (*8 - Strength*)
    77
Archetype Evaluation and Reward (*20
    - Judgement*) 149
Archetype Fate and Destiny (*10 -
    Wheel of Fortune*) 89
Archetype Justice (*11 - Justice*) 95
Archetype Rebirth (*13 - Death*) 107
Archetype Sacrifice (*12 - The Hanged
    Man*) 101
Archetype Satisfaction and Wholeness
    (*21 - The World*) 155
Archetype Spiritual Leader (*5 - The
    Hierophant*) 57
Archetype the Anima (*2 - The High
    Priestess*) 37
Archetype the Child (*0 - The Fool*) 25
Archetype the Father (*4 - The
    Emperor*) 51
Archetype the Hero (*4 - The Emperor*)
    51

Archetype the Moon (*18 - The Moon*)
    137
Archetype the Mother (*3 - The
    Empress*) 45
Archetype the Soul (*6 - The Lovers*)
    65
Archetype the Star (*17 - The Star*) 131
Archetype the Sun (*19 - The Sun*) 143
Archetype the Trickster (*1 - The
    Magician & 15 - The Devil*) 31, 119
Archetype the Warrior (*7 - The
    Chariot*) 71
Archetype Union of Opposites (*14 -
    Temperance*) 113
Archetype Wise Old Man (*9 - The
    Hermit*) 83
archway 366
armour 53, 72, 108, 109, 214, 277,
    278, 310, 342, 402, 412
Artemis 139
Asclepius 85
astral world 157
Astrology (*see sidereal and tropical*) 2,
    3, 4, 5, 10, 11, 47, 85
asymmetrical 226
auras 282

B

baboon 6
Baccus 258
bandage 202
barefoot 374
batons 7
bat wings 120
belt 26, 32, 72, 102, 210, 214, 226,
    362, 378
Bible 47, 79, 92, 120, 126, 134, 157
birds 6, 26, 134, 338, 342
Blavatsky, Madame Helena 6, 7, 8
blindfold 302, 326
Builder, The (*King of Pentacles*) 411
bull 92, 157, 412
butterflies 346, 350

C

caduceus 115, 238
cardinal virtues 77, 79, 83, 95, 113
cardo 79
cat 220
celestial power 45, 101, 155, 177, 213, 241, 277, 305, 341, 365, 401
central theme 21
chakra 2, 12, 13, 32, 39, 85, 97, 150, 288, 334
Chakras 12
chalices 115, 238, 246
Chariot, The 71, 72, 75, 129
checkerboard pattern 60, 178
Christianity 39, 79, 115, 121
Christmas 8, 157
Church window 374
circle 2, 32, 59, 73, 90, 91, 97, 115, 210, 214, 226, 412
cloud 27, 66, 92, 170, 297, 306, 314, 322, 338, 342, 346
coffins 151, 310
Coleman-Smith, Pamela 6
collective unconscious 2, 9, 91, 133
Comte de Mellet 5
cosmic consciousness 49, 101, 104, 105, 138, 159
court cards 1, 13, 164
Court de Gebelin 5
crab 72, 139
crescent moon 38, 39, 72, 262, 302, 350
crossed keys 59
Cross of St. Andrew 174, 254
cross saltire 174
Crowley, Aleister 6, 7, 16
crutches 374
Crystallizer, The (*Queen of Swords*) 345
Cupid 346

D

dark moon 39
David 40, 68, 72, 85, 121
Death 54, 55, 107, 110, 111, 139, 335
Decider, The (*Knight of Swords*) 341
Demeter 60
desert 210, 215, 220
Devil, The 68, 119, 120, 123
dissolution 91
divagating iii, 1, 17
dog 27, 139, 187, 394
dove 234
dragon 258
Druid 5, 8

E

Egypt 4, 5, 14, 210, 215, 220
Egyptian 5, 6, 38, 40, 52, 73, 91, 394
Eight of Cups 261
Eight of Pentacles 385
Eight of Swords 325, 428
Eight of Wands 197
Elusian 60
Emperor, The 9, 51, 52, 53, 54, 55, 60, 111
Empress, The 9, 45, 49, 104, 159
equinox 77, 90, 131, 197, 261, 325, 385
esoteric 7, 9, 25, 27, 39, 59, 132, 174, 221, 349, 366, 394
etheric 59

F

Feeler, The (*Queen of Cups*) 281
first card in a reversed position 16
Five of Cups 249
Five of Pentacles 373
Five of Swords 313
Five of Wands 185
flowing water 47, 109, 250

Fool, The 9, 21, 25
Four of Cups 245
Four of Pentacles 369
Four of Swords 309, 428
Four of Wands 181
fox 220
France 4
freemason 121
Freemason 5, 60, 127
Freemasonry 47, 97, 127, 326
French 5, 6, 7, 14
fruit 144, 242, 391, 408
full moon 38, 39, 262

G

Gaia 91
geometrical symbols 157
globe 174
Gnostic 47
goat 408
Golden Dawn 5, 6, 7, 26, 60
grain 47
grapes 182, 394
grape vines 390
Greek 39, 60, 91, 115, 126, 150
Greek cross 150
gypsies 4, 266

H

halo 103, 115, 170, 234, 297, 358
Hanged Man, The 49, 101, 104, 159
Harris, Lady Frieda 6
Healer, The (*Knight of Pentacles*) 401
heart 12, 47, 52, 78, 85, 97, 163, 231,
    282, 288, 302, 306
Heart pierced 306
Hebrew 5, 6, 14, 91, 127, 139, 151,
    170, 298
Hecate 150
Hera 91
Hermes Trismegistus 4, 14
Hermeticism 4

Hermit, The 9, 79, 83, 84, 85, 87, 141
heterodox 4
Hierophant, The 7, 57, 58, 59, 60, 62,
    117
High Flyer, The (*Knight of Cups*) 277
High Priestess, The 37, 41, 42, 99,
    152, 153
Hippocrates 85
hoe 382
holly 8
hooded falcon 390
Horse and rider 402
Horus 73

I

ibis 6, 134
individuation 157
initiation 60, 109
instincts 27, 39, 41, 80, 92, 108, 120,
    139, 140, 141, 145, 190, 214, 215,
    220, 221, 278, 279, 288, 342, 343,
    390, 394, 402, 408
Iris 115
Italian 4, 5, 6, 7, 14
Italy 4, 7

J

jagged clouds 314, 342
James, William 3
jewelled crown 52
Jewish mysticism 81
joy 21, 32, 89, 114, 143, 144, 146, 206,
    213, 220, 269, 270, 334, 409, 413,
    428
Judgement 41, 42, 99, 149, 150, 152,
    153
juggling 362
Jung, Carl 9
Jungian terms 85
Justice 16, 41, 42, 77, 79, 83, 95, 96,
    97, 98, 99, 113, 152, 153

K

Kabbalah 4, 5, 6, 14, 55, 127
karma 7, 26, 92, 140
keys 59
King of Cups 287
King of Pentacles 411
King of Swords 349
King of Wands 225, 227, 427
Knight of Cups 277
Knight of Pentacles 401
Knight of Swords 164, 341, 427, 428
Knight of Wands 213
Kundalini 32, 96

L

lake 115, 132, 133
lantern 85
Latin letters 151
laurel wreath 26, 73, 238, 258, 412
leminscate 362
lilies 59, 174, 234, 274, 358
lingam 73
lotus 40
Lovers, The 65, 68, 123, 428

M

Macgregor-Matthews, S.L. 5
Magic 32
Magician, The 9, 31, 34, 93, 146, 147
mandala 26
mermaids 282
mistletoe 8
moon, crescent. *See* crescent moon
moon, dark. *See* dark moon
moon, full. *See* full moon
Moon, The 72, 87, 137, 138, 141
moon, waning. *See* waning moon
moon, waxing. *See* waxing moon
myrtle 46
Mystic Rose 108

N

Native American 126
Neo-Platonism 4
new moon 38
Nine of Cups 265
Nine of Pentacles 389
Nine of Swords 163, 329
Nine of Wands 201
Norse 126
Number Eight 77, 197, 261, 325, 385
Number Eighteen 137
Number Eleven 95, 209, 273, 337, 397
Number Fifteen 119
Number Five 57, 185, 249, 313, 373
Number Four 51, 181, 245, 309, 369
Number Fourteen 113, 225, 287, 349, 411
Number Nine 83, 201, 265, 329, 389
Number Nineteen 143
Number One 31, 169, 233, 297, 357
Number Seven 71, 193, 257, 321, 381
Number Seventeen 131
Number Six 65, 189, 253, 317, 377
Number Sixteen 125
Number Ten 89, 205, 269, 333, 393
Number Thirteen 107, 219, 281, 345, 407
Number Three 45, 177, 241, 305, 365
Number Twelve 101, 213, 277, 341, 401
Number Twenty 149, 155
Number Twenty one 155
Number Two 37, 173, 237, 301, 361
Number Zero 25

O

oak leaves 182
occult 2, 3, 5, 59, 358
ocean 174, 362
Oedipus 73
Old Testament 79

olive branch 298
Ophiuchus 85
orb 47, 52, 412
ouroborus 210, 214, 226

P

Page of Cups 273
Page of Pentacles 397
Page of Swords 337
Page of Wands 209
palm tree 39
Pan 120
path 108, 127, 139, 234, 358
pearl 47
pentagram 121
Persephone 39, 60
physical consciousness 133
pip cards 163
Plato 4, 6, 14, 79
ploughed field 174, 206, 398, 403
pomegranate 39
prudence 77, 79, 83, 95, 113, 407
pyramids 5, 210, 215, 221
Pythagorean 4

Q

Queen of Cups 281, 427, 428
Queen of Pentacles 407, 427, 428
Queen of Swords 345
Queen of Wands 219, 221
Querent 14
question 13, 73, 195, 334, 417, 423, 425, 426, 427

R

rabbit 408
rain 306
rainbow 115, 270
rain clouds 306
ram head 53

rams 53, 412
rebirth 108, 287
recluse 84, 85
red lions 220
Revolutionary, The (*Knight of Wands*) 213
Rider-Waite (*Smith*) 6, 15, 16
Rolling seas 362
Roman 126
Romany 4, 266
rose 26, 46, 59, 108, 174, 330, 358, 366
ROTA 91
round disc 115, 234

S

salamander 210, 214, 226
salt 90, 91
Sanskirt 12, 73
sarcophagus 310
scales 97, 378
scarf 378
sceptre 59
sea 47, 174
Seeke, The (*King of Wands*) 225
Seer, The (*Queen of Wands*) 219
self-actualization 157
serpent 67, 210, 214, 226
Seth 73
Seven of Cups 257
Seven of Pentacles 381
Seven of Swords 321
Seven of Wands 193
ship 58, 109, 178, 289, 362, 394
shuffling 14, 16, 427
sidereal 11, 85
Six of Cups 253
Six of Pentacles 377
Six of Swords 317
Six of Wands 189
skeleton 108
smoke 127, 198, 322
snail 391

snake 32, 91, 96, 258
snakes 96
snow 27, 86, 374
Socrates 79
Sol 220
solar disc 38, 73
Solomon 40, 85
solstice 8, 120, 156
sphinx 73, 91
spirals 156, 220, 238, 391
square 53, 54, 97
square broach 97
staff 84, 85
stained glass 310
St. Ambrose 79
Star of David 68, 72, 85, 121
Star, The 81, 131, 132, 135
St. Augustine 79
staves 7
Stonehenge 5
stream 47, 170, 198, 278
Strength 16, 77, 78, 79, 80, 81, 83, 95, 113, 135
St. Thomas Aquinas 79
Succeeder, The (*Queen of Pentacles*) 407
sulphur 90, 91, 103, 156
sunflowers 144, 145, 220
Sun, The 34, 78, 93, 143, 144, 146

T

tarrochi 4
Temperance 62, 77, 79, 83, 95, 113, 114, 116, 117
Ten of Cups 269
Ten of Pentacles 393
Ten of Swords 110, 333, 335
Ten of Wands 205
tetragrammaton 91
Thinker, The (*King of Swords*) 349
third eye 13, 39, 97
Thoth 6, 134
Three of Cups 241

Three of Pentacles 365
Three of Swords 305
Three of Wands 177
Tora 39
Tower, The 75, 125, 128, 129
transmutation 151, 238
Tree of Knowledge 67
Tree of Life 6, 66, 127
triangle 68, 85, 103, 115, 156, 307, 366
tropical 11
trumps 4, 6, 7, 21
twin motive 59, 73, 109, 115, 133, 139
twisting path 139
Two of Cups 122, 237
Two of Pentacles 361
Two of Swords 301
Two of Wands 173
two pillars 40, 59, 96, 139
Typhon 91

U

undines 282

V

Venusians' plant 46

W

Waite, Arthur E. 5, 6, 7, 15, 16, 60, 163, 326
wall 129, 145, 174, 330, 394, 413
wallet 26
waning moon 38
waxing moon 38
Westcott, Dr. William Wyatt 5
wheat 47
Wheel of Fortune 34, 89, 92, 93, 146, 147, 157
white horse 108, 145, 190, 278, 342
wind 338, 342, 374

windy 338
wine 250, 258
winged icons 92
winged lion 238
winged solar disc 73
wings 66, 92, 114, 120, 150, 278
wolf 139
womb 67, 73
World, The 49, 92, 104, 105, 155, 156,
   158, 159
wreath 26, 73, 78, 145, 157, 190, 238,
   258, 282, 394, 412

Y

Yod 91, 127
Yoni 73
Yule 8

Z

zero 25
Zeus 60, 91
zodiac 1, 11, 26, 66, 85, 330
Zodiac 25, 31, 37, 45, 51, 57, 65, 71,
   77, 83, 89, 92, 95, 101, 107, 114, 119,
   125, 131, 137, 143, 149, 155, 157,
   330